HOW TO READ THE BIBLE

How to Read

THE BIBLE

HARVEY COX

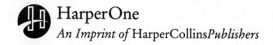

HarperOne
An Imprint of HarperCollins*Publishers*

HarperOne

HarperCollins books may be purchased for educational, business, or sales promotional use. For information please e-mail the Special Markets Department at SPsales@harpercollins.com.

HarperCollins website: http://www.harpercollins.com

HarperCollins®, 🏭®, and HarperOne™ are trademarks of HarperCollins Publishers.

FIRST EDITION

Designed by Janet M. Evans

Library of Congress Cataloging-in-Publication Data
Cox, Harvey.
    How to read the Bible / Harvey Cox. — First edition.
        pages cm
    Includes index.
ISBN 978–0–06–234315–4
1. Bible—Criticism, interpretation, etc. I. Title.
BS511.3.C695   2015
220.6'1—dc23   2015001457

15 16 17 18 19   RRD(H)   10 9 8 7 6 5 4 3 2 1

This book is dedicated to all the
friends, preachers, teachers, priests and nuns,
colleagues, professors, students, and scholars, pastors,
believers and atheists, writers, poets, and filmmakers,
who have in countless ways helped me to appreciate the Bible.
In particular I dedicate it to the memory of
my teacher, colleague, dean, and personal friend:
Krister Stendahl (1921–2008)

Contents

HOW TO READ THE BIBLE

Introduction

I did not grow up in the "Bible Belt." My parents were only occasional churchgoers. I never saw either one of them pick up a Bible, let alone read it. Nonetheless, I was born, as many of us were, in a Bible-drenched country. Take, for example, the movies I went to on Saturday afternoons: *King of Kings, The Robe,* and of course *The Ten Commandments,* among many others. The one that sticks in my mind most was *Samson and Delilah,* featuring Victor Mature and Hedy Lamarr, which suffused the biblical epic with an erotic quality sure to stir the glands of an adolescent boy. But I also knew the Bible was serious stuff. It was the volume witnesses placed their hand on to swear an oath. Soldiers reported they had been saved from death by the New Testament they carried in their breast pocket. In Protestant America, with its historic aversion to "idols," the Bible was the only universally recognized sacred icon. In a sense the whole of America was a Bible belt, although how much people knew about what was *in* the Bible was another matter.

At some point I did discover that there was in fact a Bible, a large one, in our home. Covered with dust, it lay at the bottom of a set of shelves containing several volumes of the old brown- and gold-bound *Colliers Encyclopedia.* No one ever opened the Bible or, as far as I can remember, the encyclopedia either. But one day, driven by curiosity rather than piety, I looked inside the Bible. It contained some colorful pictures of people who appeared to be wearing bathrobes and towels. Gold margins bordered the first chapters of some of the books. But, looking through it, I soon discovered that for our family its main function was to serve as an archive for the dates of births, marriages, and deaths of previous generations, inscribed in different colored ink, some of it now fading, in a section just before the book of Genesis.

I think of my personal history with the Bible as unfolding in three stages, each with its own way of reading it. The first stage I call the "narrative" stage. Like many people, I simply took the Bible at face value and more or less literally, although even as a youngster I had my doubts about some of the accounts that seemed improbable. The second phase of my evolving understanding of the Bible might be called the "historical" one. It began when I was in college and continued through seminary and beyond. In this period my emphasis was on the context in which a particular biblical book was written, for and to whom, when and why. The third stage, which has been developing slowly during my adult years, I would like to call the "spiritual" stage. I do not, however, mean "spiritual" in a narrow or merely inward sense, but in a holistic one that includes inner and outer, personal and social. I will have more to say about all these modes in the rest of this book.

In retrospect I do not believe these three stages—the narrative, the historical, the spiritual—or the manner of studying the Bible each implies can be sharply differentiated. Just as we all carry features of earlier stages in our psychological development with us as we grow older, all of these ways of grasping the Bible remain part of my repertoire. But I believe they need to supplement and complement each other in order to get the most from any reading of biblical texts. This is something I attempt to do throughout this book.

THE NARRATIVE STAGE

As a child, along with my siblings, I was dutifully dispatched to the Baptist Sunday school next door to our home by my religiously indifferent parents, in part to keep up appearances, but also—I suspect—to get us out of the house, so they could savor a second cup of coffee and peruse the *Philadelphia Inquirer*. Seated in Sunday school on hard wooden chairs under the tutelage of a series of well-intentioned but only sketchily informed lay teachers, I heard the *stories* of the Bible. I found them fascinating, if frequently not quite credible. There was the nasty fight between Cain and

Abel. And there was the aforementioned Delilah, who entrapped a muscular Samson with her sultry charms. There was Noah and his menagerie aboard the ark. I especially liked the one about David, the cheeky little kid who slew the big bully. And there were also all those stories Jesus told—the parables—and the ones people told about him.

We did not just hear these stories. We also sometimes acted them out. As a child I often pulled on a bathrobe, wrapped a towel around my head, and gripped a stick in my hand as a character in a Nativity play ("We have seen a star in the East . . ."). When as a teenager I began to attend church, mostly to sing in the choir, I always noticed the huge black leather Bible that lay open on the varnished pulpit, its gold edges glistening and its purple page marker dangling. It was the biggest book I had ever seen, so I knew it must be important. Sometimes the preacher read from it, but more often he read from a much smaller one placed on top of the big one. What little I remember about the sermons I heard from that pulpit is that they were made up mainly of anecdotes and allegories intended to illustrate the points the preacher was making. Years later I still remember many of these illustrations, but hardly any of the points they were supposed to dramatize. For a kid in a church that had no formal creeds, the Bible was not a handbook of doctrines. It was a compendium of stories, and for that I am grateful.

Those were the days before the U.S. Supreme Court ruled that the practice of reading the Bible in public schools was unconstitutional. Consequently, I heard the Bible read every day for years. At that time state law mandated that ten verses of the Bible be read aloud, but "without commentary," so that is exactly what our teachers, and later the students selected for the task, did. What we heard 90 percent of the time were Psalms from the King James Version: "Lift up your heads, O ye gates; even lift them up, ye everlasting doors; and the King of glory shall come in" (24:9). I liked the cadence of the words, but what king was entering and where those gates were were never explained. Still, it is remarkable how, after so many years, those verses still resonate through my synapses. If at Sunday school I encountered the Bible mainly as stories, in the public school it spoke to me primarily as poetry.

In my teens I became more involved with our small church, was elected president of the youth group, and as such was even invited to preach once when the pastor (along with nearly everyone else in the congregation) was on vacation. As a high-school student and as I began to read the Bible on my own, I began to realize that, as endearing as the stories I was learning were, they represented only a carefully culled sample drawn from many more, some of them apparently deemed not suitable for Sunday school, such as the ones about Noah's drunken nakedness or the prostitute who concealed Joshua's spies. It also occurred to me that the laypeople who taught us had no inkling and, maybe no curiosity, about when and why any of these stories were first told. In short, the "story stage" of my introduction to the Bible was also largely a literal stage.

When I went to college, I majored in history, but took a couple of religion courses, neither of them on the Bible. I was not, however, unexposed to the Bible during my undergraduate years. A conservative Christian organization called the Inter-varsity Christian Fellowship sponsored student-led "Bible studies" in different campus buildings and sometimes in dormitory rooms, where some of the students crouched on the bed or the floor. At first I found these sessions intriguing and attended several of them. But I soon noticed that the questions I raised were often treated with smiling dismissiveness by the student leaders. For them the kinds of queries we were taught to ask in our history classes—like the dating of a document or the trustworthiness of a source—were just not appropriate. Inquiries about when a given book of the Bible was written or for whom it was originally intended were politely ruled out. We were supposed to focus exclusively on what God was saying to us now in a particular passage. I tried, but I eventually lost interest, not in the Bible, which continued to fascinate me, but in the way it was approached, at least in these Bible study groups.

I have always been grateful that through my childhood exposure to the Bible I learned to regard it as a compilation of stories. True, this was a way of thinking that was innocent and unsophisticated. But it also taught me to appreciate the Bible as basically an anthology of different kinds of narratives, letters, and poetry, not as a handbook of doctrines I was expected to subscribe to. I continue to believe what this "narrative" approach gave me is a good foundation on which to build a more adult way of understanding it. But it only goes so far. Once I was introduced to the pleasure and the discipline of studying history in college, I could not be happy with the constraints of the dorm Bible study. I was looking for something more. Then in seminary, although it was not an easy step for me, I gradually came to see that studying the Bible historically is not something foreign we force on it. I began to appreciate the Bible as a gift that comes to us from and through history, and that a more than superficial reading of it demands we approach it, at least in part, from a historical perspective.

THE HISTORICAL STAGE

When I graduated from college, I was undecided at first whether to begin doctoral studies in order to pursue my deepening interest in history or to enroll in seminary, learn more about religion and the Bible, and maybe become a minister. In the end I decided on seminary. That was where my next "take" on the Bible began. My professors called it the "historical-critical method." What it amounted to was an attempt to apply the methods then current in "scientific" historical studies to the text of the Bible. Without knowing the terminology, I saw that this might well be what I had been looking for, given the questions I was discouraged from raising in the dorm Bible study. Still, when I found myself suddenly confronted by such a radically different way of viewing the Bible, it came as a rude shock.

Even though I was an adult by then, my attitude toward the Bible when I first arrived at seminary was a bit naive and what might now be called "precritical." Suddenly I heard about the multiple sources of the Pentateuch, the priority of the Gospel of Mark, and the question of how many of the Pauline Letters Paul himself really wrote. I will return to some of these matters later in my discussions of the biblical books. But I want to recall here that, although the new knowledge I was acquiring was often exciting, it also troubled me. I was in no sense a fundamentalist, but I wondered how or even whether this "historical-critical" vivisection of the Bible could be reconciled to the personal importance it had come to have for me. It was not an easy time. Still, in the end it was worth it, and it has made me deeply sympathetic toward people who are going through the same difficult transition. Another purpose of this book is to help them negotiate it.

Study Tip

There are now numerous online Bible commentaries on books of the Bible that take current research into consideration. There are just as many that either reject or ignore it. Among the former some are designed for preachers and theological students, others for thoughtful nonspecialists. Consequently, one must be careful in choosing. Here are three from the former category I consider reliable.

The International Critical Commentary is now available online through Logos. It is creatively arranged to allow readers to check different translations and compare interpretations.

BibleGateway lists authors and commentators to choose from if readers would like to compare and contrast different commentaries.

Hermeneia is perhaps the most prestigious commentary. It includes English translations of recent articles in French and German. It may at times be a stretch for nonspecialists, but a stretch well worth taking.

THE SPIRITUAL STAGE

Just as I had found the literal story stage not enough as I got older, I began to see that the historical approach, although important, was also not enough either. Then came the next transition in my take on the Bible. It began in September 1963 and is still continuing. That month I was arrested along with forty other civil rights demonstrators, thirty of them young black kids and a few of their parents, in a small city in the American South. We were apprehended for taking part in a peaceful protest march organized by the local chapter of Martin Luther King's Southern Christian Leadership Conference. Inside the jail, once we were photographed and fingerprinted and had surrendered our wallets and belts, the warden separated the white protestors from the black ones. But those of us in the white cell block could hear the young black prisoners singing. Sometimes we sang back in response, if not quite as lustily.

On the Saturday after we were incarcerated, the warden, a mild-mannered middle-aged white man, paused in front of our cell.

"Well," he smiled, scratching his head, "them colored kids been asking for a Bible, so's they kin have Sunday school and church tomorrow." Still smiling, he shook his head. "So I gave 'em one," he said. "Can't do no harm, I guess."

"No harm?" I thought. What the warden clearly did not know was that the reason these youngsters were in his jail was that they had been listening to Dr. King and some of his co-workers teach and preach from that harmless Bible. They had learned that they were children of the same God who created white people and that they had an equal right to dignity and equality. The warden did not realize that, from Exodus to the Gospels to Revelation, the Bible talks about freedom and has stoked more than one revolutionary movement in history.

Sure enough, on Sunday morning the black adolescents "had church." They alternated preaching, mainly from Exodus, praying, and singing. I wished I could have joined them, but as I sat on my narrow cot in the cell listening from down the hall ("Go down, Moses, way down in Egypt land. Tell old pharaoh, let my people go . . ."), I realized that for those kids the

Bible was more than a collection of beguiling stories from long ago, and also much more than a quasi-historical document to be parsed, analyzed, dated, and classified. They had never heard about any historical-critical method. For them the Bible was a summons to be all they were meant to be. It was a living link to the long history of liberation movements, of which theirs was only the most recent. And it was a powerful assurance that, as Dr. King had told them, history was on their side and, somehow, one day they "would overcome." It was not just a story; it was *their* story. They read it in the full-orbed holistic way I have termed "spiritual."

After I was released on bail and got back home, I thought again about the dusty Bible on the bottom shelf in our living room with its fading birth and death inscriptions. And I thought about the big Bible on the pulpit in church. I thought about the Bible as stories. And I thought about the classes I had taken on the historical-critical method. I did not regret either phase of my encounter with the Bible. It *is* after all in large part a collection of "narratives," as the current idiom has it. It *is* also a patchwork of documents by many writers that has come down to us through a complicated historical process. It did not drop out of the sky. And we need to know about that process. But what I learned in the jail cell is that the Bible is something much more. It is an invitation, a living record of an open-ended history of which we can have a part. It is a still unfinished story.

What does my personal "growing up with the Bible" have to do with the question implied by the title of this book? How do we read it today? And perhaps more pointedly, *why* should we read it today?

We live in what has been called a "secular age," but reading and studying the Bible has obviously not disappeared. If anything, more of it than ever seems to be going on. Year after year the Bible remains the leading global bestseller. Why does this bulky mosaic of ancient Hebrew and Greek legends, prophecies, poetry, parables, letters, and visions continue to fly off the shelves and into shopping carts? In an age of breakthroughs in brain science, electronic telescopes, cloning, and CAT scans, why is this disparate amalgam of prescientific writings still translated into new languages every year, 392 languages and dialects so far and counting?

One answer, of course, is that perhaps our age is not as secular as some people think. God, despite premature eulogies, seems not to have died after all. The dramatic resurfacing of gods and goddesses, to say nothing of angels, vampires, and apparitions, and not the death of God or the withering away of religion, has become the hallmark—for blessing or for bane—of the early twenty-first century. Yet something has undoubtedly changed in the global culture of spirituality. Are we denizens of this twenty-first century becoming more secular, but still carrying with us traces of our previous religiousness? Are we more religious, less religious, or, more likely, religious in a new way?

Is it possible that the whole secular-religious dichotomy is woefully deficient? I am in many ways a thoroughly "secular" person, and also in many ways a "religious" one, but I do not find these two identities totally at odds. They overlap, interact, and blend into each other. As a secular man, I am nonetheless shaped and informed by a religious tradition I see no reason to shed, even when I find myself disagreeing with many of its elements. As a "religious" person, I still thrive on living in whatever is meant by the "secular age," with its celebration of democracy, human rights, and relishing life in this world rather than hankering for the next. Furthermore, I am not alone. That is who most of us are, or are becoming. The dominant ethos of the twenty-first century consists of an intermingling of the sacred and the secular. Some are calling it "postsecular." But, then, there is the Bible. What can we make of its stubborn persistence in this new secular-religious age?

Large numbers of people not only buy the Bible; many continue to read and study it. Thousands of Bible study groups meet regularly in America today. Some huddle in church basements, some in homes, and others in dorm rooms, prisons, and offices. It has been reported that Bible study groups meet in the Pentagon and in the cubicles of Goldman Sachs. For those who participate, these groups obviously have a real value. They often combine the reading and discussion of a passage with personal sharing. They are in part "support groups," and in today's fast-paced, depersonalized society they serve a highly beneficial purpose. I hope that this book will help those who lead or participate in such groups to enhance their experience in them. True, professional historical-critical scholars of the Bible often sniff at these diminutive Bible study clusters, because of what the scholars view as the inept and subjective way the texts are sometimes examined. But, as I will try to demonstrate below, the experts and the amateurs have something important to learn from each other.

Please note that "Bible study" is not the same as "biblical studies." The small groups just described are what is meant by "Bible studies." Biblical studies, on the other hand, is what hit me in seminary: a specialized branch of historical research that scrutinizes the Bible with the same methods used to examine secular texts. Its objective is to learn more and more about such things as when the various books of the Bible were written and by whom and to uncover what their original sources, audience, and purpose were. It employs grammatical tools, philology, semantic and rhetorical investigation, and comparative analysis. It also draws on archaeology and paleontology and more recently on the comparative study of cultures, in short on anything that will bring investigators closer to what a given text originally meant and how it has been interpreted since.

What, then, is the relationship between the "Bible study" that groups do and the "biblical studies" that researchers do? One of my teachers, the late Krister Stendahl, once said that the two great questions about any Bible passage are "What *did* it mean then?" and "What *does* it mean now?" For a number of years this formula made sense to me. The "What did it mean then?" question obviously fell in the realm of biblical studies. The "What does it mean now?" question belongs to Bible study, preaching, and spiritual formation. This seemed like a reasonable separation of two distinct tasks. But after my short stint in the jail cell and some other experiences that followed it, I began to find the bifurcation prescribed by Stendahl's formula no longer credible.

The first postjail experience that shaped my developing view of the Bible came from Latin American liberation theology. This vigorous movement grew from the bottom up, out of thousands of "base communities" from Guatemala to Chile and from Brazil to Peru, in which ordinary people with little knowledge of "biblical studies" gathered to share food and sing, but mainly to read the Bible and discuss its significance for their lives. Whenever I sat in on one of these groups, I noticed that, like the black youngsters in the next cell block, these people heard the biblical stories as continuous with their own. They read them not just as "literature" and not as texts to be analyzed; they read them looking for insights and encouragement in their ongoing campaigns against predatory landlords and corrupt government officials. Their interactions with the Bible were rough and tumble, never merely compliant or saccharine. They were expecting something.

Sometimes they disagreed with what they found. I remember a base community in a *favela,* or slum, near São Paulo in which the participants were hashing over the account of Jesus's last supper with his disciples in Luke. Suddenly an older man with a weather-beaten face shook his head. "Why in the world," he asked, "did the Lord talk so openly, when he suspected there was an informer at the table?" He added that he had had experience with police spies and he certainly would never have done that.

His question might seem naive, but I believe scholars can learn something from the stance these amateurs bring to the Bible. Academically trained biblical researchers often try to distance themselves from any personal stake they might have in what they discover. They think it should have no bearing on their research. They do not want to be considered unscientific, so they sometimes hide any personal investment in their work, even from themselves. They try to take themselves out of the picture. This at least was the reigning methodological formula of a previous generation of academic historians, and many biblical scholars emulated them. Now, however, this situation is changing.

More and more today thoughtful historians, including those in biblical studies, know that complete "objectivity" was never obtainable and was always probably undesirable. It often served as a convenient fiction to mask the personal stake that scholars know they have in their research. Even the most allegedly neutral history always serves some goal outside the scholarly realm, often a political or ecclesiastical purpose. But now a newer generation of historical-critical scholars knows full well that they are not disembodied entities examining a historical event or a biblical book from a fully detached perspective. They cannot get themselves totally out of the picture. This is a positive change.

Those of the new generation realize that real knowledge of a historical personage, period, or biblical passage demands the cultivation of a kind of give-and-take. Also in doing their work, they are increasingly aware that they are not only writing *about;* they are also writing *for.* They have a purpose for doing it. They are human beings with fears and hopes, and they select their topics, direct their research, and frame their writing with some audience and some goal in mind. The result is that *objectivity* is fading from view, and a candid awareness of one's personal *objective* is becoming more conscious.

The truth is that it is neither possible nor desirable to get oneself completely out of the picture, and this applies especially to anyone who reads and studies the Bible, whether in a living-room group or a scholar's library. It is a book that informs our faith communities, our culture, and, whether we like it or not, our own psyches. We carry it under our skins, imbedded in our languages and modes of thinking, even before we open it. And when we do open it, we have a genuine stake in what we find. The difference between participants in a base community or Bible study group and scholars is that the lay groups freely acknowledge this realization, while some professionals are still puzzled about how their personal involvement can be reconciled with their scholarly discipline. But they now realize that the quest for total objectivity is dead, and they struggle strenuously with that realization. The study of history has changed radically since I majored in it at college. It was fascinating then, but it is even more fascinating now.

I am grateful that this lively conversation among biblical scholars is under way. Because as the third, the "spiritual," phase of my ongoing life with the Bible unfolds, I know that, although my earlier narrative and later historical-critical phases were of indispensable value, they had to be incorporated into yet another phase. The key insight I gleaned from listening in on this lively conversation is this: "what it *meant*" and "what it *means*" *cannot really be separated.* Whether we are fully aware of it or not, we all go to the Bible *looking for something,* and what we are looking for is shaped by who we are, how old we are, our class, the racial and gender composition of our society, and even by the temperament of the era in which we live. Young black inmates in a Southern prison cell hear the story of Moses and the pharaoh quite differently from the way the warden does. Impoverished Brazilian peasants read the Sermon on the Mount, with its promise to the poor and its dire warnings to the rich, from a different angle than that of the landowner. Women read those passages in Paul's Letters that mandate their silence from a perspective many men simply do not share.

The emerging consensus of this conversation about how to approach the Bible is that we should put aside any pretense of total objectivity as illusory and self-serving. The way ahead is what my colleague Elisabeth Schüssler Fiorenza aptly terms "self-conscious relativity."[1] This requires our being quite explicit about "where we are coming from" and what we hope to find as we read the Bible, and that we expect others to be just as candid. Little about the past reveals itself to a supposedly detached and "value-neutral" spectator, and this includes biblical passages. Christians claim that God continues to "speak" to us from the Bible, but the Bible "speaks to us" only when we come to it with honest questions and real hopes, not as distanced outside observers. On this count the nonexperts who gather in Bible study groups demonstrate an important insight.

But members of Bible study groups can also profit from the hard work of people who engage in scholarly "biblical studies." Regrettably, just as biblical scholars sometimes sneer at Bible study groups, the people who attend these groups often view biblical scholars as long-winded pedants who make unnecessarily complex interpretations in tomes that are dense and incomprehensible. Unfortunately, the images these two groups of people have of each other have some truth in them. Still, the two groups have something vital to learn from each other. The scholars could pick up hints from the mind-set that participants in Bible study groups and base communities bring to the Bible. But these participants ignore to their disadvantage the knowledge of the Bible accumulated over the past century by the historical-critical researchers. Finding out as best we can where the writer of a particular book of the Bible is "coming from" and to whom it was addressed are key elements in hearing what the Bible says to us today.

Simply stated, it is essential to take the historical dimension seriously, but it is even more important not to get stuck in it. Consequently, I have decided in the pages that follow not to describe these technical, historical ways of examining the Bible as "critical," even though many of its practitioners do. My reason is that in ordinary language, as opposed to scholarly discourse, the word "critical" carries unavoidable negative overtones. It often means to "disparage" or "denigrate," but I do not believe that at their best this is what the historical-critical scholars of the Bible intend to do. They want readers to understand the Bible better.

My hope in writing this book is to construct a bridge between "Bible study" and "biblical studies" in the light of a "spiritual" approach to the Bible. My objective is to help nonspecialists glean from the sometimes intimidating work of biblical scholars perspectives they can use in their own study of the Bible and at the same time to encourage professional scholars to appreciate the insights they can gain from Bible study groups. My plan is to discuss several books of the Bible selected in part because they span the entire scripture and in part because of what each one can teach us about how to integrate Bible study with biblical studies. I would add that I believe God's reality is ultimately inexpressible and certainly cannot be captured by our human gender distinctions, so I support current efforts to render hymns and prayers into gender neutral language. However, to avoid the clumsiness of "he/she" in citing the words of a biblical text, I will follow the original usage. In this case, I prefer the archaic to the awkward.

Here are the biblical books I will discuss, together with the particular mode of historical research each one illustrates:

- *Genesis* provides an excellent opportunity to investigate "source analysis," the attempt to identify the traditions, written and oral, that were patched together to compile the book.

- *Exodus* gives us a chance to learn how the most recent techniques of biblical archaeology augment our understanding of a biblical text.

- *Joshua* requires that we learn from "narrative theory" how to distinguish between history, legend, and saga and the values of each genre.

- *Job* invites us to apply literary theory to the Bible as well as to compare the original with recent fictionalized versions.

- The *Prophets* can best be understood if we are familiar with "form analysis," the study of the external shapes and internal structure of given passages.

- In reading the *Gospels* we will see how what scholars call "redaction history" (editing), the careful comparison of the Gospels with each other, and "translation studies" give us a more rounded picture of Jesus and his ministry.

- To see *Paul's Letters,* which he wrote as he traversed the Roman Empire, in a clearer light, we will use a more recent method called "empire studies."

- Finally, for *Revelation,* one of the most perplexing parts of the Bible, we will see how the history of "canonization" (of why and how it is in the Bible) and the history of its use enable us to overcome some of the difficulties it poses.

In addition to these research methods, I will also discuss a highly instructive way of reading the Bible that has been especially helpful to me. It is sometimes called the "history of interpretation" approach. Its thesis is that how people read the Bible in centuries past, from its earliest interpreters to its more recent ones, has something important to tell us about how to read it today. In a way it enlarges the circle of our Bible study group or of our fellow historical analysts by bringing in people who studied it at different times under different circumstances. It frees us from the "tyranny of the present," widens our perspective, and sometimes jars us out of our unexamined assumptions. We can accomplish a similar stretching of our take on the Bible by reading the works of commentators from another culture, gender, or ethnic situation, with different life experiences.

Underlying the way I call on all the methods of biblical studies discussed in this book is an approach that might be termed "dialogical," because it requires us to interact with a biblical passage the way we might with another human being. When we want to get to know a person, perhaps we try at first to find out as much as we can *about* him or her. But if we really want to get to *know* the person, we cannot just observe, however intently, disclosing nothing of ourselves. We have to open up. We listen, we speak, we may argue, we listen again. We try to fathom the way the person thinks. We may test our impressions with others who know the same individual. Most important, if we enter this process in a spirit of dialogue, we must be ready to hear things we do not want to hear and, after listening carefully, to agree or disagree with what we hear a given text saying. The path continues. It does not end.

But as we get ready to begin at the beginning, our question is, "How do we start down this route?" When I answer this for myself, I go back to the three stages of my life with the Bible: the narrative, the historical, and the spiritual. This means that the best way to read any passage in the Bible is to incorporate all three elements.

First, never forget that the *story* is utterly fundamental, even in a letter or a psalm. Ask, "What is happening here?"

Second, become an amateur *history* detective and uncover the "who, when, where, and why" about a particular text. Find out something about what people from other eras and other standpoints say about it. I will include some "Study Tips" throughout the book to assist with this step.

Then, move to the *spiritual* stage. Start to engage the text in a no-holds-barred wrestling match. Listen, and be ready to change, but also to argue. Respect the right of the text to say what it says and not what you would like it to say. But don't be cowed by it. Insist on your right to see things differently, if you do. This is what I mean by "dialogue," and if you open both your mind and your heart to it, the spiritual *meaning* for today of any text will find its way across the centuries. I guarantee it.

Study Tips ————————————————————————

When reading any book of the Bible, first read it all the way through to follow the story line, which in many cases is packed with multiple actors and numerous side plots, but which usually has a definite beginning, a middle, and a climax.

Next, find out something about where and why this book was first written, by whom and to whom. This is called authorship and "provenance." With most biblical books this step is fairly easy, since countless scholars have been doing the spadework for years.

Then consult two or three translations to free yourself from the tyranny of textual literalism. (It might even be useful to employ these different translations in the initial reading.)

Next, find out why this text was included in the Bible at all. For some books that is not so obvious. The technical term for this is the "history of canonization," and I will be introducing some suggestions for finding out about it.

Next, look into the way this portion of the Bible has been interpreted in previous generations and the various, often wildly conflicting ways it is being interpreted today, especially by people from different cultures and social strata.

Finally, get to the main point. What, if anything, does this book have to say to us today and exactly who is the "us" to whom it does or does not speak?

1

Serpents, Floods, and the Mystery of Evil

The Book of Genesis

In the beginning God created the heavens and the earth. The earth was without form and void, and darkness was upon the face of the deep; and the Spirit of God was moving over the face of the waters. And God said, "Let there be light"; and there was light. And God saw that the light was good; and God separated the light from the darkness. God called the light Day, and the darkness he called Night. And there was evening and there was morning, one day.

GENESIS 1:1–5, RSV

"In the beginning" are the first words of the first book of the Bible. Even though most scholars now agree that Genesis was written and compiled well after some of the other biblical books, there are still good reasons to begin with it. When the rabbis who initially arranged the order of the books of the Hebrew Bible placed it first, they knew just what they were doing. Genesis is a collection of stories by four or five different authors assembled by an editor, who may well have added some elements of his own. The book is also a compelling one, packed with action, drama, and a host of lusty characters. Perhaps the rabbis sensed that, if readers began with Genesis, they might find it hard to put the rest of the book down.

In Genesis we meet the wily serpent, which Milton thought so captivating that in *Paradise Lost* he made him a suave, smooth-talking Don Juan. Here also is Cain, who bludgeoned his brother, Abel, to death because his own sacrifice was not accepted by God, thus committing the first, but—alas—not the last slaying inspired by a religious dispute. Here is the chronicle of Noah and the great flood, the dove, the rainbow, and the embarrassing aftermath of the old man's unzipped drunkenness. Here is the saga of Abraham, the "father of faith," a founding figure for Jews, Christians, and Muslims. Here is Jacob, cheating his brother, Esau, out of his rightful heritage, wrestling all night with an angel (or God), and then courting the lovely Rachel. But most gripping of all, here is the epic of Joseph and his jealous brothers, which Thomas Mann spun out into one of the great novels of the twentieth century, *Joseph in Egypt*. To be unfamiliar with these characters and plots exacts a cost. It makes one an outsider to some of the best literature ever written.

In addition to the engaging stories we find in it, there is another reason to begin with Genesis. We are trying in the present book to deepen our appreciation of the Bible by seeing it in the light of modern biblical studies. By stepping into Genesis we tread on scarred turf, over which many hard-fought scholarly battles have been waged, not just fights between literalists, historical critics, and symbolic interpreters, but internal fights within all these camps. And there are still unexploded mines here.

I also have a personal reason for starting with Genesis. It was in studying it that I was first introduced to contemporary biblical scholarship and had to cope, given my evangelical background, with how this analytic scalpel first seemed to threaten my own faith, but eventually helped strengthen it. Consequently, my approach here will be to select from the many nuggets Genesis offers some that will best illustrate my basic purpose.

Here is how it happened to me. Genesis is a *collection* of stories by *different* writers. But when I went to seminary I had no inkling of such a thing. At that time, however, the "multiple-source hypothesis," though hardly new, was still regnant. Our Old Testament professor told us all to buy a box of colored pencils, so we could draw vertical lines in the margins of our Bibles to mark which parts came from the "Yahwist" source (blue), which from the "Priestly" source (red), which from the "Elohist" (yellow), and so forth. These different writers, he explained, can be identified not only by what they call God ("Yahweh" or "Elohim"), but also by their different vocabularies, their varying approaches, and even their disparate theologies. The consensus at the time held that the Yahwist source, which is now referred to as "J" (for the German *Jahweh*), dates from sometime between 950 and 800 BCE. The Elohist source, "E," was said to come from about a hundred years later. A third source, called "P" for "Priestly," was dated to a 150 years after "E." (In recent studies all these dates have been sharply contested.)

I dutifully bought the pencils and drew the lines. I am sure our professor thought this was a useful exercise, and in retrospect I admit he was probably right. But at the time it was a little disquieting. I wondered what all this mincing and slicing would do to the voice of Genesis, to its overall narrative and to its spiritual power. But I also realized that the multiple-source theory did help explain why there are different accounts not just of creation, but also of the flood, God's promise to Abraham, and the moving drama of Hagar and Ishmael. The interweaving of these disparate strands also explains why at times the surface of Genesis exhibits a certain jerky, discontinuous quality. The seams sometimes stick out. Little by little I decided that recognizing Genesis as the work of many hands did not diminish its spiritual significance. It deepened it.

I still have on my shelf that edition of the Bible, with its multihued marginal markings, its covers now missing. But I had not been out of school long before another way of studying the Hebrew scriptures assumed front stage. It was called the "narrative approach." Some of its supporters questioned or even rejected the multiple-source theory. Others claimed that focusing on it too much, with or without colored pencils, could make one forget that at some point *someone* put all these pieces together, and that the overall trajectory of the whole edited work was what really mattered. Still others claimed that Genesis had grown by a kind of accumulation process, not by calculated editing and pasting. These newer modes of study were especially favored by people, including some evangelicals, who had always been suspicious of "chopping the Bible up," but many others found them sensible too. In my view, it is immensely helpful to be familiar with the sometimes inconsistent sources of Genesis, but also that we enjoy its matchless narratives.

Subsequently the narrative method has been complemented by at least two other approaches. One is derived in part from literary studies, and its proponents call it "rhetorical criticism." This means reading a book or passage and asking questions such as: To whom is the writer or editor aiming this text? Who is he or she trying to convince or refute, and why? What is being left out and why? This is also an especially helpful approach, because it enables us to see not only that the different writers of the Bible *differed with* each other, but also that they *argued against* each other. Think of Genesis as a kind of panel discussion in which the panelists (drawn in this case from different centuries) present their divergent views on some of the persistent questions of human life, such as guilt, responsibility, death, suffering, jealousy, family tensions, and our relationship to God. In the end you see that, although they differ, their views also overlap, and all of them agree that what they are talking about is of pressing concern.

Another recent mode of study is called "effect history." It focuses on the question: How has this text been used, applied, or deployed in the centuries since it was written? This method makes sense to many people, because it takes seriously the question the average person might well ask about any part of the Bible: What difference has it made? We will see later how this method is especially helpful in studying the last book of the Bible, Revelation.

Not everyone needs to master the ins and outs of these tempests among the scriptural literati. The net result is that we can not only appreciate the Bible as a long conversation, even as a series of ongoing quarrels; we can also view our own reading and study as a continuation of this conversation. The Bible not only presents multiple points of view; it invites multiple interpretations, and generations of its readers have joined this uninterrupted colloquy.

For me, the discovery of the profusion of biblical voices and subsequent interpreters was a welcome one. It still is. In an age of both religious conflict and interfaith dialogue, to find that the Bible itself, beginning with the book of Genesis, fosters a kind of pluralism is refreshing and timely. Indeed, when one looks carefully at the deity described in Genesis, it seems that God smiles on miscellany rather than uniformity in the world.

This becomes even clearer when we learn that the Hebrew word most translators have rendered with the word "create" actually carries a somewhat different significance. The Hebrew term is *bara,* and it is used in the Bible exclusively for the activity of God. It does not mean "to make" in the sense of "to build" or "to construct." There is another word for that. Rather, *bara* has the sense of "to order" or "to assign a place or role." It seems that God's work in "creation" is to compose a symphony of diverse sounds and tonalities that is intended to be a harmonious whole, complete with counterpoint and minor chords. But unlike the old deist conception of the clockmaker God, who constructs an intricate mechanism and then leaves it to run on its own, the biblical image of God is more like that of a composer-director-performer who constantly rearranges the balance if the trumpets or the bass violins start to drown out the flutes and the violas. Further, he must do so delicately while the orchestra continues to play. To extend the metaphor, in this creation God enlists the musicians in continuing to compose what still remains an "unfinished symphony." Now with this biblical research in hand, let us begin with "in the beginning."

THE CREATION STORIES

As we peruse the familiar accounts of the creation stories (1:1–2:4a; 2:4b–31) with the help of what biblical studies have contributed, we immediately recognize important discrepancies among the different strands. And if we consult commentaries, we will also become aware of a large dose of disagreement among competent scholars, not just on what a particular verse *means,* but even on what it actually *says.* This variation of opinion starts with the first verse. Although standard English translations render it, "In the beginning God created the heavens and the earth," most experts on the original Hebrew agree that the words mean, "In the beginning *of God's creating* the heavens and the earth . . ."[1]

The dispute may at first appear it to be merely grammatical, but it is more than that. Was God doing something else before he started his "creating of the world"? The second verse ("The earth was without form and void, and darkness was upon the face of the deep") raises equally puzzling dilemmas. Did God generate the world out of nothing (*ex nihilo*), or did he shape it out of some preexisting chaos of "formless matter"? These questions may seem esoteric, but they allow us to foresee a theme that will recur time and again throughout the Bible, from Genesis to Job to the book of Revelation: the mystery of evil.

The answers scholars give to the *ex nihilo* or non–*ex nihilo* question are complicated, but the consensus is that "P," the writer of the account that appears in chapter 1, may have wanted to depict a God-shaping-chaos scenario, while the second, "J," preferred the creation out of nothing (2:4b–5). If "P" is right, with his God-shaping-chaos description, where did the chaos come from? Did God also create that as well? This becomes a critical question for generations of philosophers, because this chaos (not God) is often interpreted as the source of evil and disorder in the world. But if the second version ("J"), the *ex nihilo* account, is right, then we are left with the question of where this disorder and evil came from.

Theologians have faced a strenuous test trying to explore this ambiguity. Those who opt for an *ex nihilo* version do so in part because they are concerned that if there was "something there" along with God before the creating began, then what was it (a "formless void"?) and, most important, who created it? Or was it "always there"? Both the supporters of "J" and those of "P" want to steer clear of a dualistic theology. They want to avoid any hint of two creators, a good cop and a bad cop.

A dualistic theology was present in the world in which the biblical creation narratives were written. It assumed classical form in Zoroastrianism, which appeared in Persia in about 1000 BCE. In it, two equally strong deities, the good, illuminating deity Ahura Mazda and the bad, destructive god Angra Mainyu, were locked in endless combat. The editors who pasted Genesis together were aware of the Zoroastrian religion, and they wanted to spell out a quite different view of God: as one who is *not* the source of evil. But did they succeed? God no sooner creates men and women and places them in a luxuriant garden than the serpent appears. And where did he come from? We will return to this snake below.

The mystery of the source of evil has troubled thoughtful human beings from the beginning. At first it was thrashed out in the language of myth, as in Genesis. The discussion continued. Think about the book of Job, in which God strikes a deal with Satan to torment a righteous man to test his faith. Think about the demonic forces Jesus contended with or the "principalities and powers" Paul mentions. Think of the terrible horses with lions' teeth and scorpions' tails conjured up in Revelation 9. In all these instances, the writers grapple with the riddle of evil using the language of symbol and myth.

When scholars of religion use the word "myth," they do not mean something that, unlike a "fact," is simply untrue. Rather, "myth" is a narrative that, although not necessarily factually accurate, is nonetheless true in a deeper and more significant sense. A myth is *essentially true* because it is a symbol, and a symbol is something that points beyond itself to a truth that might be difficult or impossible to express in ordinary language. In this sense a myth is a *narrated* symbol just as a ritual is an *enacted* symbol. For example, when we say the Adam and Eve story is a myth, we suggest it is a story that is not empirically factual, but one that nonetheless illuminates a profound truth about the human condition. Much of the difficulty we have in reading the Bible today results from literalism—when we mistakenly look for facts instead of recognizing and appreciating the profound truth of myth.

After the Bible the argument about evil waxed more philosophical, but has continued to attract novelists, playwrights, and poets. It is a question that has aggravated theologians for centuries. It still does. The twentieth-century Russian Orthodox theologian Nicholas Berdyaev preferred a view of creation that does not see God making something out of nothing. He favored a God who struggles with *me-on,* Berdyaev's Greek term for an unformed void that was and still is the source of anxiety, anguish, and sin in the world. Brilliant and original, Berdyaev was, however, regarded with profound suspicion by many of his fellow theologians. Still, when I was a theological student, Richard Niebuhr, a professor who had a special interest in the problem of evil, recommended him to me. I remember sitting up half the night engrossed in his book *The Destiny of Man*.[2]

Today I still think Berdyaev may have had something. As I will mention later, I am not satisfied with the *ex nihilo* interpretation of the creation account, which implies a God who is utterly omnipotent and therefore does not have to struggle against evil as we humans do. Nor am I comfortable with a cosmic dualism. Consequently, I am glad the Bible allows for, indeed encourages, a range of views on this subject. I find it appropriate that the Bible says some quite contrasting things, even about some weighty matters, *from its very opening*, because this tips us off that for some sixty-five books to come there will be more of this divergence. In reading the Bible, get ready not for unanimity, not for a single cadence, but for what the New Testament Letter to the Hebrews calls a "great cloud of witnesses."

In any case, let us be clear that neither of the writers of the two creation stories was trying to formulate some proto-scientific theory of how the universe came into being or how the various species of animals appeared. These accounts are not relevant, one way or another, to the stale creation-versus-evolution argument that still ruffles school boards and textbook writers in some parts of America. The writers of Genesis had a different purpose in mind. They were also not concerned about what one philosopher has recently suggested is the fundamental question of all philosophy: Why is there something and not nothing? (Or why does the world exist anyway?) Genesis does not assign a single verse to this intriguing riddle. Some of the earlier Near Eastern myths the biblical writers drew on had this puzzle in mind, but the writers of Genesis were interested in something else. They had three objectives.

First, they wanted to sharply differentiate God both from pantheism (the idea that the world itself is divine) and polytheism (the idea that there are a number of equally powerful deities). Thus they insisted that the sun, moon, and stars, which some neighboring religions considered gods, were decidedly not. They were creations of God, not gods themselves, and therefore not appropriate for worship. As we will notice later, the Bible does at points allow for the existence of other "gods," but they are not in the same league with the one God, who "created" (in one way or another) heaven and earth.

Second, the writers of Genesis were focused on their own times. They were not antiquarians, peering curiously into the dim recesses of some primeval past. Rather, in looking at the world around them, they wondered why human life seemed to be so nasty, brutish, and short. If God is good, and God declared the world to be "very good," then why is there evil in the world and in us? These writers advanced their reasoning about violence and disorder not by turning to history or psychology, but by using mythic language, which can be a powerful way of speaking about the here and now at the deepest level. They obviously thought the mythic idiom was a more potent way to portray the reality they wanted to convey. But, like us, they found no satisfying answer. Is this why they give us not one, but two accounts of the creation?

Third, the Genesis writers were interested in something in addition to these perennial questions. This concern has recently been brilliantly explored by the Israeli scholar Avivah Gottlieb Zornberg, who outlines her own interpretation of the creation story. Pointing to the first day of creation in the biblical version, when God "separated the light from the darkness," she suggests that the first action attributed to God is one of *decentralization*, a process that continues in the following days as well. In other words, as she explains in her insightful book on Genesis, from the beginning God busied himself breaking up his unitary and monolithic power into other centers. God's work, she writes is one of "increasing complexity," of "primal disintegration." Paraphrasing the great medieval rabbinic commentator Rashi, she continues, "The main business of that [first] day was the radical transformation of reality from the encompassing oneness of God to the possibility of more-than-one."[3]

Rashi and Zornberg give us clearer insight into what the writers of Genesis wanted to convey. More than simply arguing for his oneness, they wanted to describe the *character* of God. They wanted to show how he exercises his divinity in a radically different way than did the king or tyrant gods of their neighbors. They pictured a God who is intent on compromising his oneness, on sharing his rule by arranging a universe with independent centers of power, even to the point of giving the human being the responsibility to name the animals. The portrait that emerges is of a God who wants to dismantle his monopoly both of being and of power, so much so that the creation became capable of opposing him, which in turn opened the door for both bane and blessing.

Here, then, is another point where source analysis becomes a useful tool for understanding Genesis. In this instance the comparison of sources is not restricted to the various writers of the book itself, but includes the prebiblical Babylonian and Egyptian religions these biblical writers knew about and drew on, but with which they sharply differed at important points.

The vexing issue of evil, which casts its shadow over the first verses of the Bible, bleeds over from the creation narratives into everything that follows. It throbs as a basso continuo under the chapters on Adam and Eve, Cain and Abel, Noah, Jacob and Esau, and Joseph and his jealous brothers. We start, of course, with Adam and Eve.

ADAM AND EVE AND THE SERPENT

Evil rears its slithery head almost immediately after the creation (3:1). Adam ("Man") and Eve ("Life") live in a paradisiacal garden. In Hebrew "Eden" means "delight." They were naked and unashamed, all their wants lavishly provided for. But they soon became impatient with being merely mortal; they longed for complete supremacy. They were not content to be human; they wanted to be "like God" (3:5). Ironically they craved to possess precisely the kind of total control God had just been relinquishing.

One reason to recognize the spiritual objective of Genesis, and not to read it as an attempt at a prescientific cosmology, is so that we waste no time trying to compare it with the big-bang or string theory. These tactics may be popular, but they allow *us* to slip out of the picture too easily. Genesis is about the present, not the past. Adam and Eve are not some remote forebears. They are us. We are not cursed by their sin or the juice of their fatal apple; we are enmeshed in the fruits of our own collective narcissism and irresponsibility. Nor can we pass the blame on to others with either

"The serpent told me . . ." or "That is not my department." We have to assume the responsibility. Consequently, we are the exiles who now dwell "east of Eden." Our world today is hardly one of sheer delight.

Even though Adam and Eve no longer reside in the garden, generations of poets, artists, writers, and philosophers have been unable to stay away from it. It has remained a paradise for imagination, speculation, elaboration, and blaming others. Male interpreters have seized on the statement that Eve was the one who first gave in to the serpent's wiles (and as we have pondered above, where did that seductive snake come from in a world God had just declared "very good"?). Everyone blames everyone else. Nobody takes responsibility.

Consider also John Milton's famous retelling of the story in his *Paradise Lost*. Milton raises an old theological and philosophical question, the notion of the "fortunate fall" (*felix culpa*). This idea implies that the primal couple are better off than they would have been, had they continued to snuggle in the garden of innocent bliss. They had to grow up, as we all must (remember, this is us as well). They were expelled from infantile naïveté into the harsh but necessary landscape of adulthood. And in this adult phase they now had to cope with the deepest mystery, namely, death. Would the two have died eventually, even in Eden? Some theologians speculate that they might not have. Others opine that they would have died eventually, but that after their expulsion things got worse, because they had to live with the daily realization that they were mortal. Still, one might ask, is that realization a punishment or a blessing?

Reading the Adam and Eve story inevitably raises in many people's minds the question of "original sin." Have all generations since them had to pay the price for their disobedience or irresponsibility? Do we still live under their "curse"? In reading what Genesis might tell us about this question today, it is important to remember that the term "original sin" does not appear in the Bible. It is a concept invented by theologians in an effort to explain the frustrating dilemma in which we often find ourselves in our efforts to live a good life; we are trapped by both society's expectations and our own and contradictory impulses. Thinking about this we recognize ourselves to be both the *inheritors* of the distortions of past history and also, often despite our best intentions, *contributors* to the continuation of those distortions. Like Adam and Eve in the story, we still find ourselves eager to be in full control of ourselves and others (to be "like God"), and like them we tend to palm off responsibility for our actions on something or someone else ("The serpent told me . . .").

For the Protestant theologian Reinhold Niebuhr, the underlying meaning of "original sin" is that, as both nations and individuals, we tend to identify our own view of what is right or good with what is right and good for everyone. Giving it a more philosophical import, the German theologian Paul Tillich writes that original sin refers to the sense of "alienation" we experience as finite beings separated from our essential nature. For both men, because we are ensnared in what sometimes feels like a vast spiderweb, our thrashing around only makes it worse. We need something from the outside to help us, and thus—as we will see in subsequent chapters in this book—the biblical concept of "grace," expressed in different ways throughout the Bible, enters the picture as God's benign response to the idea that "original sin" seeks to express.

Like many other doctrinal formulations that have arisen over the past centuries, the doctrine of original sin may once have helped clarify our human situation, but unfortunately it also produced some negative by-products. One was the belief that sin was passed on biologically from parents to children like a genetic disease, and this mistaken view sometimes led to a suspicion of sexuality itself. But this is a theory hardly any theologian of any tradition would defend today. An even more destructive idea derived from the notion of "original sin" was a kind of fatalism, the conviction that we are wholly determined by "Adam's fall" and therefore cannot be held accountable for our own behavior. Ironically, this attitude mirrors the excuses offered by both Adam and Eve in the story when they blamed the serpent for what they had themselves decided to do.

Our challenge in reading Genesis today is how we can translate the book's valid insight into human reality in a way that both preserves the truth "original sin" points to, but avoids the pitfalls and detours it has created. One theologian, Hans Ott, proposes that "original sin" might more accurately be termed "tragic enmeshment." This proposal may or may not be helpful, but it rightly suggests that we need to continue to search for a more resonant and faithful way of articulating the truth that is both expressed and distorted by the idea of original sin.

After Eden, Adam and Eve knew they were going to die. This suggests that our uniqueness as human beings lies not in our reason or imagination or in our use of language. Nor does it lie in our mortality. Many animals display a certain kind of reason and even speechlike behavior. And all animals, humans included, must die. Rather, our uniqueness as humans may lie in our *awareness* of our mortality, which does seem to be specific to our species. As a youngster I used to speculate, as many of us did and maybe still do, on what it might be like not to have to die. At some point it dawned on me that endless life might eventually become unbearably boring. Much later when I asked a class I was teaching how many of them, given the chance, would choose to live forever, only one student raised her hand. After a hundred, a thousand, ten thousand years, wouldn't we all be ready to call it quits?

As a theologian I have continued to be interested in just how special our awareness of our mortality is. When I talk with colleagues in anthropology and zoology about this, some anthropologists suggest that one of the first evidences of the emergence of *Homo sapiens* from our simian forebears is the appearance of burial mounds and markers. Even the most advanced primates do not make them. A mother chimp may cling to a dead infant for a while, but in time she simply discards it. Animals know when one of the herd or pride is dead, but do they realize that one day they too will die and be left behind? It is impossible to say, but there is no evidence that they do. What about the legendary "place where elephants go to die"? A zoologist who has studied pachyderms assured me that it was just that, mere legend.

The point here is that the human awareness not just of mortality in general, but of one's own inevitable death may be the primal source of art, culture, and religion, from the cave paintings at Lascaux to the great cathedrals. I am not suggesting here that our awareness of mortality inevitably produces the longing for an afterlife (though it may), but that it raises the fundamental question of the meaning of *this* life. Without the "fortunate fall" this question might never have arisen.

We will now examine how the rest of Genesis plays out this preoccupation with evil, how it surfaces in a range of human relationships, and the creative ways both God and his human creature have coped with it. Among these, we turn first to the story of Noah, one of the most familiar in all of scripture.

NOAH, THE ARK, AND THE DELUGE

Here, as with the creation stories, the Hebrew writers had heard the epics of deluges told by their Sumerian and Babylonian neighbors in the ancient Near East. The most intriguing of these is the one found in the Babylonian tale of Gilgamesh, the hero who becomes paralyzed by the fear of his own death and so sets out to find one of his ancestors who, he believes, has achieved immortality. The ancestor, named Utnapishtim, recounts to Gilgamesh how he and his wife found the secret. It seems that when the gods decided to destroy the world, one of them told him in a dream to tear down his house and build a ship in which he could save himself and "the seed of all living things." Utnapishtim then loads the vessel with his family, both tame and wild animals, and men skilled in crafts (presumably to be on hand when the rebuilding of the world began). Then the rains poured down, the rivers flooded, bursting their dikes, and thunder roared so fiercely that even the gods (who were apparently on board along with everyone else) were so terrified, they "cowered against the walls of the ship." Eventually the storm ended and Utnapishtim sent out two birds, a dove and a swallow, which returned to the boat, and then a raven, which did not. Finally, a god named En-lil arrived on the scene and rewarded Utnapishtim and his wife with immortality. End of story.

Today when readers of the Hebrew Bible read or hear this hoary old saga, they respond in a number of ways. Some are confused, because it bears so many similarities to the Noah story. Others have seized upon it to try to demonstrate the historicity of a universal flood. I have another, and I think more valuable, reading to suggest. First, the Gilgamesh legend does not establish the historicity of the great deluge. True, there are such accounts in other ancient literature, but the story is missing in vast areas of the world. More important, reading it as history diverts our attention from the most significant consideration: noticing how the Hebrew writers transformed it so that the Noah story delivers a radically different spiritual message.

In the Hebrew version God decides to punish the world because of its moral corruption and violence. In the Babylonian epic, the gods are more like the Greek deities. They cheat and deceive and express no apparent reason for wanting to destroy the world. And they cower in terror in the hold of the ship, as they become victims of their own destructiveness. When the flood subsides, Utnapishtim and his wife are transformed into immortal gods. Noah and his sons, on the other hand, are told to "be fruitful and multiply, and fill the earth." God then places a rainbow in the sky and declares that he will never destroy the earth again.

> *Then God said to Noah and to his sons with him, "Behold, I establish my covenant with you and your descendants after you, and with every living creature that is with you, the birds, the cattle, and every beast of the earth with you, as many as came out of the ark. I establish my covenant with you, that never again shall all flesh be cut off by the waters of a flood, and never again shall there be a flood to destroy the earth." And God said, "This is the sign of the covenant which I make between me and you and every living creature that is with you, for all future generations: I set my bow in the cloud, and it shall be a sign of the covenant between me and the earth. When I bring clouds over the earth and the bow is seen in the clouds, I will remember my covenant which is between me and you and every living creature of all flesh; and the waters shall never again become a flood to destroy all flesh. When the bow is in the clouds, I will look upon it and remember the everlasting covenant between God and every living creature of all flesh that is upon the earth." God said to Noah, "This is the sign of the covenant which I have established between me and all flesh that is upon the earth." (9:8–17, RSV)*

But after this glorious spectacle something both ordinary and extraordinary takes place. Noah does not become a god. As if to underscore his ordinary humanity, he knocks back a little too much of his own homegrown wine and gets drunk. Utnapishtim is the one who becomes a god, not Noah. Not only does Noah get sloshed; he lets his clothes fall off and becomes an embarrassment to his sons. After that, as if to underscore his mortality, the biblical account concludes: "All the days of Noah were nine hundred fifty years; and he died" (9:29).

Comparing the flood stories of Gilgamesh and Noah is highly illuminating. They share a common thread, but the moral and spiritual insights they impart differ radically. The God of the Genesis version has little in common with the Babylonian gods. The biblical God's anger is kindled by the violence his creatures wreak on each other. And after the flood has passed, he expresses regret about what he had done and vows not to do it again. The Babylonian gods do not repent. In short, the story of Noah, like the parts of the Bible that precede it, is about morality and the mystery of evil in a world that God declared to be good. It is a question that still haunts us today, and this is what makes Genesis such a strangely contemporary book.

Study Tip ───

In "The Flood," in vol. 2 of *The Interpreter's Dictionary of the Bible* (ed. Keith R. Crim and George A. Buttrick, 5 vols. [Nashville, TN: Abingdon, 1981]), J. H. Marks presents a fair and balanced summary of earlier epics, including Gilgamesh, and provides a useful bibliography.

───

I say "contemporary" in a quite immediate sense. One hundred years ago, before the twentieth century's titanic world wars, death camps, and gulags and its relentless bombing of civilian populations, what had previously been called the "problem of evil" almost disappeared from the philosophical agenda. If, at least for some people, a benevolent deity was no longer in the picture at all, then the old way of formulating the issue (how could a good and powerful God allow for innocent human suffering?) was now moot. Some even assumed that evil was the product of human ignorance and superstition and that with the advance of science and education it would gradually disappear. But after that horrendous century had unfolded its chilling display of hatred, cruelty, and unprecedented destruction, this callow conjecture was no longer credible. A new chapter in the history of philosophical reflection on evil began with Hannah Arendt's controversial *Eichmann in Jerusalem,* which she subtitled *A Report on the Banality of Evil.*[4] In that book Arendt argued that in our time evil is not merely a question of bad or malevolent people; it has to do with our not being attentive to how our seemingly small roles in complex and intricate societies can result in unspeakable evil. Eichmann claimed that all he did was to fulfill the responsibilities of his job and remain loyal to his government. He made sure the trains ran on time. The fact that those trains were crammed with innocent men, women, and children being transported to Auschwitz was not his department. Since Arendt's book, new information about Eichmann has emerged, raising questions about his seeming naïveté. But her work served an important purpose. Since it was published, a small library of books on the topic of evil has appeared, and once again the themes of the book of Genesis are back on the table. But it is well to remember that that is where the discussion started.[5]

ABRAHAM AND HIS WIFE/SISTER

The story of Abraham, Sarah, and the pharaoh is one I never heard in Sunday school. Nor have I ever heard a sermon about it, even though it is told three times in Genesis, each with its own twist (12:10–20; 20:1–18; 26:1–11). The version "J" tells (12:10–20) is the most unvarnished. Abraham (still Abram at the time) took his wife Sarah to Egypt, because "there was a famine in the land." Because Sarah was so ravishing, however, he was afraid the locals would lust after her and possibly kill him to get her. So he instructed Sarah to tell people she was his sister. Sure enough, when they arrived, the Egyptian princes noticed her loveliness and even reported it to the pharaoh, who immediately had her brought "into [his own] house." In plain words she became a part of his harem. She apparently pleased the ruler a lot, because in gratitude he plied Abram with gifts and rewards. But God was displeased with what the pharaoh had done, so he infected him and his household with plagues (a prelude to the Exodus story?). Somehow—we are not told how—the pharaoh learned that Sarah was actually Abram's wife, and that he had been duped into doing something wrong. So he sent for Abram, upbraided him for his deceit, and sent him and his wife packing.

It is hard to sort out what is most disconcerting about this saga. Was Abram an unprincipled coward who was willing to lie and then to reap the pharaoh's benefits for his wife's services in his royal boudoir? Or was he just being canny, maybe even preserving his and his wife's lives, so that they could fulfill God's promise by producing descendants who would eventually outnumber the stars in the skies? Did he feel any discomfort at receiving all the sheep and oxen and camels and slaves he got from the pharaoh for acting as his procurer? Is there something we are missing here?

Before delving further into the moral enigma contained in this story, we might notice that whatever else it does, it provides us with three invaluable insights. First, it should disabuse us of the innocent notion that the Bible is a reliable source of moral paradigms we can hold up to our children as ethical models. The late Rabbi Marshall Meyer, an astute teacher of the Torah, once remarked to me that there is scarcely one figure in the entire Hebrew scripture we would want our children to emulate. That may be an overstatement. Another rabbi, Nahum M. Sarna, who wrote the commentary for the Jewish Publication Society's volume on Genesis, puts it this way: "The biblical heroes are not portrayed as demigods or perfect human beings. They are mortals of flesh and blood, subject to the same temptations and possessed of the same frailties as are all other human beings."[6]

Second, the three versions of this one story tell us something about the character and predispositions of the three writers that will be useful when we encounter them later. Readers will form their own individual opinions about them, but here is mine:

1. "J" (12:10–20) is the Ernest Hemingway of the lot. His prose, here as in other passages, is terse and even at times plodding. He spares us too many adjectives. His God is a rather human character who gets angry, changes his mind, regrets what he has done, and otherwise acts the way most of us do. "J" has no interest in making Abraham look good. His portrayal is candid and unapologetic.

2. "E" (20:1–18), who is writing perhaps a hundred years later, displays a more delicate style and sensibility. He is a bit prudish. He changes the venue from Egypt to Gerar, a frontier town southwest of Canaan, and the royal personage is no longer the pharaoh, but Abimelech, a local king. Further, God intervenes to preserve Sarah's honor before the king has sex with her; and to save Abraham from appearing to be a liar, Sarah turns out to be his sister (well, half sister; same father, but a different mother) and also his wife. To top it off, the king heaps his favors (again the sheep and oxen and slaves) on Abraham not as a payment for sharing his wife/sister, but as a kind of reward for his honesty. He also throws in a thousand pieces of silver to sweeten the deal and allows the couple to stay in Gerar.

3. When we get to the third version of this troubled script (26:1–11), we cannot even be sure who the writer is. Is it "P," who worked another hundred years after "E"? Or is it, as many scholars argue, yet another "later source"? In any case what now appears is a scrupulously cleaned-up version. If the first was X-rated and the second suitable for minors accompanied by adults, this third one is certified as squeaky clean for even the most finicky. It is the family version. The location is still Gerar, but now Isaac and Rebekah have replaced Abraham and Sarah as the lead characters. The king does not get the heroine into his house, let alone into his four-poster. He merely glimpses her out a window as she is being hugged (the text says "fondled") by her husband. Deducing that she could not be his sister as announced,

which would have bordered on the incestuous, he confronts Isaac, who explains the whole thing. (Why he is fondling his wife in public is not explained.) The Peeping Tom king does not hold it against him and allows Isaac to live and prosper in his domain. Camera draws back, music swells, happy ending.

Attentive readers who are not aware of the different sources the ultimate editor drew on in pasting Genesis together might be understandably puzzled by these three chunks of material. Are they three separate incidents? When one considers the famine-migration-deception-discovery motif they all have in common, that seems highly unlikely. What we have here is a tiny gem of folk tradition polished by several hands. And remember that neither "J," "E," nor "P" (or whoever the final "late" writer was) knew they would one day be bundled together by an even later editor who was reluctant to cut anyone out.

This is an excellent example of how historical research into the Bible enlarges our appreciation of it. Now that we know about these multiple sources and have even been able to size up its different writers, we can read Genesis in a new way. Since we do not have a single version of something as central to the Hebrew religious tradition as the lives of Abraham and Sarah, Isaac and Rebekah, we should not expect a single version of anything else either. We can greet the different voices with gratitude. These stories prepare us for the contending voices we will meet throughout the Bible, the argument between Deuteronomy and Job, for example, and the four Gospels.

A third reason to treasure this somewhat unsavory libretto about a central figure in the Bible is that we can use it to illustrate the fabulous imagination of the rabbis in inventing what the Jewish tradition calls *midrashim*. *Midrashim* are stories not found in the Bible itself. They are imaginative elaborations and extensions of biblical episodes, invented and passed on over the generations, intended to render them more vivid and make them applicable to the present. A famous *midrash* (singular) of the Abraham and Sarah story is particularly rich. It goes like this:

God knew Sarah found herself in a compromising situation and he wanted to protect her virtue. So he summoned one of his angels and sent him down to hover over Pharaoh's canopied bed. Each time Pharaoh tried to remove one of Sarah's garments, the angel struck him a hard blow. When he tried to unbutton her blouse, the angel hit him on the head. When he sought to pull her slippers off, he punched him in the stomach. This went on all night, so that by dawn a bruised and battered Pharaoh sensed that something was awry. It was then that he discovered Sarah's true identity, and the rest is history.

This perils-of-Pauline snippet may help explain why I am an unapologetic aficionado of the *midrashim*. There are thousands of them (and we will refer to a few more in the course of this book), and they serve a wonderful purpose. They demonstrate the Bible's power to spark the imagination. They remind us that, like all good jokes and stories, the ones in the Bible call forth more jokes and stories.

JOSEPH AND HIS BROTHERS

The final chapters of Genesis (37–50) are devoted to the long saga of Joseph, the eleventh son of Jacob. As with previous parts of this first book of the Bible, the narrative seems to consist of a collection of legends about him that were eventually collected. Other than to David, more pages are devoted to Joseph than to any other figure in the Old Testament.

Joseph's life is marked by defeats and victories from start to finish. Apparently his father's favorite, he did not hesitate to flaunt his position. According to a *midrash* he was a bit effeminate and more than a little self-centered. Most people know the account of his being attacked by his brothers when he goes out to visit them as they tend the flocks, thrown into a pit, and eventually sold in Egypt as a slave. His spectacular rise to vizier in charge of the food supply, his temporary fall, and his restitution are the stuff of high drama. The description of his stalwart resistance to the seductive wiles of Potiphar's wife serves both as comic relief and proof positive of his unwavering moral fiber. Also, his large-hearted forgiveness of his brothers when they are forced by a famine to come to Egypt in search of food certifies to his character. If anything, Joseph may come across just a tad too perfect. Did he have any real flaws, as the *midrash* implies? How might David, for example, have responded to the come-hither allurements of Potiphar's wife? Given what we know about his escapade with Bathsheba, might he have been less resistant to her charms?

Genesis ends with a depiction of Joseph, still in Egypt, in his old age, his satisfaction at seeing his children's children, and his death at the age of 110. Before he dies, he makes his fellow Israelites swear that when God eventually leads them to the "promised land," they will carry his bones along with them. He was duly embalmed, which was the Egyptian custom, and according to Exodus 13:19 Moses took his body along with him when the Israelites left Egypt, and he was eventually buried in Shechem (Josh. 24:32). The link, in life and in death, between Egypt and Palestine is thus forged, and we are ready for the next chapter.

Following the Footsteps of Moses

The Book of Exodus

Then the LORD said, "I have observed the misery of my people who are in Egypt; I have heard their cry on account of their task-masters. Indeed, I know their sufferings, and I have come down to deliver them from the Egyptians, and to bring them up out of that land to a good and broad land, a land flowing with milk and honey, to the country of the Canaanites, the Hittites, the Amo-rites, the Perizzites, the Hivites, and the Jebusites. The cry of the Israelites has now come to me; I have also seen how the Egyptians oppress them. So come, I will send you to Pharaoh to bring my people, the Israelites, out of Egypt."

EXODUS 3:7–10

In the previous chapter I suggested that reading Genesis in recognition of the different sources that were sutured together to compose it enhances its spiritual value. Genesis also provided a transparent example of how discovering the way writers responded to prebiblical accounts, such as the creation of the world or the flood, by adopting, trimming, and converting them for their own purposes enables us to read it in a more meaningful way. Otherwise we can easily miss the book's real contribution. As we turn now to Exodus, its sequel in the Hebrew canon, we will find, similarly, that our appreciation of its significance is enriched if we read it with at least a passing knowledge of another important subfield in biblical studies, namely, biblical archaeology. In the case of Genesis it was the careful analysis of the text itself that uncovered its multiple sources and opened the book to a more intimate understanding, but archaeological research assumed a relatively small role. Despite occasional extravagant press reports, no one has discovered the location of the Garden of Eden or the spot where Noah's ark came to rest. No archaeological expedition has ever found the stone on which Jacob laid his head when he had the dream of the ladder connecting heaven and earth.

With Exodus, however, it is different. Textual analysis plays a role, but archaeology holds a much more prominent place, and thoughtful readers of the Bible need to know something about it. This is not a daunting challenge. Achieving a layperson's grasp of biblical archaeology is not difficult. It can be an absorbing undertaking, and numerous resources are easily at hand to help. In fact, recent developments in this field have made it one of the most exciting in current biblical studies. By employing contributions from cybernetics, X-ray photography, isotopic residue analysis, DNA research, and radiocarbon dating, archaeologists have shed the image they once had.

The field has changed dramatically. We all remember the old stereotype: earnest folks slathered in sunblock, in pith helmets, with pickaxes, placing shards of pottery from ancient ruins into wicker baskets. Now most trained archaeologists try to avoid removing anything from a site. Rather, combining X-ray and digital contour photography, they can leave most artifacts where they are, even under the surface, and subject them to scrutiny on a computer screen later in an air-conditioned lab. Leaving these articles in place signals a significant change, since taking even a tiny fragment of a vase or a pedestal away from the stratum in which it was found deprives it of its usefulness for reconstructing the social history of the era. Also, these ancient objects, rather than being lodged in a museum, can now be viewed by people all over the world in a virtual museum on their television screens.

Some of the newer breakthroughs are astonishing. Using recent techniques, archaeologists can now even reconstruct the diets of people who lived ten thousand years ago; this means that not just temples, but latrines, with their promising store of petrified feces, become an invaluable resource, something that might come as a shock to the founders of the discipline. Taken together, these advances have led to the creation of a new field called cyberarchaeology, which combines computer science, engineering, religious studies, and history with elements of classical archaeology.

It is not hard to see how much this revolution in archaeology can enhance understanding of the Bible. What did the Canaanites and the Philistines eat for lunch before they flung themselves into battle? What did the inside of a long-buried shrine used by the Jews before the construction of the Temple in Jerusalem look like? One example illustrates this value. Some historians had recently come to doubt whether the Jews in the tenth century BCE, at the time of King Solomon, really had the resources and skills to construct a temple of the dimensions mentioned in the Bible. Recent cyberarchaeological findings, however, demonstrate that they did.

On the other hand, what if some of the findings seem to contradict biblical accounts? An amusing example of this possibility became news recently when the *New York Times* published an article entitled "Camels Had No Business in Genesis."[1] It reported that archaeologists using radiocarbon dating had determined that camels were only domesticated in the tenth century BCE, long after the era of the patriarchs, the exodus, and the kingdom of David. Hence, when Abraham's servant set out to find a wife for Abraham's son hundreds of years earlier, he probably made the journey by donkey or on foot, not on a camel, as stated in Genesis 24:10. Also our fond images of the Jews fleeing Egypt on camelback will have to be corrected.

The archaeological findings reinforce what any informed readers of the Bible will soon learn, that many of the Old Testament books were either written or compiled centuries after the happenings they record. And those who did this work understandably added some colorful details that have now proven to be anachronisms, like camels. However, it is important to remember that these tiny flaws need not undermine either the spiritual message of these books or, in some cases, even their overall historical value.[2]

There is little doubt that this breakthrough in archaeology poses some of the most intriguing questions in current biblical scholarship. But appreciating it does require one to move beyond a literalistic view of the Bible to a more mature comprehension. For many people this is not an easy transition to make. But once made, it is immensely rewarding and brings the Bible alive in a new way.

IN THE FOOTSTEPS OF MOSES

I discerned how tricky this progression can sometimes be a few years ago when I found myself traveling with a group of alumni from our university on a trip designed to retrace the exodus, the trail of Moses and the Israelites from the Nile through the Sinai Desert to the Jordan. The Alumni Association had invited me to accompany a mixed group of modern Bible reenactors, mostly of retirement age, and give them some lectures about the historical background of what they were seeing as we traversed the storied landscape where the Jews had wandered for forty years.

Our itinerary would take us from the Nile, in which Pharaoh's daughter is said to have found the baby Moses floating in a basket of bulrushes, to the foot of Mt. Sinai, the soaring peak where God handed him the Ten Commandments, and then on to the eastern bank of the Jordan and Mt. Horeb, where Moses was permitted to glimpse the promised land he never entered. We would then cross the river ourselves (over the Allenby Bridge) and wind up visiting the Western Wall, Masada, the Church of the Holy Sepulchre, Nazareth, and other pilgrimage sites in Israel.

I was informed that the sojourn was scheduled to begin in a couple of months. We would all fly from the United States to Cairo and start from there. Local guides would fill the group in on the touristic specifics, and I was to draw on my background in religious studies to "broaden and deepen" their experience. Would I be interested?

I hardly hesitated a minute before accepting the invitation. I had never been to some of these places, and I was eager to see them, so I set to work preparing the talks I would offer. Immediately, however, I saw that my assignment would not be an easy one. As we moved from place to place, perusing the text of Exodus and exploring the sites that are mentioned in it, the travelers could not avoid noticing the conflicts that have arisen in recent years in archaeological research between, as one scholar in the field calls it, "what's in the text and what's in the ground."

MIRACLES AND SCIENCE

I was a bit apprehensive about how my fellow travelers would take this. They were all thoughtful and well-educated people, but they had gleaned their knowledge of the events of the exodus from what they had read in their Bibles or heard in sermons, from the narrative recited at the Passover seder, or, more often, from Cecil B. DeMille's *The Ten Commandments*. How would they react to the often quite different picture of those events that the shovel-and-spade crews had dug up (or failed to find) in recent decades? I wanted to inform them as best I could, but not spoil their enjoyment or subvert their faith.

However, as I pondered my dilemma, I also recognized that anyone who reads the Bible, in this case the book of Exodus, would also be somewhat aware from magazines and TV of the often dramatic results of archaeological research, and that this might already have posed a challenge to their spirituality. I could not pretend that such a challenge did not exist. I knew it could not be ignored. But what, exactly, was—or is—the nature of the challenge? And how could I help my fellow sojourners to think about it constructively?

By the time I arrived at the Cairo airport I had decided to come clean. I would tell my fellow pilgrims about my own initial unease with the historical approach to the Bible and how I eventually came to a satisfactory resolution. Before we had even boarded the bus, I started by describing how my personal view of scripture had grown as I had traveled through the thorny desert from naive literalism first to historical understanding and then to spiritual appreciation. Then I asked them to talk about how their own views of the Bible had evolved over the years. I mentioned that, like most of them, I had started by simply taking the Bible at face value, albeit with certain skepticism about passages like Joshua's stopping the sun and Balaam's talking donkey. I told them about my first encounter with the historical-critical method and how it appeared to be a lethal threat to biblical truth, a cynical undercutting of religious faith, mine and that of many other people. Then I asked them to recount their own personal odyssey with the Bible.

It worked. Everyone, it seems, has a stash of memories and anecdotes, favorable and unfavorable, about their relationship with the Bible, and as we sat on cushions around a low table laden with figs, eggplant, falafel, lentil soup, and other Egyptian delicacies in a restaurant overlooking the pyramids, they talked about them freely. The conversation was lively, and it also gave me some insight into the various mentalities represented in the group. One of the guests, a charming elderly gentleman named Mr. Clemens, assured us that he had done a lot of reading in preparation for this trip. He quoted some of the well-meaning articles one sees now and then that attempt to adduce an allegedly scientific explanation for the miracles—the parting of the sea, the manna from heaven, and others—depicted in the book of Exodus and thus presumably to rescue it from scoffers.

The formula is predictable. Maybe the sea was divided, they say, but doesn't the text mention a "great wind"? Such winds do blow in the desert, and one might have opportunely come up just as Moses and the Israelites stood stymied on the shore with the Egyptian chariots in hot pursuit just behind them. Water from a rock? Well, there are underground springs in the desert, and hitting a rock hard enough just might uncover one. What about quails to eat and manna from heaven? Travelers have reported that flocks of birds do fall to the ground from exhaustion. Also, sometimes a spongy white doughlike substance is exuded from desert plants. In other words, if we look long and hard enough (and are not afraid of a little speculation), we can rule out the miraculous entirely from Exodus. *Science,* it seems, *can explain it all.*

I told Mr. Clemens I appreciated the preparation he had made. He added that he was not naive, and that some of these theories seemed quite far-fetched. The pillar of cloud by day that led the Israelites poses no problem. There are lots of clouds in the desert and, like clouds everywhere, they move, depending on the wind. The pillar of fire by night requires a bit more of an effort. Still, reflections on a cloud bank of fires on the ground or lightning flashes must be considered. I knew that Mr. Clemens and I would be having some good chats as we wended our way toward the Holy Land. But I hoped that, by the time we parted, he might have discovered a different way to read this old but timeless account.

Talking with him reminded me that in one stage of my changing association with the Bible I also sought out these well-meaning explanations. I *wanted* the Bible to be "true," but I had my doubts about God dropping fowl and bagels on the wilderness migrants. But I now believe that, well intentioned as they surely are, such pseudo-scientific conjectures misfire entirely. They are still trying to read Exodus as a historical account in our modern sense of "historical." They have not done the preliminary but indispensable job of locating what *genre* of literature they are reading, and they forget to take into account the mentality of a people who, however gifted in so many other ways, lived two millennia before the appearance of modern science. It may not have been an "age of miracles," but it was surely an age in which people believed in miracles and saw the world through their own lenses, not ours. The meaning of the "miracles" of Exodus is that these people believed that it was through God's grace and justice that they were escaping from slavery, and they told their story in their own idiom. Mature and imaginative students of the Bible try to get inside that worldview. They do not simply reject it as superstitious or recast it in terms of modern, if often improbable, scientific rationalizations.

Still, I was glad to hear from Mr. Clemens. I could see that for some of my companions the inward intellectual journey, along with the geographical one, would be a little harder than it was for others. There was one friendly couple, George and Gladys MacDonald, who had obviously arrived with a fairly straightforward understanding of Exodus, and they knew the biblical text better than anyone else. In keeping with the announced purpose of our trip, nearly all the travelers had brought along their own copies of the Bible. But most of the couples had usually packed only one. The MacDonalds, however, each had one.

This turned out to be very helpful, since their Bibles were two different translations. Mr. MacDonald had the Revised Standard Version, his wife had the Jerusalem Bible, and this helped me to show the group how essential it is to compare translations. Doing so immediately loosens the grip of literalism by enabling us to see that the same original Hebrew passage can be read in different ways. Before that trip, when I led a Bible study session, I always suggested that we consult two or more translations, and I continue the practice. I was glad the MacDonalds were along. They sometimes raised questions I suspected were lingering in the minds of others who were reluctant to voice them. And they were serious and open. Little by little, as the dunes receded and we talked, they all began to see what I was driving at.

Study Tip ————————————————————————

Comparing the accuracy and readability of the different translations of the Bible can be confusing, but it is important. A helpful guide is Dan Brunn's *One Bible, Many Versions: Are All Translations Equal?* (Downers Grove, IL: Inter-Varsity, 2013). Brunn skillfully reviews twenty different English renderings of the Bible from the Amplified Bible to Young's Literal Translation, including the American Standard Version and the Revised Standard Version. He explains the trade-off between, on the one hand, literal "accuracy," exemplified by the New American Standard Bible, which, given the way words change their meanings, often produces a misleading translation, and, on the other hand, the more vernacular versions like *The Message*, which in their enthusiasm for up-to-dateness sometimes stray rather far from the original text.

Again I drew on my own experience. As a college student at Penn, I often attended a church in Philadelphia where the towering and eloquent figure of a well-known fundamentalist preacher named Donald Grey Barnhouse presided. Week after week he chided the "modernist" critics of the Bible and reassured the congregation that whatever calumnies these impious rogues churned out about the scripture would sooner or later be refuted by fundamentalist scholars. "Just wait. You'll see!" The people in the pews in that church seemed comforted, but I remained skeptical.

I was happy with the group that had assembled for this sojourn. There were Catholics, Protestants, Jews, and "no preferences" among them. Exodus states that the ragtag throng Moses led out of Egypt was a "mixed multitude." Our busload of modern wanderers was too, and we were on our way.

TACKLING "OUR STORY" ON THREE LEVELS

In this book we are also on our way through Exodus. I will be relying on the combination of story, history, and spirituality that I have already described. This means we do not read it as a flawed attempt at what modern people would call "history." Rather, we read it as a saga more like the *Iliad* or the *Odyssey*. Those classics of Greek civilization, like the book of Exodus, also have a historical core, in their case the Trojan War, which was hidden in the remote past, but was drawn upon many centuries later in the composition of the timeless masterpieces. Likewise, Exodus was written probably six hundred years after the events it recounts, but it is different from the Greek classics in one important way. Exodus is *our* story. However much we may marvel at the Greeks, as much as we may be stirred by Antigone and dazzled by the Parthenon, and even though the Greeks developed a limited form of democracy, their contribution to our civilization is not as fundamental or pervasive as that of the Hebrews through the Judeo-Christian tradition.

Let us then enjoy Exodus at all three levels. First, the *stories* themselves are absorbing. Whenever we retell them at our family Passover seders, I realize this afresh. They are just plain good yarns. Initially, we should just soak them in without opening our historical-analytical tool kit. But, then, *historical* inquiry also comes in. Finding out where and why it was written, far from diminishing its religious power, enhances it, and luckily in recent years we have come to know a lot about this. But then there is another stage. Reading this book in a *holistic spiritual* manner involves putting ourselves in the shoes of the Jews who, in about 600 BCE, compiled the legends and folk stories the book incorporates. It requires us to ask why they did it and who they were trying to speak to, and it enables us to ask what it means for us today. By employing all three approaches we can grasp the core message of Exodus, and when we do, it will afford us a priceless glimpse into the psyche of a people whose understanding of God and human history has left a permanent imprint on our own psyches and our institutions as well.

This mature approach is the one I *hoped* my fellow trekkers through the intimidating sands of the Sinai and through the convolutions of biblical scholarship and archaeological digs might come to grips with as we faced the text-versus-ground dilemma. But I also realized that we had only two weeks to work through it. Still, I also knew that mastering this task would eventually enable my charges to apply the same approach to other parts of the Bible. I quickly learned that these pupils, most of whom had reached "senior citizen" status, were ready and eager for the adventure.

Study Tips

The bimonthly *Biblical Archaeology Review* is especially designed, according to its website, to "connect the academic study of archaeology to a broad general audience seeking to understand the world of the Bible." First issued in 1975, it is accessible for nonspecialists and keeps readers informed on both old and new digs and disputes.

Neil A. Silberman's *Digging for God and Country: Exploration, Archeology, and the Secret Struggle for the Holy Land, 1799–1917* (New York: Random House, 1982) clearly demonstrates how difficult it is to do archaeology in the Holy Land without becoming entangled in politics.

Silberman also cooperated with Israel Finkelstein in writing *The Bible Unearthed: Archaeology's New Vision of Ancient Israel and the Origin of Its Sacred Texts* (New York: Free Press, 2001), the best and most readable of all the many books on this touchy subject. Its main strength is that it is neither an exposé nor a cover-up, but shows how historical research heightens our appreciation of the biblical text.

It is intriguing to look at the events recalled in Exodus from an Egyptian perspective (even though the Egyptians seem to have taken little notice). The best resource, albeit somewhat demanding, for this is an essay by D. B. Redford, "An Egyptological Perspective on the Exodus Narrative," in *Egypt, Israel, Sinai: Archaeological and Historical Relationships in the Biblical Period*, edited by A. E. Rainey (Tel Aviv: Tel Aviv University, 1987).

When I first began to explore what was for me the strange new world of biblical scholarship, one of the writers who appealed to me was G. Ernest Wright (1909–74). I got to know him personally years later when we became colleagues at Harvard Divinity School. Wright was encouraging, because he understood the task of biblical archaeology to be that of demonstrating, by means of "what is in the ground," that the events recounted in the Bible *actually did occur*, albeit (and this was an important point for me) maybe not exactly as the text says. He was therefore troubled by the work of the German biblical scholar Martin Noth, whose view was that much of the Old Testament is mere legend. Wright was in no sense a fundamentalist; as a Presbyterian theologian, he insisted that both Judaism and Christianity staked their claims to truth not on legends, but on historical events, and whether those events really occurred mattered a great deal. For Wright that was an utterly crucial question.

As a world-class archaeologist and a student of the famous pioneer William Foxwell Albright (1891–1971), Wright devoted his life to searching for the connections between the text and the ground. He was especially interested in the accounts of Abraham and the other patriarchs, but he also worked on later strata, including those of Joshua and the "conquest" narratives. His approach is well expressed by the title of the first book of his I read, *The God Who Acts: Biblical Theology as Recital*.[3] I cannot think of a book that would have been more helpful for someone like me at that time in my life, when I was moving from a defensive literalism to a cautious gratitude for historical biblical scholarship.

But despite the archaeological sophistication and textual excellence he brought to the task of reconciling the scripture with the shards, Wright's career ended in some disappointment. As with many great scholars, it was his own students who eventually not only went beyond him, but placed a large question mark beside his whole enterprise. One of those students was Kathleen Kenyon, and her archaeological work on Joshua and the city of Jericho was what proved to be the undoing of much of her mentor's vision. Her discoveries constitute an absorbing tale, but I will save it for a later chapter on the book of Joshua. Here it is important to follow the thread of my story by returning to Moses, the ancient Israelites, and the modern sojourners with whom I retraced the old path from Egyptian captivity to the promised land.

The problem is, however, that from an archaeological perspective *there wasn't any path to follow.* There is not a single trace of the exodus "in the ground." So we are required to think about the book of Exodus in a new way. Therefore let us begin with the story itself.

THE PLOT

Everyone knows the general plot. The Israelites are held in cruel captivity in Egypt, but their numbers increase ("They multiplied and grew exceedingly strong, so that the land was filled with them"; 1:7). Consequently, Pharaoh orders the firstborn of their male children to be drowned. But Moses's mother hides him in a makeshift raft and floats him on the Nile. From here on the narrative follows the formula of a classic hero tale. The child is discovered by the daughter of Pharaoh, who takes him home and raises him, with the convenient assistance of the child's sister, as a "prince of Egypt." Cosseted in royal privilege, one day the young Moses sees an overseer beating an Israelite slave. He intervenes and kills the brutal taskmaster. Now he must go into hiding, so he flees into the hills, where he becomes a shepherd and marries the non-Jewish daughter of a local king. (It has become a matter of some discomfort among some Jews today, understandably concerned about the growing rate of intermarriage, to discover that Moses himself was involved in such a misalliance.) Walking through the sandy hills, one day Moses comes upon a bush that is "blazing," but "not consumed." A voice speaks to him and the encounter becomes a turning point in his life. Here is that famous passage:

> *Moses was keeping the flock of his father-in-law Jethro, the priest of Midian; he led his flock beyond the wilderness, and came to Horeb, the mountain of God. There the angel of the LORD appeared to him in a flame of fire out of a bush; he looked, and the bush was blazing, yet it was not consumed. Then Moses said, "I must turn aside and look at this great sight, and see why the bush is not burned up." When the LORD saw that he had turned aside to see, God called to him out of the bush, "Moses, Moses!" And he said, "Here I am." Then he said, "Come no closer! Remove the sandals from your feet, for the place on which you are standing is holy ground." He said further, "I am the God of your father, the God of Abraham, the God of Isaac, and the God of Jacob." And Moses hid his face, for he was afraid to look at God.*
>
> *Then the LORD said, "I have observed the misery of my people who are in Egypt; I have heard their cry on account of their taskmasters. Indeed, I know their sufferings, and I have come down to deliver them from the Egyptians, and to bring them up out of that land to a good and broad land, a land flowing with milk and honey, to the country of the Canaanites, the Hittites, the Amorites, the Perizzites, the Hivites, and the Jebusites. The cry of the Israelites has now come to me; I have also seen how the Egyptians oppress them. So come, I will send you*

to Pharaoh to bring my people, the Israelites, out of Egypt." But
Moses said to God, "Who am I that I should go to Pharaoh, and
bring the Israelites out of Egypt?" He said, "I will be with you;
and this shall be the sign for you that it is I who sent you: when
you have brought the people out of Egypt, you shall worship God
on this mountain."

   But Moses said to God, "If I come to the Israelites and say to
them, 'The God of your ancestors has sent me to you,' and they
ask me, 'What is his name?' what shall I say to them?" God said
to Moses, "I AM WHO I AM." He said further, "Thus you shall say
to the Israelites, 'I AM has sent me to you.'" God also said to
Moses, "Thus you shall say to the Israelites, 'The LORD, the God
of your ancestors, the God of Abraham, the God of Isaac, and
the God of Jacob, has sent me to you': This is my name forever,
and this my title for all generations." (3:1–15)

Before resuming the plotline, I should note that our group also had an encounter with that bush, which, even though it did not change anyone's life, did alter the tone of our conversation about Exodus. Here is what happened. Our bus stopped at the ancient Monastery of St. Helen, located in the Sinai Peninsula at the foot of what is now called the Mountain of the Ten Commandments. One can still scale the peak, but in order to make it up and down before the fierce heat of the desert sun begins to beat down, one is strongly advised to get out of bed at 2:00 A.M. and start up right away in order to be back by 7:00. One rugged member of our company tried it, but scrambled back down before he reached the summit. I decided to forgo the privilege.

The monastery property encloses a somewhat dubious showpiece. Egyptian guides (not the monks) point to a large shrub on the edge of the grounds and inform any audience that will listen that *this is the original burning bush*. My companions were unconvinced. Some wondered how the bush, which figured into an earlier phase of Moses's life, just happens to be at the foot of Mt. Sinai. Others wondered how it had lasted for three thousand years. I seized the opportunity. The "burning bush" gave me a chance to chat with them about legends, how stories take on a life of their own, and how certain oral traditions often get attached to particular places. This in turn contributed to their growing understanding of the stories found in Exodus. We had taken a big step on our way to the promised land.

Back to Moses. When he saw the bush, he stopped. At this point the story spirals to a new level, a turning point not just for Moses, but for the Hebrew people and for hundreds of millions of people ever since, because God introduces himself at the burning bush not just as the creator, but as the liberator. A voice speaks to Moses from the burning bush, commanding him to go back down into Egypt and unshackle his fellow Israelites from their captivity. Hesitant and fearful, Moses tries to dodge the order and asks, quite sensibly, "Who shall I say has sent me?" There follows one of the most important passages in the entire Bible:

> God said to Moses, "I AM WHO I AM." He said further, "Thus you shall say to the Israelites, 'I AM has sent me to you.'" (3:14)

What the voice replies ("I am who I am," RSV, NRSV) is famously difficult syntax to untangle. It may even be in part a pun or wordplay, and it still befuddles even the most expert Hebrew language scholars. It is therefore a valuable exercise for serious readers of Exodus to spread four or five different translations of the Bible on a table open to this passage. The King James Version makes it "I am that I am," but many scholars insist that this mistranslates the phrase and makes God too static, belying the dynamic nature that characterizes him in the rest of the Bible. In a footnote, the Revised Standard Version (1952) suggests it might mean "He causes to be what he causes to be." The New Revised Standard Version (1989), comparing it to Exodus 33:19 ("I will be gracious to whom I will be gracious"), says it could mean, "I will be whatever I will be." My favorite rendering is that of the crack Hebrew scholar Everett Fox:

> God said to Moshe, "EHYEH ASHER EHYEH, I will be-there howsoever I will be-there. You shall say to the children of Israel, EHYEH/ I-will-be-there sends me."[4]

There is little point in asking, "But what does it *really* say?" The un-settled dispute about what one of the key passages in the whole Bible actu-ally says renders any literal interpretation impossible. But this is good news. Since the ongoing dispute enables us to see how the most renowned experts do not agree, it also frees us from being boxed into a single unam-biguous definition of God. And maybe that is exactly what God intended.

In any case, Moses does return to Egypt and, with the assistance of his brother, Aaron, confronts Pharaoh: "Let my people go!" Pharaoh refuses. God sends a series of plagues—lice, mice, boils, frogs, and so on—culminating in the death of the firstborn sons of the Egyptians. Pharaoh finally relents. The Israelites depart in haste; there is no time to permit the bread to rise before it is baked. Stymied by the Sea of Reeds (still popularly but mistakenly called the Red Sea), they are saved when God opens a path-way through the waters for them and then closes it over the pursuing Egyptian army. They wander for forty years in the desert, led by a cloud by day and a pillar of fire by night and fed by "manna," which God sends. They grumble and complain, and at one point some try to organize a re-volt against Moses. At Mt. Sinai Moses climbs to the top and God hands him the tablets of the law, which Moses smashes into bits when he climbs back down and discovers that his people have been worshipping a golden calf during his absence; God gives him a second set. Eventually the so-journers arrive at the Jordan River. But because he has disobeyed God during the long trek, Moses, who we are told has now reached the age of 120, is not permitted to enter.

It is hard for many people to read this account without thinking of Martin Luther King's famous "last sermon" given at Mason Temple in Memphis the evening before his death. Standing at the pulpit, a weary King declares to the congregation, "I've been to the mountaintop. . . . And I've *seen* the promised land." He then goes on to say, "I may not get there with you," which of course he did not. That dramatic moment naturally comes to mind, but it is only a particularly vivid example of the enormous impact the figure of Moses has had on history, and on American history in particular.

The Moses story is about the role of God in the liberation of a politically, religiously, and economically oppressed people. When Benjamin Franklin was asked to design the original great seal for the new American republic, he chose a scene depicting Moses standing on the shore while the waters of the sea were rolled back so that the Israelites could escape Pharaoh's tyranny. As it turned out, Franklin's design was not selected (the eagle clutching the arrows won out), but Moses and the exodus continued to be major themes in the American experience. For black slaves he was, next to Jesus, the most important figure in the Bible:

Go down, Moses, way down in Egypt land.
Tell old pharaoh, let my people go.

There were also songs about "crossing over Jordan" and other Moses-related themes. But for people of all castes and colors, the idea of America as a "promised land" was a powerful one.

Moses died and was buried just on the edge of the promised land. And the Bible states that "no one knows his burial place to this day" (Deut. 34:6). This last stern note is vitally important. Exodus presents Moses as a kind of antipharaoh. It is God, not Moses, who leads the captive slaves out of Egypt. The pharaohs were buried in colossal pyramid tombs, and centuries later people still know where their mummified bodies lie. Not Moses. He was not even permitted to enter the promised land. Just what sin he and Aaron had committed that exacted such a severe penalty is not at all clear.

Possibly the painful, indeed heartbreaking punishment stems from something he did at Meribah, when the Israelites were complaining about their hunger and thirst. The incident, which is described in Exodus 17:1–7, is also recounted in Numbers 20:2–13 and mentioned in passing in Deuteronomy 33:8. These are the passages in which the Israelites are in a nasty mood, threatening rebellion, and Moses is nearly at his wits' end. The desert wanderers complained that they were thirsty. Moses's people were parched, and they snarled at Moses, so God tells him to call forth water from a rock by striking it with the same rod he had held over the Sea of Reeds, where—ironically—it had not been a question of too little, but of too much water. Moses seems to follow God's command. He picks up the staff and strikes the rock twice, and water flows out. But in the next instant God warns Moses: "Because you did not trust in me, to show my holiness before the eyes of the Israelites, therefore you shall not bring this assembly into the land that I have given them" (Num. 20:12).

Today's readers of this episode must swallow here before going on. Just what had Moses done? Was he castigated because he had not made it clear to the people that it was God, not Moses, who was providing the life-giving water? Was it because he struck the rock too hard, too many times, or in the wrong way? Was it because Moses called the Israelites "rebels" (Num. 20:10)? Modern commentators disagree.

There is another possibility, a rather grim one. Exodus 32 recounts the famous incident in which, while Moses is on Mt. Sinai, the people melt their rings, make a "golden calf," and worship it. When he returns and discovers what they have done, this is what happens:

> Then Moses stood in the gate of the camp, and said, "Who is on the LORD's side? Come to me." And all the sons of Levi gathered themselves together to him. And he said to them, "Thus says the LORD God of Israel, 'Put every man his sword on his side, and go to and fro from gate to gate throughout the camp, and slay every man his brother, and every man his companion, and every man his neighbor.'" And the sons of Levi did according to the word of Moses; and there fell of the people that day about three thousand men. And Moses said, "Today you have ordained yourselves for the service of the LORD, each one at the cost of his son and of his brother, that he may bestow a blessing upon you this day."
> (32:26–29, RSV)

There is no doubt that this is an appalling account. It certainly does not appear in any of the children's Bible stories, and it is skipped over or not mentioned in most Passover celebrations. It sounds more like the vengeful tactic of an SS officer in a Nazi-occupied country. But there it stands in the scripture, and we must at least try to come to terms with it, even though we may never succeed. One might think, well, they were re-volting against him and against God weren't they? But this punishment seems vindictive in the extreme. Why did God, speaking through Moses, choose it? And for which of these actions was Moses denied his entry per-mit into the land of milk and honey?

There is just no satisfying answer. Once again the Bible simply lacks closure. Other parts of the Bible are not very helpful either. In Deuteron-omy 32:50–51 God tells Moses he has to die before entering the promised land, because he "broke faith" with him. But just how had he broken faith? We are left to wonder.

BUT DID IT HAPPEN?

No one can deny that Exodus is an impressive epic, one of the greatest ever spun. But what my alumni travelers, like so many other people, wanted to know was, *Did it really happen?* In their chapter "Did the Exo-dus Happen?" Israel Finkelstein and Neil Silberman demonstrate, in *The Bible Unearthed,* that it could not have, at least not at the time, or in the places, or with the vast number of Israelites (six hundred thousand) the Bible reports. The book of Exodus does not give the name of the pharaoh under whom the escape from Egypt took place. But it does name the city they were toiling to build (with "bricks without straw") at the time of their hasty departure: Rameses. Firm archaeological evidence about the city of Rameses places it in the thirteenth century BCE. But the problem arises when we try to trace the Israelites' trail after they left Egypt and wandered into the Sinai. As Finkelstein and Silberman put it rather bluntly:

> *Not a single campsite or signs of occupation [from this period] has ever been identified in Sinai. And it has not been from lack of trying. Repeated archaeological surveys in the region of the penin-sula, including the mountainous area around the traditional site of Mt. Sinai near St. Catherine's Monastery, have yielded only negative*

evidence: not a single shard, no structure . . . no trace of an ancient
encampment.[5]

Some of my fellow pilgrims found this a bitter pill to swallow. When I read my charges this paragraph, I could almost hear the air go out of the room. What? They had flown all the way to Egypt to follow the route of the exodus, and it had never happened? I was afraid some might demand their money back. One man voiced an understandable objection. The Sinai Desert is a vast space, he pointed out. How could archaeologists possibly have scoured the whole thing? And it was so long ago, so maybe the traces have been lost. But the fact is that modern archaeological technology does allow the survey of such vast spaces. Besides, traces of extinct encampments and villages from a thousand years earlier and hundreds of years later have been found, just nothing at all from the time the Bible dates the exodus.

To complicate matters further, the biblical text does name actual places in the Sinai at which the Israelites are said to have stopped, sometimes for long periods, such as the town of Kadesh-barnea, where Moses is reported to have struck the rock with his staff. This should be helpful to those searching for "history." But it is not. The difficulty is that Kadesh-barnea did not exist at the time. Nor did any of the other desert sites mentioned in the text. They all date from centuries later.

Finkelstein and Silberman's conclusion is unavoidable. Many sites mentioned in the Exodus narrative are indeed real. Some were occupied in centuries before the exodus or at a much later time, but not anywhere near the thirteenth century BCE:

> *Unfortunately for those seeking a historical Exodus [these sites]*
> *were unoccupied precisely at the time they reportedly played a*
> *role in the events of the wandering of the children of Israel in the*
> *wilderness.*[6]

So where does that leave us? Fortunately, Finkelstein and Silberman do not just abandon us. Their way forward is to remind readers that these places were thriving and well known six hundred years later, in the seventh century BCE, when other evidence suggests the book of Exodus was written or edited in the form we have it today. This is precisely the clue we need. If we ask the questions I suggested earlier—When was Exodus written? For what purpose? For whom?—then both the historical and the spiritual significance of the narrative become clearer. When we combine what is in the text with what is in the ground, it enormously amplifies our understanding of this timeless tale.

As it turns out, six hundred years after the biblical date of the exodus, during the seventh century BCE, a strong king named Josiah ruled over Judah, and he was intent on expanding its borders. But Egypt had also become newly resurgent and powerful. The Israelites, endeavoring to integrate a rabble of disparate tribes at home and facing the looming threat from across the Nile to the south, longed for a renewed injection of piety and patriotism. Drawing on patchy stories from many centuries before, the priests in Josiah's court plaited them together into this epic, then sewed into the fabric the names of current places to lend a note of contemporary realism. The result was the biblical book we were rereading twenty-five hundred years later as our bus sped through the desert. The goal of these writers was never to fashion a "historical" record of events that had long since faded into dim memories. Rather, it was to craft an inspiring saga that would imbue the Israelite people, who often felt threatened and fragmented, with a sense of unity and hope.

It was a case of retrieving past memories to buoy up present hopes. As the book of Exodus was being written in the seventh century, just across the Nile Egypt was being ruled by strong pharaohs such as Psammetichus I (664–610 BCE) and Necho II (610–595 BCE). Both these monarchs consciously modeled themselves on the great pharaohs of their ancient history, and both harbored expansionist dreams. But the Israelites reasoned that if their great past leader, Moses, could challenge a proud pharaoh eons before, then they could stand up to one today. Just as millennia later Cecil B. DeMille took the book of Exodus and reshaped it into a forceful filmic celebration of the "free world" at the height of the Cold War (*The Ten Commandments*), the writers and editors of the original Exodus deployed old stories of liberation from Egyptian tyranny to bolster current national and religious purposes.

I have written in a previous chapter that reading the Bible today requires a leap of imagination, putting oneself "inside the text," not just examining it at arm's length. What the text-and-ground approach makes clear is that in the case of the book of Exodus our leap of imagination should begin with the simple pleasure of telling and hearing stories about the Israelites of the thirteenth century BCE. We can read it the way we might read a gripping modern historical novel. But we cannot stop there. We must then make the imaginative jump forward to the seventh century BCE when the book was being written. Only when we get a feel for the life of the Israelites at that time of threat, can we look back—in a double imaginative leap—to how they creatively reappropriated and refashioned that previous era to infuse meaning into their own.

Nations, peoples, religions, families, and even individuals frequently search the past to shed light on the future. Barack Obama took his oath as president on two Bibles, one of Lincoln's and one owned by the family of Martin Luther King. People visit historical museums in order to find what someone once called "a usable past." The practice is especially prevalent in religion. Indeed, the Haggadah, the book Jews use to observe Passover, explicitly instructs the participants to imagine themselves present at the time of the exodus, but also to think and talk about what that struggle for human liberation requires of us today.

By now my charges, skeptical at first, had begun to see how they might start to look at the Bible in a new way. There were a couple of holdouts. As she sipped a brandy in the ship's bar on the Gulf of Aqaba, one matronly traveler glanced over her shoulder, leaned toward me, and whispered that the secret to the whole thing was that one day when he was a little boy, Moses "looked down" and saw that in one respect he was different from the little Egyptian boys he played with. Then when he saw some Jewish boys (she did not elaborate on where and how), he knew that he "was a little *Jewish* boy." From then on, she assured me, he was intent on liberating his enslaved people. I chose not to argue with her. It's a nice story. Why spoil her day?

After a couple of days in Amman, the capital of Jordan, our bus rolled westward, the same direction the Israelites had taken, until we reached the Jordan River, the border with the Israeli-occupied West Bank. There we stopped to pass through security at the bridge the Jordanians call the King Hussein Bridge, the Palestinians call the al-Karameh Bridge, and the Israelis call the General Allenby Bridge. The different names for this short span highlighted the fact that we were indeed in disputed territory, and also that the various peoples in the area read and interpret history, both ancient and modern, in different ways.

The collapsing of the long ago and the not so long ago could not escape our notice. Edmund Allenby was the British general who led the troops of the Egyptian Expeditionary Force through the Sinai and into Palestine during World War I and entered Jerusalem in December 1917, prompting the newspapers in England to exult that "the Holy Land was back in Christian hands after four hundred years." The bridge that bears Allenby's name is only ten miles east of Jericho, the city the Israelites first conquered after they crossed this same river.

We were also close to the place in modern Jordan where the aged Moses clambered to the top of Mt. Nebo so that he could at least see the "promised land," which God would not permit him to enter. A stone monument stands there today with inscriptions in Hebrew, Arabic, and English, reminding visitors that just as Jews and Muslims both trace their lineage back to Abraham, both (and Christians, of course) also honor Moses. As we have noted above, Moses never made it into the "land of milk and honey" toward which he had led his people for so many years. When they were reminded of this bittersweet twist in the story we had been retracing, some of my fellow passengers confessed that this seemed to them an unnecessarily harsh punishment. I could appreciate their sentiments, but the Bible does not specialize in happy endings.

As we sat on the bus, listening to both Arabic and Hebrew on our portable radios, and waited while the Jordanian and then the Israeli border authorities checked our papers and searched through some of our luggage, we had a chance to pull together what we had learned during our trek. Could we now read the Exodus account not as flawed history, but as something else possibly much more meaningful? One of the travelers gave an excellent answer. He said that now we could read it in a couple of ways. We could read it as an absorbing historical novel set in the thirteenth century BCE. But we could also read it as a moving testimony to how a real people in real time (the seventh century) can gather threads and patches from a remote past and weave a testimony to human liberation for their own, and all time. And we could continue to think about the huge impact this book has had on so many subsequent generations. We were now ready to "cross over Jordan" and also to begin to read another difficult, even grisly, biblical story, the account of the conquest of the promised land as told in the book of Joshua.

3

Battles and Burlesques in the Conquest of Canaan

The Book of Joshua

After the death of Moses the servant of the LORD, the LORD said to Joshua the son of Nun, Moses' minister, "Moses my servant is dead; now therefore arise, go over this Jordan, you and all this people, into the land which I am giving to them, to the people of Israel. Every place that the sole of your foot will tread upon I have given to you, as I promised to Moses. From the wilderness and this Lebanon as far as the great river, the river Euphrates, all the land of the Hittites to the Great Sea toward the going down of the sun shall be your territory. No man shall be able to stand before you all the days of your life; as I was with Moses, so I will be with you; I will not fail you or forsake you.

JOSHUA 1:1–5, RSV

The book of Joshua was composed as a sequel to Exodus to describe the conquest and settlement of the "promised land." But it is different in at least one important respect. In packing up and leaving Egypt, the Israelites may have deprived the pharaoh of his workforce and even caused some of his army to be drowned, but they did not invade another people's turf or decimate its population as they do in Joshua. Get ready for a violent and wrenching saga.

The biblical scholar Regina M. Schwartz tells of teaching these books in a course on the Bible and extolling them as a celebration of freedom and liberation. A student raised his hand and asked, "Yes, but what about the Canaanites?"[1] This is a question that continues to rankle, one that we will return to below. It is raised more systematically by Robert Allen Warrior, a member of the Osage Nation of Native Americans, whose ancestors had to contend with another people laying claim by divine mandate to their forests and prairies.[2] It might be a useful exercise for today's readers to follow the Joshua story not just from the Israelite perspective in which it is presented, but from the point of view of the various Canaanite peoples who were its victims.

The plot of Joshua picks up where the story of Moses ends, but it also offers us an opportunity to introduce another mode of biblical studies. This one is called "narrative theory," which addresses itself to the questions that arise when someone writes a description of events that occurred a long time before the writing and when we read that account a long time, perhaps a very long time, after it was written. This mode of biblical studies is derived from literary criticism and is often blended with historical analysis into a composite method. It therefore does not focus exclusively on questions of historical accuracy, date of composition, or authorship. Rather, it examines a document to locate literary genres such as romance, tragedy, satire, comedy, and even farce, all elements present in Joshua, as ways of penetrating the surface and getting to its purpose.

The scholar Mario Liverani expresses the underlying premise of narrative theory: "When we read a narrative history, what we are reading is not a source for the events depicted, but a source for understanding the author(s) and the community and era they represent."[3] Clearly this method is also applicable to Exodus, but even more so to Joshua, as we will see below. (This is a hint to keep in mind in reading many biblical books, but is especially important for the various "historical" books in the Old Testament such as 1 and 2 Samuel, 1 and 2 Kings, Judges, and Joshua.)

THE PROMISED LAND

As the story in Joshua begins, Moses is already dead. He has died at the edge of the promised land. Now God is calling upon his assistant, Joshua son of Nun, to lead the people over the Jordan to conquer and settle the land, so the text asserts, God has already promised them. The centuries-long persistence of the idea of a "promised land" makes it one of the most enduring themes in history. It not only shaped Jewish thought, but later became integral to the identity of European settlers in America and of the Dutch "Voortrekkers" in South Africa. It still inspires some of the West Bank settlers in Israeli-occupied Palestine, who often point to the "conquer and settle" motif in Joshua as the divine command they are trying to fulfill today.

Time and again the Israelites and their descendants, the Jews, have been displaced from *Eretz Israel* (the land, as distinct from the people, of Israel), and time and again they, or some of them, have returned. But as the book of Joshua tells it, the Israelites did not originally take possession of "the land" in a vacuum. They are depicted as defeating and virtually destroying the previous inhabitants. Joshua and his fighting men did battle with "Amorites and Canaanites" and other peoples who were not convinced that somebody else's god had given their land to this wandering tribe. Also, the way the Israelites treated the people they were conquering has been a troublesome question for a long time, and it remains so today. We will return to this point below.

We also have to bear in mind while reading Joshua that we should not be looking for ethical models or moral norms. From that perspective the book is a horror. Joshua is about the "conquest" of the area later called Palestine and Israel. But this is hardly an ordinary imperial conquest in which a conqueror seeks to augment territory, gain trade concessions, or control raw materials and markets. This is a conquest of attrition and slaughter. And it is a holy war. According to the command of Yahweh, for the most part faithfully executed by Joshua, the indigenous Canaanites are to be annihilated and their sacred places and altars torn down and burned. The report makes for gruesome reading, and we will return to it below. But first let us pick up the script where the compilers of Joshua do—with a comic prelude (2:1–24).

SPY STORIES

When they reached the river Jordan from the east the Israelites found themselves in what is now the Hashemite Kingdom of Jordan. Joshua then dispatched two spies to reconnoiter the city of Jericho and size up what kind of opposition they would be facing. The story of sending out spies must have been one the Hebrews were fond of, since it is told in three other places: Numbers 13; Joshua 7:2–5; and Judges 18:2–10. In fact, its fourfold location invites a comparative reading, since each version uses the same account for a somewhat different purpose. This illustrates both the practice of editing and reworking, which we see in so much of the Bible, and the thesis of narrative theory, which suggests that we should not rely on such a text to inform us about the events it depicts, but about the religious and political purpose for which it was composed. When we have understood this principle, it helps us read it in a more rewarding way.

Why is the story of Rahab and the spies so appealing? Can it be because it combines suspense with a slightly racy aroma, giving it something of a James Bond flavor? It seems the spies, having looked around in Jericho, decide to spend the night in the house of a woman named Rahab, who is explicitly identified as a prostitute. The possibilities for a vivid 007 episode almost leap from the page. Why, among the beds and couches that might have been available to them, did these espionage agents choose this bordello in which to hide from view? Was Rahab a beautiful lady of the evening, wearing her own distinctive scent? Did she already secretly favor the Israelites? Or was it just that they might not be expected to hide out in a house of ill repute?

Since we are told nothing, our imaginations can soar. The plot thickens when the king's counterspies knock on the door and question Rahab. But she has hidden the infiltrators amid "stalks of flax" on her roof, and she lies blatantly, perhaps batting her eyelashes, assuring the king's men the spies have already left (and adds that these border patrol agents had best get after them right away). It is a tense moment, but the pursuers do not find the spies. We can breathe more easily. Now Rahab tells her guests that she and her neighbors have heard how fierce the Israelite warriors are, and that this made their "hearts melt," a valuable bit of intelligence for Joshua's scouts. But Rahab also tells them that, since she has saved their lives, they must promise her that, if they invade Jericho, she and her family will be spared. The promise made, she lowers them out her window. By agreement she leaves a long red cord hanging there, so that when the Israelites return in force, they will know which household to spare. It sounds a bit far-fetched, but some commentators claim this length of crimson yarn is the origin of the term "red-light district."

After the incident with the spies, we are not finished with Rahab. She keeps reappearing like a favorite character in a TV series. In Matthew 1:5 she is listed among the ancestors of Jesus. Hebrew folklore says she married Joshua after the conquest and gave birth to the prophet Jeremiah.

OLD STORIES FOR NEW PURPOSES

When reading a book called *How to Read the Bible*, readers are entitled to know that, since the Bible is an anthology of widely different types of writing, we should read it in different ways. For example, do not expect to gain deep spiritual enrichment from reading the register of tribes catalogued in Numbers. In this dinner-theater fluff piece that might be called "Rahab and the Spies," we find something we can read mainly for entertainment. It is a titillating episode complete with some zany details. We can imagine the infiltrators holding their breath under the piles of flax and listening while Rahab charms and misleads their pursuers downstairs. But this is comedy with a purpose. We learn that a lot of people in Jericho are already terrified of the approaching Hebrew fighters. When the scouts promise Rahab that she and her family will be spared the sword, we get the queasy feeling that no one else will survive. And we learn that God can use unlikely characters, including this inventive madam, to protect his own people. But this is all a brief, light touch to prepare us for the awful things that lie ahead.

In reading Exodus and now once again in Joshua, we discover how stories garnered from the past are retrieved and deployed for current purposes. Indeed, this is a vital key to understanding hosts of biblical texts. Here in Joshua we have a dramatic example. In order to cross over the river Jordan and begin the conquest and settlement, the children of Israel must first be persuaded that Joshua is indeed the legitimate heir to Moses. But they also have to get across the river, long before the Allenby-Hussein Bridge was constructed. In one dramatic gesture God solves both problems at once. He instructs Joshua to perform an act that will temporarily dry up the Jordan, so the Israelites can cross over dry shod. Sound familiar? And when this miracle happens under Joshua's direction, could there be any further question that he is the God-appointed successor to Moses?

Once across the river, the invading army proceeds to Jericho. There God again displays his miraculous powers by telling them they do not need to attack the city. The story (6:1–27) is a familiar one. Following God's instructions, the Hebrews march around the city for six days led by six priests bearing the ark of the covenant. On the seventh day they march around it seven times, the people shout, and, as the spiritual goes, the walls "come a-tumblin' down." So far this has been a bloodless victory for Yahweh and for Joshua, but not for long. After the ramparts have fallen, the Hebrews swarm into the city and "devote to destruction by the edge of the sword all inside the city, both men and women, young and old, oxen, sheep, and donkeys" (6:21). Only Rahab and her family escape.

After the fall of Jericho, Joshua leads his battalions to the city of Ai to look for another divinely sanctioned victory. On the way, however, there occurs an ugly incident in which one of the Israelites, a man named Achan, steals some of the silver and gold booty of Jericho that was to have been totally devoted to Yahweh and hides it in his tent. Found out by Joshua, Achan and his whole family, along with his oxen, donkeys, and sheep, are dragged out of town and stoned to death by the Israelites (7:24–25). Joshua then moves on to the city of Ai, which he captures by putting into operation a tactical trick, a fake retreat and an ambush, suggested by none other than God himself, who has now become a tactician as well as the supreme commander. The city falls, and once again the Israelite victors finish by "slaughtering all the inhabitants" (8:24).

After this triumph Joshua repeats what Moses had done; he offers a sacrifice and then reads all the words of the covenant to the people. This is not just a pious afterthought to a bloody episode. It points us to at least one of the motives the composers of Joshua had in mind: that utter dependence on and obedience to God was their only hope. It is also important to notice that Joshua himself, not the priests, is in charge of the ritual. Since this book was composed when King Josiah was trying to center all Hebrew religious activities in Jerusalem (which in Joshua's time was not yet in the Israelites' possession), its message is clear: the top man (then Joshua, now Josiah) is in charge not only of the political realm, but of the religious realm as well.

Now comes another episode of comic relief, this time in the form of what some writers have termed a satire (9:3–27). It seems that when the inhabitants of Gibeon, a neighboring city, heard about the destruction of Jericho and Ai, they "acted with cunning." They organized a charade, dressing in worn-out clothes and patched sandals and loading their donkeys with ragged sacks. For their provisions they took along dried and moldy food. Thus rigged out in these ridiculous props, they presented themselves to Joshua at Gilgal, told him they had journeyed "from a far country," and begged him to make a treaty with them. They even elaborated their "far country" ruse by showing him the moldy bread, which they said had been fresh when they set out, and the raggedy cloaks and sandals, which they claimed had worn thin from the journey.

Joshua, the text says, on the advice of his advisers, made a treaty with them. Significantly, the Bible explicitly tells us that Joshua did not ask God what to do. Maybe he decided this was not such a difficult decision. He soon learned, however, that he had been hoodwinked, that these shabby folks "from afar" were actually next-door neighbors. Still, having made the treaty, albeit under false pretenses, he observed it. But because they had deceived him, Joshua decreed that the Gibeonites could continue to live among the Israelites, but as "hewers of wood and drawers of water," in other words, as a permanent underclass of servants.

Now Joshua's enemies, hearing about this new alliance, quickly banded together and attacked, but the Israelites defeated them with the timely assistance of another of Yahweh's miracles. At Joshua's appeal, God makes the sun stand still, so Joshua can complete the massacre, and then unloads stones from heaven on the heads of the fleeing enemies (10:1–14).

Let us remind ourselves of what I have written above: *we are not looking for history here.* There is not only no archaeological evidence of such a conquest of Jericho. The research proves that such a city did not even exist at the time. Rather, what we have is probably a folk legend about the ruins of a small abandoned mountain outpost that long antedates the arrival of any Israelites. The composers of Joshua scooped it up, along with other local legends, and wove it into the story perhaps to demonstrate that Yahweh did not even need an army to work his conquests, just devoted followers who would do exactly what he commands, even if it means doing something that (if it indeed happened) must have appeared ridiculous to the Hebrews at the time, namely, marching around Jericho blowing horns. As for the blood-soaked defeat and destruction of Ai, no archaeologist has yet to discover any evidence that such a city existed, then or since. Once again the composers have appropriated a legend from a long time before the arrival of the Israelites to make a point: one should never oppose the awful power of Yahweh either from within (the hapless Achan) or from without (the luckless residents of Ai).

As for the deceptive and scruffy Gibeonites with their rancid bread, this part of the story serves two purposes. First, once one makes a treaty in God's name, it must not be broken. Second, the story explains why the Gibeonites, who continued to live among the Israelites, had been reduced to servant status: their duplicity was being punished. The story does indeed have a satirical thrust. It makes the Gibeonites, with their purposely shredded cloaks, look farcical.

Multiple attempts to explain the stopping of the sun, some of them absurdly far-fetched, have been advanced from time to time. A comet threw the earth's rotation temporarily off balance? An unusually bright moon? All these ploys fall into the same category as the pseudo-scientific theories I referred to in the previous chapter on the exodus. All ignore the fact that ancient peoples had no inhibition about attributing miraculous deeds to God. So our task remains the same: asking the *intent* of the authors. Their purpose seems transparent. They want to equate Joshua with Moses and the conquest of Canaan with the escape from Egypt. If God could supply a pillar of fire by night and a cloud by day then, why not a short pause in the sun's arc? If he could send manna from the skies to supply food, why not a shower rocks on the heads of enemies?

After the conquest of Jericho and Ai and the parodying of the Gibeonites, the book of Joshua returns to its dismal recitation of conquest and murder:

> *Joshua attacked and captured Makkedah and its king that day.*
> *He put everyone in the city to death; no one was left alive. . . .*
>
> *After this, Joshua and his army went on from Makkedah to Libnah and attacked it. The LORD also gave the Israelites victory over this city and its king. They spared no one, but killed every person in it. . . .*
>
> *After this, Joshua and his army went on from Libnah to Lachish, surrounded it and attacked it. The LORD gave the Israelites victory over Lachish on the second day of the battle. Just as they had done at Libnah, they spared no one, but killed every person in the city. King Horam of Gezer came to the aid of Lachish, but Joshua defeated him and his army and left none of them alive. (10:28–33, GNT)*

From Lachish, in sickening repetition, Joshua led his army to Eglon ("they . . . put everyone there to death"; 10:34–35), and then to Hebron ("they killed the king and everyone else in the city as well as in the nearby towns. Joshua condemned the city to total destruction. . . . No one was left alive"; 10:36–37), and then Debir ("Joshua did to Debir . . . what he had done to Hebron and to Libnah"; 10:38–39, GNT). Note that this is not just a campaign of mass destruction; it is also a holy war, and the objective of the massacres was also religious. As one of the final verses of this section says, "This was what the Lord God of Israel had commanded" (10:40, GNT).

Scholars place Joshua in a block of material called "Deuteronomic," which means one of its purposes was to illustrate how the rules set forth in God's covenant were to be carried out. The grounds for the behavior of the Israelites were not just irrational or impulsive. They believed they were obeying God's command, or at least this is what the biblical writers want us to believe they were doing:

> And when the LORD your God gives them over to you and you defeat them, then you must utterly destroy them. Make no covenant with them and show them no mercy. Do not intermarry with them, giving your daughters to their sons. . . . But this is how you must deal with them: break down their altars, smash their pillars, hew down their sacred poles, and burn their idols with fire. (Deut. 7:2–5)

I do not believe it is necessary for current readers of the Bible to slog through all these grisly verses. It does not take long to discover what is going on. But it is both painful and important to recognize that for centuries many people, not just the Israelites, have perpetrated horrendous crimes believing they were doing God's will. Crusaders swung into their saddles shouting, *"Deus vult!"* ("God wills it!"), as they galloped off to murder Saracens. German soldiers in World War II marched into battle wearing belt buckles with the inscription *Gott mit uns,* "God with us." American airmen bowed their heads in a prayer led by a chaplain before they flew off to incinerate sixty thousand men, women, and children in a single blast at Hiroshima. If it teaches little else, the book of Joshua should remind us to be cautious about people who are sure they doing exactly what God wants them to do; and this includes us.

After all this mayhem, the next chapters are something less than riveting. They spell out in numbing detail which territories are allotted to which of the tribes of Israel and establish the borders between them. The single bit of relief comes in chapter 20, in which God instructs Joshua to set apart cities of refuge, cities to which anyone who has killed someone unintentionally may flee and be protected from anyone seeking revenge, presumably a family member intent on retribution, even though the death was unintentional. The invaluable idea of certain sacred places, including churches, as sanctuaries from law enforcement officers traces back to this section.

In the final chapters, "when the LORD had given rest to Israel from all their enemies all around, and Joshua was old and well advanced in years" (23:1), the old warrior assembles all the people for a kind of farewell address. He reminds them once again that it is God who has given them all these victories, and that now that they dwell in the promised land, they should keep two things firmly in mind. First, they should not in any way honor, swear by, or bow down to the gods of these defeated people. Second, they should not intermarry with them.

The old man makes some particular specifications. First, they should not continue to serve the gods they served in Egypt and before they arrived here (24:14–15). Does this mean the Israelites had not all been devoted monotheistic worshippers of Yahweh before they crossed the Jordan? It seems so, and many historians believe, on this and other evidence, that the worship of one God was still just taking hold among them. Jewish monotheism was still a work in progress. Also, they should not worship the gods of the Amorites, among whom they were living. This is clearly a warning against the constant temptation all immigrants face: taking up the religious and cultural patterns of the people with whom they would henceforth live. It is a tension that refugees and migrants have had to cope with ever since.

Finally with all the people assembled one last time in Shechem, Joshua recaps their entire history, their deliverance from Egypt, their crossing of the sea, their wanderings in the wilderness, and their conquest of the land. In the course of his recital he reminds them that their ancestors, Abraham, Isaac, Jacob, and Joseph, had already dwelt in this land and that Jacob was buried there. To seal this connection, the bones of Joseph, which had been brought from Egypt, were transferred here, all of which strongly implies that the conquest Joshua has just led was seen as a kind of "return" to a land to which the Israelites already had ancestral claims. The assembly now swears that they will obey only this God, the one without whom none of this would have been possible. Joshua sets up a huge stone to remind them of this solemn covenant. Then he dies at the age of 110.

What can contemporary students of the book of Joshua take away from a reading of it? We do not learn much "history" in our current sense of the term. In fact, there are scholars who contend that not only did the conquest not take place in the manner in which it is described here, but quite possibly no conquest at all ever took place. In his book *The Tribes of Yahweh,* Norman Gottwald argues that the "Israelites" never invaded or conquered Canaan. They were also Canaanites who had been living there all along in dispersed extended family units that eventually formed a coalition that overthrew the ruling elites in the cities. The book of Joshua, in his view, was written down centuries later during the reign of the reforming king Josiah, who was both threatened by Assyria and was also trying to centralize all worship in his capital city of Jerusalem.[4] This suggests that we might compare Joshua with Virgil's *Aeneid,* which was written to lend the upstart Roman Empire and its ruler Augustus some mythic and historical gravitas. No one reads the *Aeneid* to learn about empirical Roman history, but we do read it, and English schoolboys once committed whole sections of it to memory. Still, it does tell us something about the spirit and mentality of Rome that we can garner nowhere else. We might consider reading Joshua in the same frame of mind.

But what if Gottwald's domestic uprising thesis is wrong? Many scholars disagree with him. Indeed, as Regina Schwartz has pointed out, interpretations of the "conquest" story sometimes seem to reflect the politics or the nationalism of the scholars who write them rather than "what in fact happened." Left-leaning historians tend to prefer Gottwald's account of subjected peoples rising up to overthrow their oppressors. German scholars have sometimes advocated the idea of a gradual settlement, a *Völkerwanderung* that sees the Israelites drifting into Canaan over many years. Most Americans have favored an invasion-by-outsiders picture.[5]

In this battle among the scholars, it can hardly be expected that average lay readers of the Bible can venture anything but a guess. Instead, it would be better to think about a more basic issue: the function of conquest narratives as such. Again Schwartz's insights are helpful. What if in fact there was no conquest, and the process was one of internal revolution or peaceful settlement? The fact is that the *book* of Joshua, and not these alternative accounts, has been handed down to us as scripture and therefore carries with it a certain authority. The conquest virus has found its way into the bloodstream, and it continues to serve a variety of purposes, most of them destructive. I am not suggesting that we tear its pages out of the Bible, but I think it is important to read it for what it is, a document composed centuries after the events it depicts and written for particular religious and political purposes, what we would now correctly term "propaganda." Reading it now poses the blunt question of whether in a world armed with weapons of mass destruction we can continue to permit conquests of any sort, or ideologies and religions that validate them.

Study Tip ──

When reading the biblical book of Joshua, you should have a map in hand. Most Bibles designed for study purposes, including *The HarperCollins Study Bible,* have such maps. They are invaluable, because Joshua teems with geographical place-names. It is not important to remember all or even most of them. But it makes reading the book more enjoyable and more realistic. It is also virtually impossible to read this book and look at the map without also seeing one of the maps we so often glimpse in newspapers today—of Israel, the West Bank, and their neighbors.

Talking Back to God
from the Garbage Heap

The Book of Job

There was a man in the land of Uz, whose name was Job; and that
man was blameless and upright, one who feared God, and turned
away from evil.

JOB 1:1, RSV

Here is something different. When we open the book of Job, we can
lay aside most of the historical research techniques we have met so far.
There are three reasons why. First, this book has an utterly timeless quality, so its dating, intended audience, and authorship, although interesting,
are not of primary importance. It dives headlong into a perennial subject,
the mystery of human suffering, especially the suffering of the innocent.
Why is there such evil in a world God has created, or at least "shaped," and
then declared to be good? The book articulates a response (*not* an answer)
that is different from anything that has come before in the seventeen
books from Genesis to Esther or anything that will come later in the re-
maining books of the Old Testament or in the New Testament. Job is a
classic. It could probably stand on its own without being a part of any
scripture.

The second reason we can read it in a different manner is that Job is
explicitly *fictional*. It opens with the Hebrew equivalent of "once upon a

time." It does not claim to be history, and very few scholars would suggest that Job the man was ever an actual person. This is an especially important feature of the book, since it allows those readers who hold to a literal view of the Bible and therefore constantly grapple with whether what they are reading corresponds with archaeological data or documentary discoveries to relax. They can read Job with a different attitude and recognize that God speaks through legends, sagas, and stories. And this can provide an invaluable lens through which to look at other biblical books.

Third, the book of Job is poetry. In fact, it is soaring poetry. Hebrew scholars rate it as the best in the entire Bible, of such quality that its lyricism can be felt even in translation. But there is a more fundamental reason why Job is in poetry: it is the best idiom in which the issues it takes on can be expressed. The literary critic Moshe Greenberg, in his discerning essay on Job in *The Literary Guide to the Bible,* puts it this way:

> *Poetry allows stark and untempered expression that, while powerful in impact, awakens the kind of careful reflection that leads to the fuller apprehension of a subject. Moreover, the density of poetic language, compelling the reader to complement, to fill in gaps, fits it peculiarly for representing impassioned discourse, which by nature proceeds in associative leaps rather than by logical development.*[1]

All this means that poetry is not only the preferred vehicle for plumbing the tangled and anguishing ideas found in Job; it may be the only vehicle with any chance of conveying them.

TRANSLATION ISSUES

Before plunging into the text of Job, a couple of notes are needed. First, although I have said that historical methods are not important in Job, the issue of translations does matter. The book is written in a type of Hebrew studded with words derived from Arabic and Aramaic that puzzles even veteran linguists. Rendering it into English has involved a lot of speculation and guesswork, so it is even more vital to have two or more translations in hand to read it intelligently. One of my favorites is the visceral version of Job by the poet Stephen Mitchell.[2] Here is an example of Mitchell's coarse but effective style, taken from Job's first speech (3:1–5), compared to the more genteel New Revised Standard Version. First, here is the NRSV:

After this Job opened his mouth and cursed the day of his birth.
Job said,

> *"Let the day perish in which I was born,*
> *and the night that said,*
> *'A man-child is conceived.'*
> *Let that day be darkness!*
> *May God above not seek it,*
> *or light shine on it.*
> *Let gloom and deep darkness claim it.*
> *Let clouds settle upon it;*
> *let the blackness of the day terrify it."*

Here is Mitchell's translation of the same passage:

> *God damn the day I was born,*
> *And the night that forced me from the womb.*
> *On that day—let there be darkness;*
> *Let it never have been created;*
> *Let it sink back into the void. (Job 3:1–4)*

This is not one of those times in which a debate over the literal accuracy of either translation is relevant. In the case of poetry, the question should be: Which best captures the energy and emotion of the original? Whenever someone tries to translate poetry, the result has to be in large part the creation of the translator. If a classic has to speak to many generations, and if language is an evolving reality, then no translation is ever the final one. I will say more about the poetry of Job below.

Study Tip ————————————————————————————

> Compare Job's protest against being born with a similar one by the prophet Jeremiah (20:14–18). It is intriguing to ask if one is dependent on the other or whether such a nihilistic outcry was part of a common stock of angry phrases in Hebrew culture that both writers drew on.

————————————————————————————

Second, put out of your mind the phrase "the patience of Job," which I heard many times as a child ("Yes, poor Mrs. Ewing, with that terrible husband. Why, she must have the patience of Job.") The patience phrase comes from the King James Version of the Letter of James:

> *Behold, we count them happy which endure. Ye have heard of the*
> *patience of Job, and have seen the end of the Lord; that the Lord*
> *is very pitiful, and of tender mercy. (5:11)*

Instead of "patience," recent translations of the Epistle use the word "perseverance" or "steadfastness," which, although they may be better than "patience," still do not characterize the petulant, sometimes furious man we meet in this book. Job the man is anything but patient. He is irritable, insolent, and provocative. He might be better described as "impatient."

Also, the phrase "Job's comforters" has come into wide use, but it usually designates something closer to the original meaning. The friends who come to sit with Job and converse with him after his many catastrophes hardly comfort him. They berate and needle him. So the phrase "Job's comforters" carries an ironical ring, which is the way it is commonly used today. It means a person who may or may not intend to "comfort" someone in distress, but ends up making the situation worse.

THE PLOT

After its overtly fictional "Once upon a time" opening, the book of Job places the story in the "land of Uz," which is briefly mentioned in some other biblical books, but always as a far-off and unknown realm. It suggests something like what the "Land of Oz" or "a faraway land" might mean to modern readers, further underscoring the imaginary quality of the tale. But its fictitious character does not make Job less serious or less credible. Rather, it endows it with a timeless quality and therefore makes it even more relevant both to those who first read it centuries ago and to those of us who wrestle with it today. The man Job, like Adam (Heb. *ha-adam*), is us, a human being trying to come to grips with the most besetting enigmas of life.

Most people are familiar with the outline of the story. Job is portrayed as "a blameless and upright man, one who feared God and turned away from evil." Besides that, he is rich, indeed very rich. The lush description of his herds of "seven thousand sheep, three thousand camels, five hundred yoke of oxen, five hundred donkeys" (1:3) reaches for poetic hyperbole to make the point. Besides that, he is an exemplary family man with seven sons and three daughters, whom he treats generously and teaches piety. He gets up early every morning to pray and offer sacrifices to God. He also has a large retinue of slaves. All in all he seems unusually well fixed and perhaps just a tad too well satisfied with himself.

Now, however, the plot thickens and the trouble begins. God is depicted as meeting with . . . whom? The New Revised Standard Version of the Bible calls them "heavenly beings," but a footnote informs us that in Hebrew the words mean "sons of God." Are they angels, demigods? We are not informed. But the passage seems to point to issues we have raised before about the gradual emergence of what we now call "monotheism." Here, however, that is not the issue, for among these heavenly beings assembled before God stands one called in Hebrew *ha-satan*, rendered in the NRSV as "Satan." But this is problematical. Most scholars prefer to call him simply "the Accuser" (or "the Adversary"), since at this point the idea of Satan as a developed personality still lies far in the future. In a charming note one NRSV study Bible describes him as a kind of secret agent in the imperial service of God, "something like a CIA agent."[3] What is significant in this disagreement about the exact word to use is that the *ha-satan* is not an independent or semi-independent source of evil. He is clearly one of God's staff, in His Divine Majesty's Secret Service, so to speak.

God now stirs the pot by boasting to this cloak-and-dagger agent about his exemplary servant Job. The spy, however, tells God in effect that Job's virtuousness is largely the result of all the blessings God has lavished on him and suggests that if he did not possess all these perks, he might turn out to be a different kind of person. So God gives the Accuser the right to take all this away from Job, but, unlike 007's license to kill, explicitly denies him the right to lay a hand on Job's body.

The Accuser takes his job seriously, even ferociously. In catastrophe after catastrophe Job is deprived of all those camels, sheep, oxen, and donkeys. After this comes the death of all ten of his children. A messenger, who has already relayed to Job the bad news about the animals (all killed by Sabeans or Chaldeans), now tells him, "Your sons and daughters were drinking wine and eating in their eldest brother's house, and suddenly a great wind came across the desert, struck the four corners of the house, and it fell on the young people, and they are all dead" (1:18–19). The desolate Job now goes into mourning, sitting on a dust heap (the Greek translation makes it a dung heap), but he never turns against God. On the contrary, he murmurs words that are often spoken today at funerals: "The LORD gave, and the LORD hath taken away; blessed be the name of the LORD" (1:21, KJV). So far God's parental pride in this righteous servant has been vindicated.

Now, however, the Accuser tells God that the reason his righteous servant Job has remained so faithful is that his body has not been touched. "Just let me get at that," he pleads, "and you'll see. Your exemplary citizen will denounce you!" Once more God yields to the Accuser's callous plea and allows him to afflict Job's physical form. The wretched man is suddenly afflicted with boils and suppurating blisters from head to toe. He crawls off and crouches on his dung heap, scratching his itchy limbs and torso with a broken pottery fragment.

At this point three of his friends hear of his misfortune and come to pay a visit, sitting with him in silence for seven days. Incidentally, neither Job himself, nor these three, later four, friends—Eliphaz the Temanite, Bildad the Shuhite, Zophar the Naamathite, and Elihu—have Hebrew names. It seems they are all Gentiles. In fact, it is not even clear that the poet who wrote Job was Jewish, with the peculiar result that one of the best known parts of the Hebrew Bible is not "Jewish" except by its adoption into the Hebrew scriptures.

Just here, at 3:1 in the book of Job, a sudden transition occurs. It has started as a simple morality tale, the sources of which some historians trace back to 2000 BCE, but now we listen in on a conversation between Job and his friends and eventually a theatrical intervention by God. We leave the surface and plunge into the depths of an enduring and inescapable question. Prose becomes poetry.

Here we have to pause and ask the unavoidable question that thousands of people have posed for years: What kind of a demonic or sadistic God is this who permits an innocent man to be tormented and tortured just to prove a point? The only answer is that, just as the book of Job does not—as we will see—provide a satisfactory "answer" to a perennial mystery, it does not answer the question about God either. God does make an appearance, but this is primarily a book about human beings, and one human being in particular, "Job" from the "land of Uz," grappling with an unavoidable life quandary.

The main body of Job consists of a series of statements and counterstatements by his four visitors with responses by Job, climaxed by a booming intervention in the debate by God himself speaking out of a whirlwind. The dispute between Job and his companions begins in a relatively calm tenor, an exchange of reasonable comments and disagreements, but it escalates from chapter to chapter until the participants seem to be screaming at each other. This structure suggests that one powerful way to treat this book is to parcel out the characters and to read it aloud as a drama. It lends itself easily to this kind of production. I heard it presented this way once in a college auditorium, and it was enormously effective.

It is best, therefore, to allow oneself to be drawn into the increasingly intense arguments between Job and his friends, remembering that, although these interlocutors are sometimes dismissed as smug "false comforters," their arguments are not just straw men. They state, often with eloquence, the same ideas about suffering that are voiced throughout the Old Testament and some of the New Testament as well. They rehash ideas on the subject we still hear today, and Job's responses to them become more pointed and sarcastic by the minute. It is a real debate.

I will not try to summarize the whole argument here. It would not only be unfair to the participants; it would amount to yet another futile effort to transpose poetry into prose. Still, some initial acquaintance with the "comforters" will help us recognize that they not only differ from each other, but that a certain amount of "character development" occurs. They change their tone noticeably as the conversation goes on. In addition, some familiarity with the often convoluted structure of the give-and-take that unfolds will help us to read it more appreciatively.

Eliphaz the Temanite opens what will soon deteriorate into a testy squabble on a fairly genteel note. He admits that all human life is marked by misfortune. He commends Job for how he has helped people in the past who have undergone similar calamities and encourages him to call on those same resources now that he is the victim. But he also voices the theme that all the friends keep harping on, that God is just and therefore Job must have done something truly awful to have merited such castigation, but that if he repents God will restore him to health and prosperity.

Job now replies to Eliphaz, setting the pattern for the rest of the argument, in which the speeches of each of the comforters are followed by his replies. In this first response Job already betrays impatience and irritation with his interlocutors. Picking up on Eliphaz's note about the misery of life, he still wonders why he—not people in general—has been meted out such a dreadful chastisement. He demands his day in court and insists on being informed of the charges against him. He declares: "I will argue my case before him. Through this I will gain victory" (13:15–16, Mitchell).

Now the next two friends turn up the heat. Bildad the Shuhite begins, "How long will you go on ranting, filling our ears with trash?" (8:1–2,

Mitchell). Then he turns the blade in the wound by suggesting that Job's children also must have done something for which they were justly punished. Now Zophar the Naamathite agitates things even more. He tells Job that his punishment is probably even less than the one he deserves, but piously adds—repeating what the previous two companions have said—that if Job would only stop playing the innocent and fess up to his wrongdoing, God will richly reward him.

By this time the "comfort" his buddies have offered, insulting him and maligning his character, is taking its toll on Job (12:13–14). He mocks their claim to wisdom, calls them liars and "worthless physicians," and tells them that the smartest thing they can do is just to shut up. But he knows that his real argument is with God, not with these know-it-alls, so he turns away from them and blurts out a prayer that borders on despair, imploring God simply to withdraw his hand and not let dread terrify him (13:20–28).

When a second round of arguments begins (chaps. 15–20), Eliphaz leads off again. But the mild manner he evidenced in the first round is now gone. He is obviously riled by the way Job has mocked his friends' advice and cuts to a deeper level. What Job is saying, he contends, is not only wrong, but it undermines religion and morality, so now the man with the oozing skin eruptions is not only a sinner; he is also a heretic and blasphemer. The other two friends Bildad and Zophar join him in this allegation. Why is Job ignoring, even denying, the wisdom of the ages? Just who does he think he is? Carried away by their own rhetoric and trying a new tactic to get Job to repent, the three now pile on vivid descriptions of how God punishes the wicked. Bildad predicts that not only Job, but all his future generations will suffer from his sin. Zophar (chap. 20) then offers a vivid description of the torments awaiting the wicked that calls to mind James Joyce's recalling in *A Portrait of the Artist as a Young Man* of the descriptions of hell he heard at spiritual retreats in his early years. Zophar conjures details of food turning into the venom of asps as soon as the wicked eat it, of bronze arrows piercing their bodies and being drawn out of their entrails, and of all their possessions being carried away.

This time when Job replies to all three, he begins, given the harsh way he has spoken before, in a remarkably subdued tenor. He tries to answer theory with facts, received wisdom with empirical evidence. Just look around. The wicked live well, enjoy prosperity, and reach ripe old age surrounded by happy children dancing and playing their tambourines. Even their bull breeds unfailingly, and their cows always calve. The catalog of victorious vice and thriving evil goes on, and all these transgressors ask of God is, "Leave us alone! We do not desire to know your ways" (21:14). "What kind of just God might this be?" Job demands.

Job's statement seems to bring out the worst in Eliphaz. He exclaims that the colossal pride of Job in wanting to put God on trial is blasphemous. It is proof of his deep-dyed sinfulness. Eliphaz gets carried away with his own stubborn line of argument. Since God only punishes the wicked, and Job is being punished in this horrid way, then ipso facto *his* sin must be grave indeed. He then goes on to elaborate an inventory of crimes Job has committed, including stripping clothing from the naked, refusing water to the thirsty, and withholding bread from the hungry, none of which Job has actually done in reality. The argument seems to have reached a hysterical pitch.

Job also now seems to start repeating himself. He goes back to his fantasy of hauling God into court. Indeed, he is so wrapped up in this idée fixe that he even imagines appealing to a higher court:

> I would lay my case before him,
> and fill my mouth with arguments
> I would learn what he would answer me,
> and understand what he would say to me.
> Would he contend with me in the greatness of his power?
> No; but he would give heed to me.
> There an upright person could reason with him,
> and I should be acquitted forever by my judge. (23:4–7)

SOME CREATIVE INTERPRETATIONS

I began this chapter by saying that, with the exception of comparing translations, for the book of Job we can set aside most scholarly approaches to biblical texts. There is, however, another method of biblical studies that I have already mentioned and will return to later that is acutely relevant for Job. It is the "history of interpretation." This book, with its energetic argument, has evoked more debates and dispute than almost any other. A religious studies professor at the New School, Mark Larrimore, has written an engrossing history of these contradictory construals.[4] Early Christian commentators were eager to find in it premonitions of Christ's unswerving fidelity in the face of undeserved suffering. Jewish commentators, including the formidable Maimonides, were not impressed with this tactic, but they were equally eager to uncover symbolic meanings. Thomas Aquinas, Martin Luther, and John Calvin all took a crack at Job, but with results that are hardly memorable.

Modern writers have not resisted the temptation of Job either. In 1958, *J.B.*, a play in free verse by American playwright and poet Archibald MacLeish, was produced on Broadway and drew large audiences. The plot centers on a rich banker, J.B., who claims his fortune is attributable to his piety. But two circus refreshment and balloon vendors argue about whether J.B. would remain so pious if he lost everything. Sure enough, the banker's family is destroyed in accidents, and then three characters, representing History, Science, and Religion, all offer J.B. explanations for what has gone wrong. But, like his biblical prototype, J.B. rejects their rationalizations and advice. In one clever theatrical device, MacLeish introduces an offstage voice that tries to escalate these events into a cosmic religious drama, but fails to do so. This play, MacLeish seems to be saying, is not about cosmic questions, but about the situations—both sad and silly—that we human beings get ourselves into. Unlike the biblical account, J.B. is not vindicated by God, does not get all that he has lost back, and instead opts for a simple life with his ordinary wife. MacLeish's is a secularized adaptation of the biblical saga. It does not either pose or pretend to answer any large questions. But it does demonstrate the inherent power of the story itself, and the poetry of the play makes it even more potent.

It seems that no one is immune from trying to unravel Job. Some years ago I offered a course for Harvard undergraduates, "Law, Religion, and Science," with two remarkable colleagues, Alan Dershowitz, of the law school, and Stephen Jay Gould, a paleontologist and science writer. Our tactic was to pick a different topic each week, which each of us would then approach from the angle of our own field. We covered a wide range of subjects, from the nature of evidence, to when life begins, to whether torture is ever permissible. Once Gould suggested that we talk about the meaning of suffering and recommended that we assign the book of Job to the overflow crowd of students who enrolled in the course. We all thought that if Archibald MacLeish could put History, Science, and Religion on the stage to bring Job to life, why couldn't we try it with Law, Religion, and Science in Lecture Hall 3 of the Science Center, where our class met?

It turned out to be one of the best sessions of the semester. Dershowitz was delighted that Job actually wanted to haul God into court and sue him:

> *I want to speak before God*
> *To present my case in God's court.*
> *Listen now to my arguments:*
> *Hear out my accusations . . . (Mitchell)*

But he also noted that Job wanted to act as his own counsel, which Dershowitz—a recognized superb defense attorney—insisted was always a serious mistake. "Anyone who wants to act as his own lawyer," he offered, quoting an old quip, "has an idiot for a client." But Job did just this, and did pretty well for himself. Or did he?

> *For I have prepared my defense,*
> *And I know that I am right . . .*
> *Accuse me—I will respond;*
> *Or let me speak and answer me*
> *What crime have I committed? . . . (Mitchell)*

In short, Dershowitz loved Job, because it reads in part like a courtroom drama, and he felt quite at home.

I was particularly drawn to Gould's focus on what has to be recognized as an alternative to the human-centered accounts in Genesis. In Job, "man" is not portrayed as the apex of creation, not even as its principal caretaker. Human beings are one species among all the others, and a not exceptionally significant one at that. Men and women are a part of the intricate web of life, and therefore we should recognize who we are and not try to puff ourselves up into something special.

I largely agreed with Gould. But, as I have mentioned before in this book, I added that I am glad the Bible speaks in more than one voice. There are times when we need to be reminded of our humble place as one minute strand in the vast and interdependent web. But then there are times when we need to be reminded that we are also stewards of something that does not belong to us. ("The earth is the LORD's and the fulness thereof; the world, and they that dwell therein," Ps. 24:1, KJV.) Gould, a congenial colleague and a courageous man, was struggling with brain cancer during the final weeks of the last year we offered the course. Like Job, he had urgent personal reasons to ask some hard questions about suffering. But he never missed a class session, even when he had to lecture sitting down. He died just a few weeks after the term ended.

I also had the unpleasant task of trying to assuage the students' patent annoyance that God does not "answer" Job's persistent questions. Students, like most of us, want answers, even to intractable mysteries. It is hard for anyone to come to terms with the raw truth that sometimes there just are none. But I am pleased that when the rabbis assembled the Jewish canon, they admitted this sometimes quite aberrant book into it. It serves as an invaluable minority report against what are the all-too-easy answers often found in the rest of scripture. Job's question is never answered. But then neither is the question Jesus coughs out as he hangs on the cross, "My God, my God, why have you forsaken me?" (Matt. 27:46).

Discussions in our class sometimes became so lively that we carried them over to the following week. This happened with Job, so before we met again, I composed a modest updating of God's scathing speech from the whirlwind (chaps. 38–39), which Steve Gould had liked so much. It went like this:

Who is this speck of dust who is making so much noise, going on and on as though he knows something about the great mystery that surrounds us?

Where were you, my little man, when the primal nebulae exploded into being?

Have you ridden one of your puny space rockets the thirteen billion light-years to the edge of that part of the universe that you can observe?

Do you know what lies beyond the edge? Do you?

Where were you more recently when the pterodactyl and the tyrannosaurus rex roamed the steamy earth?

You actually think that nature is there for your comfort and use, to dig up and shovel around, to drain and gobble up!

Think again. Why does the rain fall and the sun shine to nourish land where no humans live?

You may think you are in charge here, or may be an indispensable caretaker. But nature and the cosmos are older and bigger, took care of themselves for a long time without you, and could do so again, maybe even better without you around to mess things up.

Even if Job does not "answer" the newly rediscovered "problem of evil" today, does it say anything significant about it? I believe it does. One of the hopeful recent developments in the human imagination is its effort—against fearful odds—to reclaim language as a living organism, not a set of inert signs. In this sense the book of Job makes an invaluable contribution. Reading it can remind us that poetry, drama, dance, and music are better vehicles for conveying spiritual meaning than is most philosophy (not including philosophers like Plato and Nietzsche, who wrote in poetry and aphorism) or even most theology.

After reading and thinking about Job carefully and despite all its pungent poetry and bold imagery, many people are left with a dissatisfied feeling. God does not answer Job's searching questions. Neither do his comforters. But maybe that is exactly the answer. Maybe trying to find some satisfying meaning in innocent human suffering is, after all, a futile endeavor. In our times the countless attempts to find some meaning in the Holocaust, or Shoah, in which millions of innocent people, most of them Jews, were killed, can serve as an example. Deeply thoughtful writers who were themselves survivors of the killing, such as Primo Levi and Elie Wiesel, insist that any attempt to impose some significance on it inevitably becomes a trivialization. Some have even suggested that we suffer today under a kind of "tyranny of meaning," a compulsion to eke some kind of import out of events that by their nature allow for no such reading. The memory of the Holocaust confronts us with titanic meaninglessness, an evil we must resist as we also must live with it, but without ever being able to get our minds around it.

THE PERSPECTIVE OF SUFFERERS

I think there is an important element of truth in this rejection of a quest for an "explanation" of innocent suffering. But the quest still goes on, and when it comes to Job's question, there is one important cluster of voices we have not yet mentioned, those who pose it from the perspective of the people who suffer themselves. Among these voices in recent decades some of the most articulate have arisen from the slums and *favelas* of Latin America. The Costa Rican poet Elsa Tamez, for example, has published a fierce *Carta al Hermano Job* (*A Letter to Brother Job*), in which she points out that the turning point for the central character comes when he realizes he is not alone in his suffering, but that the poor and outcast also suffer, although in his wealth and comfort he had scarcely been aware of it. At this point, Tamez states, Job broadens the question he has been doggedly putting to God. He no longer focuses on his own personal pain. Nor does he ask a general question like, "Why is there suffering in the world?" Rather, he now recalls the suffering of the broken and the destitute, which he now shares. Tamez sees here the reason why the hungry shantytown residents she knows so well can relate to Job. She says to Job:

The smell of death that is about you reaches our nostrils; we smell
you everywhere. Your skeletal body goads us. Shreds of your cor-
roding flesh hang from our flesh: you have infected us, brother
Job, you have infected us, our families, our people. And your look
of one who thirsts for justice and your breath that is soaked in
wrath have filled us with courage, tenderness and hope.[5]

Another Latin American, Father Gustavo Gutiérrez, has written about
Job in a book entitled *On Job: God-Talk and the Suffering of the Innocent.*[6]
A priest who has served in the most desperate slums of Peru, Gutiérrez
seems at first to be joining in a long-standing debate in academic theology
about whether it is possible to "speak *about* God" at all. Aren't silence,
awe, and humility the most appropriate ways to respond to the Great Mystery? But Gutiérrez shuffles the deck of this discussion by suggesting that
the most basic question about God-talk is not how it is formulated, but the
question of *who* is talking and *why* and to *whom.* He is not particularly
interested in God-talk in general or even with Dietrich Bonhoeffer's pressing concern: How do we speak of God in a secular age? Rather, Gutiérrez
is concerned with talking about and to God in the midst of the impoverished people among whom he lives, some of whom, he says, literally live
today in ash and garbage dumps.

His question is, "How are we as human beings to speak of God from
the heart of human poverty, hunger, and suffering?" This is not the way in
which the classical problem of theodicy has been stated. Gutiérrez calls his
approach "theology done from the garbage heap." He holds that the theme
of the book of Job is not the impenetrable human mystery of suffering, but
rather how to speak of God from the rubbish pile.

From this perspective he believes nearly all the efforts to interpret Job,
and with them the "problem of evil" (theodicy), have gone astray. These
efforts have misfired in large measure because they pose the question too
impersonally. With Job, the boil-infested man sitting on his dung heap,
the question is intensely personal. But, although it is personal, it is not
individual. Like Tamez, Gutiérrez points out that Job's breakthrough comes
when he discovers that he is not alone in his pain. This is crucial, because

suffering often turns us in on ourselves and we forget our links with other sufferers. Here Job is different. He demands from God not only a response to his own suffering, but also to the unjustified and preventable hurt that the powerful inflict on the outcast. At this point, as he catalogs the continued injustices that the higher-ups perpetrate on the oppressed, Job's language crackles with the strident tones of some of the prophets like Jeremiah and especially Amos:

> *Some move landmarks;*
> *they seize flocks and pasture them.*
> *They drive away the donkey of the fatherless;*
> *they take the widow's ox for a pledge.*
> *They thrust the poor off the road;*
> *the poor of the earth all hide themselves.*
> *Behold, like wild donkeys in the desert*
> *the poor go out to their toil, seeking game;*
> *the wasteland yields food for their children.*
> *They gather their fodder in the field,*
> *and they glean the vineyard of the wicked man.*
> *They lie all night naked, without clothing,*
> *and have no covering in the cold.*
> *They are wet with the rain of the mountains,*
> *and cling to the rock for lack of shelter.*
> *There are those who snatch the fatherless child*
> *from the breast,*
> *and they take a pledge against the poor.*
> *They go about naked, without clothing;*
> *hungry, they carry the sheaves;*
> *among the olive rows of the wicked they make oil;*
> *they tread the winepresses, but suffer thirst.*
> *(24:2–11, ESV)*

Continuing his complaint to God about injuries and inequity he now sees everywhere and not just under his own tent, he goes on to protest that

the well-fed and comfortable rich people, on the other hand, seem to prosper and grow fatter:

> *Look at me and be appalled;*
> *clap your hand over your mouth.*
> *When I think about this, I am terrified;*
> *trembling seizes my body.*
> *Why do the wicked live on,*
> *growing old and increasing in power?*
> *They see their children established around them,*
> *their offspring before their eyes.*
> *Their homes are safe and free from fear;*
> *the rod of God is not on them.*
> *Their bulls never fail to breed;*
> *their cows calve and do not miscarry.*
> *They send forth their children as a flock;*
> *their little ones dance about.*
> *They sing to the music of timbrel and lyre;*
> *they make merry to the sound of the pipe.*
> *They spend their years in prosperity*
> *and go down to the grave in peace.*
> *Yet they say to God, "Leave us alone!*
> *We have no desire to know your ways.*
> *Who is the Almighty, that we should serve him?*
> *What would we gain by praying to him?" (21:6–13, NIV)*

Notice that in this angry outburst, Job does not blame God directly for
causing this anguish. Rather he points his accusing finger at the earthlings
who profit from it while flaunting their contempt for divine justice, but
also at God for letting them get away with it. Clearly something has happened to Job. His personal experience of infirmity and deprivation has
moved him to look at the world from a different perspective. His cascading
descent from the privileges of wealth to the desolation of powerlessness has

cast the world in a new light, one he would never have known, had he lived out his life in cosseted comfort.

Job's life-changing upheaval is strikingly similar to the change that took place in the life of Dietrich Bonhoeffer, the German pastor who was executed by the Nazis in a concentration camp in April 1945 for his resistance to their tyranny. Bonhoeffer, like Job, was a member of a wealthy family in Berlin. His father was the city's most respected psychiatrist. He enjoyed vintage wines, extensive travel, and the finest music. When he was snatched away from this refined setting, locked in a cell with a filthy bed, and permitted few visitors, it took him a long time to discern any positive element in what had happened to him. Nonetheless, he eventually did. In a famous passage in his *Letters and Papers from Prison,* dated shortly before his death, Bonhoeffer muses to a friend what his years behind bars have taught him. Bonhoeffer writes:

> *There remains an experience of incomparable value. We have for once learnt to see the great events of world history from below, from the perspective of the outcast, the suspects, the maltreated, the powerless, the oppressed, the reviled—in short, from the perspective of those who suffer.*

We will return to Bonhoeffer in a later chapter. Here it suffices to say that he did not stop with this radical realization. He disclaimed any superior significance for his new point of view. He continues:

> *This perspective from below must not become the partisan possession of those who are eternally dissatisfied; rather, we must do justice to life in all its dimensions from a higher satisfaction.*[7]

At the end of the book of Job, God lashes out at his false comforters who have deployed all the traditional theological rationales for suffering, and then he praises Job who has both argued vigorously against him and recognized that there just is no satisfying answer. Job's worldview now embraces angry, impatient protest against injustice. But the mystery remains. There is a mystical dimension here, a place for wonder, in which we trust the ultimate wisdom and justice of God. In effect, Job has now combined impatience at the injustice of the world with patience in the goodness and mercy of God. But his patience with God does not make him any less impatient with the grossly degrading conditions he now sees so clearly around him.

For Gutiérrez, what he calls "contemplation" must always have a place, along with vociferous protest, in the repertoire of spiritual gifts the faithful need to cultivate. He believes we have to learn to blend the two. Too often those who know how to take action against the cruelty of the powerful forget to acknowledge the mystery, and those who dwell on the unfathomable mystery shutter themselves from the tears of the downtrodden. But as Bonhoeffer once put it, "He who does not cry out for the Jews has no right to sing Gregorian chant."

THE LANGUAGE OF COMPLAINT

The book of Job makes another valuable contribution. It gives the language of complaint a fresh validity. From other Old Testament books, including Lamentations, we can see that both complaining *about* God and complaining *to* God were acceptable expressions of prayer. This dissenting, even rebellious way of addressing God continued in Judaism. We can hear it, for example, in the tales of the Hasidic rabbis. Tevye, in *Fiddler on the Roof,* employs it in a soft-pedaled key. But it virtually disappeared from Christian prayer and liturgical practice. Calling God out about the agony of our fellow creatures has become pale and bloodless.

Recently, however, that has begun to change. And it has appeared especially in those areas where the disinherited live and "hunger for righteousness." The German theologian Claus Westermann writes: "Some of the younger churches are taking the initiative in restoring 'complaint' to its rightful place in prayer."[8]

Gutiérrez warmly welcomes this "return of complaint," but he takes another step. Not only is complaint a legitimate *element* of prayer, but the enraged outcry of the poor is also a legitimate *form* of prayer. When God speaks to Moses at the burning bush, he says, "I have observed the misery of my people who are in Egypt; I have heard their cry" (Exod. 3:7), even though these cries were not specifically addressed to him. Not only can there be a protest element in prayer; there is also a prayer element in the protest of the poor. God accepts Job's "God-talk." To the leading comforter, Eliphaz the Temanite, he says: "My wrath is kindled against you and against your two friends; for you have not spoken of me what is right, as my servant Job has" (42:7). In other words, God upbraids Eliphaz because he has not complained to him. What might be called "social complaint," as opposed to merely personal complaint or impersonal curiosity about suffering, might, it seems, be an incipient expression of a theodicy-in-the-making, a searing statement of what suffering means when it comes from the heart of the sufferers.

Christians have much to learn from Jews about the "return of complaint." The late Arthur Gold, a professor at Wellesley College, put it in typically rabbinical humorous and ironic style. In his droll retelling of the opening of the Job story, he has the *ha-satan* tweak God with the question of why he continues to put up with the Jews, this peculiar people he has chosen, even though they treat him so impertinently. They *complain* so much! Why can't they be more like, say, the Greeks, who stride erectly into whatever fate holds for them without all this grumbling? God, in Gold's retelling, answers that he prefers the Jews and their discontented murmuring. "At least," says God, "it shows that they still believe in me, and they think I could do better."[9]

A PROBLEMATIC ENDING

Job ends in a flurry of rare and opaque Hebrew words, a linguistic cryptogram that has puzzled scholars for centuries. What does Job actually say in his final response to God? The King James Version puts it this way:

Then Job answered the LORD, *and said,*

> *I know that thou canst do every thing,*
> *and that no thought can be withholden from thee.*
> *Who is he that hideth counsel without knowledge?*
> *therefore have I uttered that I understood not;*
> *things too wonderful for me, which I knew not.*
> *Hear, I beseech thee, and I will speak:*
> *I will demand of thee, and declare thou unto me.*
> *I have heard of thee by the hearing of the ear:*
> *but now mine eye seeth thee.*
> *Wherefore I abhor myself,*
> *and repent in dust and ashes. (42:1–6)*

But what a disappointing denouement this is for a character who has bravely stood up both to his comforters and to God for forty chapters! Must this all end in a defeated, ground-down Job, who seems to take back all he has said and grovel? Here differences in translation are of supreme importance. Stephen Mitchell asserts that depicting Job as fawning and kowtowing is built on "the shakiest of philological ground."[10] Further, he says, since a large measure of sheer speculation is necessarily involved in translating the unfamiliar Hebrew words, the sixteenth-century King James translators drew on their own current theologies in figuring out what Job is saying. And given those theologies, they thought he *ought* to abase himself. But the key, Mitchell says, is that Job tells God, "I had heard of you with my ears, but now my eyes have seen you" (42:5). In other words, Job has had an encounter with the transcendent, with God the unnamable, and that has changed him. What we find Job doing, says Mitchell, is not abject submission, but spiritual transformation. Nor does the reference to "dust" imply self-demeaning. It is not about self-deprecation. It is an acknowledgment of his finitude. Job's only regret is that he tried to speak about the unspeakable, when silence would have been a more appropriate response.

When the poetry ends (42:6), the book of Job returns to the prose with which it began. It also returns to the baroque hyperbole of those opening verses. God rewards Job lavishly. He is given even more oxen and sheep and camels. He is given seven sons and three daughters. His relatives (who do not appear in the narrative during his misery) now flock to his house bearing cash and gold rings. He lives to be 140, twice the traditional life span of three score years and ten. He sees his grandchildren and great-grandchildren, and when he dies, like Abraham, he is "old and full of days." As an attempt to give the story a Hollywood ending, this exaggerated effort seems overdone. Apparently the writer wants to be very sure we get the point.

Should we be sorry that Job ends on such a note of exaggeration and scholarly wrangling? I think not. The fact that the text itself does not yield a neat or satisfying answer to the question of innocent human suffering suggests that the problematical ending is entirely fitting. The difference between a "problem" and a "mystery" is that we may be able to "solve" a problem, but a mystery is something we have to live with. Like the man from Uz, we must learn to combat preventable suffering, by seeking cures for diseases and struggling against injustice. But we must also recognize that not even the most advanced medical research or the most vigorous campaigns against misrule will end all innocent suffering. Still, we have to try. This is a hard lesson, maybe an impossible one, for modern minds to come to terms with, attuned as they are to a cognitive approach to the world, but it may be exactly why the book of Job still both attracts and infuriates us.

Listening to the Voices
of the Voiceless

Amos and the Prophets

> The people who walked in darkness
> Have seen a great light;
> Those who dwelt in the land of the shadow of death,
> Upon them a light has shined.

ISAIAH 9:2, NKJV

How should we read the Hebrew prophets today? What connection is there between them and the exemplary moral leaders we sometimes call prophets today? Most students of history recognize prophecy as the most distinctive and important feature of Hebrew faith. Many Jewish scholars, however, express some ambivalence about this judgment. They feel that Christians have overrated the prophets, elevating their significance because they are so often seen as predictors of Jesus Christ. There are real grounds for their caution, which we return to below.[1]

But one of the greatest Jewish scholars of the twentieth century, Rabbi Abraham Joshua Heschel (1907–72), insisted that the prophets are indeed central and that they should not be devalued just because Christians have made use of them for their own purposes. In his famous book on the prophets, Heschel advances an idea that eventually became the keystone of his thinking. He contends that the prophets dramatize the central tenet of

Jewish faith, that God is best understood not as anthropomorphic, that God takes human form, but rather as anthropopathic—that God has human feelings. Heschel argues for the view of Hebrew prophets as receivers of the "divine pathos," of the wrath and sorrow of God over his nation, which has forsaken him. In this view, prophets do not speak for God so much as they remind their audience of God's voice for the voiceless and the forgotten.[2]

These observations also apply to the Christian idea of a God who feels the pain and anguish of humanity. In any case there are many reasons why both Jews and Christians can and should come to grips with the Hebrew prophets. For one thing, Christians need to be familiar with them if only because Jesus placed himself clearly in this tradition. It is how he introduces himself in his inaugural message in his hometown, sometimes called his Nazareth Manifesto:

> *Then Jesus, filled with the power of the Spirit, returned to Galilee, and a report about him spread through all the surrounding country. He began to teach in their synagogues and was praised by everyone.*
>
> *When he came to Nazareth, where he had been brought up, he went to the synagogue on the sabbath day, as was his custom. He stood up to read, and the scroll of the prophet Isaiah was given to him. He unrolled the scroll and found the place where it was written:*
>
> > *"The Spirit of the Lord is upon me,*
> > *because he has anointed me*
> > *to bring good news to the poor.*
> > *He has sent me to proclaim release to the captives*
> > *and recovery of sight to the blind,*
> > *to let the oppressed go free,*
> > *to proclaim the year of the Lord's favor."*
>
> *And he rolled up the scroll, gave it back to the attendant, and sat down. (Luke 4:14–20)*

The discussion about how to read the prophets goes back to a distinction we alluded to earlier about the relationship between "what it meant then" and "what it means now." I wrote that I think this distinction has been overplayed. We have to add "what it *has meant*" (the history of interpretation) and also to recognize that the meaning of any text is a combination of all three of these layers. As I have suggested in earlier chapters, I do not believe that a biblical book or passage has only one meaning, for example, the writer's original intent, even if that intent can be ascertained with any degree of assurance (which is unlikely).

Take the famous passage from the prophet Isaiah that opens this chapter as an example. When the vast majority of Christians hear this read, usually at a Christmas Eve service amid candles, wreaths, and carol singing, they understand it to be about the birth of Jesus. To tell these listeners that this was not what Isaiah originally meant may be factual, but it does not change the way people hear it today, nor should it. Once written, a classic text is like a bird released from its cage. It develops a life of its own. Its "meaning" is not locked in. Isaiah's eloquent words serve additional purposes.

This does not mean, of course, that the words can be hijacked and enlisted in any cause whatever, and here the original context helps prevent such misuse. For both Jewish and Christian interpreters the luminous words of the prophet point to the confidence that God will not abandon us to despondency and despair amid tragedy and loss. Isaiah's words are a canticle of hope, even though just how God responds differs in the two cases. Hence, it is important to be familiar with the text's original setting as best we can. And this means we need to understand the institution of prophecy in the light of its biblical setting.

THE ROLE OF THE PROPHET

What is a prophet? The Bible endows a range of people with this designation, beginning with Moses and continuing through Samuel, Elijah, Amos, Isaiah, Jeremiah, Ezekiel, and a host of "minor prophets" such as Habakkuk, Zechariah, and Malachi. In modern usage the word is also applied to inspiring moral leaders such as Martin Luther King, Jr., and Nelson Mandela. For many scholars, Hebrew prophecy may be the most important feature of Jewish faith, but like many of the other such features we have already noticed, it was not invented out of whole cloth. The word "prophet" derives from an earlier Canaanite word meaning "announcer," a *forth*-teller rather than a *fore*-teller, as the textbooks have it. Still we cannot overlook the fact that Jeremiah, Isaiah, and the other prophets seem to engage in some *fore*telling, and the Bible itself makes clear that the prophets developed out of the "seers."

Remember also that the prophets who now appear in our scripture had to contend with what the Bible itself calls "false prophets." The most celebrated of the battles between the true and false prophets is the one described in 1 Kings 18, in which Elijah has his epochal contest with the prophets of Baal on Mt. Carmel. There he ridicules their prayers and contortions and cutting themselves with knives and spears, none of which set the sacrifice on fire as Elijah's prayer did. To complicate the picture even more, something similar to Hebrew prophecy also emerged in non-Hebrew cultures, like ancient China and Greece.

As we come to the question of how to read the prophets today, I confess that this is one area of "How to Read the Bible" in which I was slow to absorb the best current biblical scholarship (for reasons I will make clear below), but eventually reading them in that light heightened my appreciation for them. My life with the prophets goes back to my boyhood, during which I learned in Sunday school to see them almost exclusively as inspired predictors of the coming of Jesus, but also to some extent as severe critics of the Jewish people for their waywardness. A change came when, as a teenager, I attended some Bible study sessions at a student conference. The teacher was a black Baptist pastor who stood firmly in the social gospel tradition, and the biblical book he led us in studying was the prophet Amos.

I have forgotten the name of the teacher, but I, like a Holden Caulfield even before *The Catcher in the Rye* appeared, had already entered a phase of rebellion against the phoniness and hypocrisy of the society around me, and Amos instantly became my favorite biblical book. Just listen to this:

Thus says the Lord:

> "For three transgressions of Israel,
> and for four, I will not revoke the punishment;
> because they sell the righteous for silver,
> and the needy for a pair of shoes—
> they that trample the head of the poor into the
> dust of the earth,
> and turn aside the way of the afflicted." (2:6–7, RSV)

Those pubescent years were for me, as they are for others in that cohort, also a time of impatience and anger about the stuffiness and rigidity of the church. And Amos addressed this sentiment as well:

> I hate, I despise your feasts,
> and I take no delight in your solemn assemblies.
> Even though you offer me your burnt offerings and
> cereal offerings,
> I will not accept them,
> and the peace offerings of your fatted beasts
> I will not look upon.
> Take away from me the noise of your songs;
> to the melody of your harps I will not listen.
> But let justice roll down like waters,
> and righteousness like an ever-flowing stream.
> (5:21–24, RSV)

Suddenly, I became a devotee of Amos. That was in the 1950s, and at that time the teacher's take on Amos also reflected mainstream biblical scholarship. The prophet Amos reigned as the blistering critic of inequality, empty ritualism, and rigid institutional piety. He was the hero of those—including me—who were fed up with smug piety and hypocritical moralism. Imagine my satisfaction in finding my dissident adolescent zeal so sharply vented in the pages of scripture itself. I also soon accepted the received wisdom of the time by which the prophets were framed as anti-cultic, antipriestly, and antiroyal. Isaiah carries on and sharpens the invective of Amos:

> *"The multitude of your sacrifices—*
> *what are they to me?" says the* LORD.
> *"I have more than enough of burnt offerings,*
> *of rams and the fat of fattened animals;*
> *I have no pleasure*
> *in the blood of bulls and lambs and goats.*
> *When you come to appear before me,*
> *who has asked this of you,*
> *this trampling of my courts?" (1:11–12, NIV)*

Is it any wonder that an inwardly iconoclastic (if outwardly rather conventional) young man should be powerfully drawn to the prophets? I read them as kind of incipient revolutionaries against all the pillars of the establishment of their day. Right on, Amos!

PROPHETS AND SEERS

As the scholarship about the prophets developed over the next decades, however, researchers questioned this flamboyant image of Amos and began to view the prophets, including Amos, as in closer relationship to both the kings and the priests than had previously been thought. One of the scholarly methods that contributed to this refocusing is the analysis of the literary and rhetorical forms through which a message is transmitted. Introduced by German biblical scholars, it was called "form criticism." But given my distaste for the overuse of the word "criticism" in biblical studies (see the Introduction to this book), I prefer to call this method simply "form analysis." The idea behind it is a simple one. Here is how it works.

The word "form" has two meanings in this method. The first refers to the structure or pattern of any biblical portion, its internal skeleton. The second refers to the genre or type of expression it is and the kind of human situation in which it might be used. Just as we know there are different types of mail in our boxes each day (advertisements, bills, magazines, personal letters, etc.), and we read each of them with a somewhat different attitude, so—as we have already noted before—there are different types (forms) of material in the Bible. There are poems, curses, prayers, narratives, songs, letters, and many more. When we read any part of the Bible, we need to be aware not just of the content of what we read, but also of what kind of material it is. This recognition keeps us from misreading the Bible by confusing legends with chronicles or mistaking parables for histories. And this in turn prevents us from falling into a kind of heedless literalism. Just as important, form analysis reminds us that the Bible is not just the product of inspired singular spiritual geniuses; it is the creation of a whole people over many generations.

How does form analysis clarify our reading of the prophets? By applying it, historians discovered that similar forms also existed in material before and around the time of the biblical writers, in both written and oral expression. Reading the Bible with this in mind helps us to recognize prophecy wherever we see it. It also sheds new light on some old dilemmas, for example, the quandary of the relationship between the prophets, the kings, and the priests. It also helped clarify whether and to what extend Hebrew prophecy grew out of the preexisting institution of the "seers."

Look, for example, at how the prophets addressed the kings. The most poignant example is Nathan's confrontation with King David, who had just sent Uriah, one of his warriors, to his death in battle, so that he could snatch his wife, Bathsheba, the beauty he had glimpsed on the rooftop while she was bathing. Nathan tells David the story of a man who owns only one little lamb, which a rich man takes from him; David, indignant at the injustice, says the rich man deserves to die. Nathan then points his finger at David: "You are the man!" (2 Sam. 12:7).

Form analysts point out that there existed a formula, a package, into which different kinds of content could be poured before the classic Hebrew prophets appeared. It consists of two parts. The first is an indictment, a catalog—sometimes a long one—of the noxious things people were doing both to each other and to God. The second part is a threat that says, in one way or another, "And this is what will happen to you, if you do not change your ways." The Hebrew prophets made use of this "form" and others, but used them for what eventually turned out to be a radical new purpose. In time the new wine put into the old wineskins burst them. Like many other qualities of biblical faith, prophecy shares some aspects with other traditions, but acquires its own distinctive voice.

This transformative use of what is already at hand is something we have seen in other books of the Bible, and we will notice it again in books we will consider later. We have seen it in the retelling, with a new twist, of previous creation and flood sagas in Genesis. We noted that the book of Job is an inspired Hebrew reworking of an old folktale that had been known for generations. In general we can begin to recognize that modern biblical research, whether in archaeology, form history, or one of the other current approaches, reveals a Bible that is clearly both in continuity and discontinuity with its religious and cultural environment. Consequently, we do not need either to opt for the Bible's utter uniqueness or to dismiss it as "pretty much the same" as what the other traditions teach. This is especially important to bear in mind as Christians find themselves in a religiously heterogeneous world, both around the globe and at home.

The prophets of Israel arose both in continuity and discontinuity with just such a spiritually hybrid world. Historians now recognize that different religions existed not just around the outside borders of the two Jewish kingdoms, Israel and Judah, but within their borders as well. When David conquered the Canaanite city of Jerusalem and made it his capital, he retained the services of its resident Jebusite priests, for whom the city was already a holy site, and they conducted their services side by side with the priests of Yahweh, David's favorite god. Solomon not only had many, many wives (the figure of one thousand may be a stretch), but also just as many "foreign" gods and goddesses in his Temple.

In this piebald context the prophets created what one historian has called a "Yahweh only" theology. They never insisted that the "foreign gods" did not exist, only that the Israelites should not worship or serve them. This idea is stated in a straightforward manner in the First Commandment: "Thou shall have no other gods before me." The prophets did indeed often rail against the worship of Baal and other deities of the time, but the thrust of their concern was not against the Baal cult itself; it was aimed at the Israelites who slid into it. Again this is an important insight for Christians, Muslims, or Jews, all of whom consider themselves to be "monotheists" living on a spiritually pluralistic planet. We need not confute or seek to invalidate the values of other faiths in order to be faithful in our own.

The prophets are most helpful to us today not because they tore down other people's altars, but because they constantly spelled out what it meant to serve Yahweh alone in the homeland. To be more specific, prophetic faith lived in continuous tension with three related religious and political institutions, each of which has its modern equivalent today. They are the following:

1. The first was the old tradition of the *seers,* who often went into states of ecstasy or alternative consciousness in which they claimed to have had an encounter with the holy; they maintained they were able to discern what the future would bring. The rough analogue of these people today can be found in the flood of mystical and esoteric movements that seem to keep arising and that, in an allegedly scientific age, still attract innumerable devotees.

2. The second were the *priests,* the cultic officials who presided over the holy sites and eventually in the Jerusalem Temple, who offered sacrifices and therefore mediated between God and the people. They could be equated with today's priests, rabbis, imams, pastors, and other clerical personages. They constituted the religious "establishment."

3. Finally there were the *kings.* The Hebrews were relatively late in establishing the institution of kingship and did so with considerable reluctance, as is made clear by Samuel's ominous

warning to them when they asked for a king (see 1 Sam. 8:10–
22). But the ancient Jews, despite these warnings, did eventually choose to have kings, and they constituted the rough
equivalent of the governments and regimes of today's national
states.

SEERS

There is undeniable evidence that the classic prophets carried with
them remnants of the ancient tradition of the seers. Ezekiel's vivid vision
of "the wheel in the wheel" and Isaiah's visions of the creatures surround-
ing the heavenly throne constitute just two of many examples. Again, the
prophets did not seem to disdain these semitrance states, but they drew on
them for different purposes.

When it comes to the place of ecstasy in spirituality, including Christian faith, it is important to remind ourselves both that it has not disappeared today, but also that it seems to be a rising tide. The mystical and
experiential dimension of religion has undergone a rebirth. Pentecostal
and charismatic people now account for one of four Christians in the
world, and they are the fastest growing wing of Christianity, especially in
the global south. And this is a movement in which ecstasy, a somewhat
neglected and even scorned element in Christian history, has made a sensational comeback. Pentecostals, whether in Africa, Korea, Brazil, or the
United States, worship with their bodies. They sway, dance, and sometimes collapse on the floor in what appears to be a trance, which they call
"being slain in the Lord." For many years disparagers labeled them "holy
rollers." They also "speak in tongues," a practice they sometimes call
"prayers of the heart," in which students of comparative religion see similarities to what they term "ecstatic speech," something found in a wide
variety of religions. What connection, if any, does prophecy have with all
of this? Does ecstasy have a place in the Christian life?[3]

If we read the Hebrew prophets carefully, we will find some illumina-
tion about these questions, but also some confusion. It seems that the

prophets both built on and went beyond the seers. But in some ways the roles of "seer" and of "prophet" continued to overlap. An especially puzzling verse in this regard appears in 1 Samuel 9:9. In this charming narrative Saul and a companion are searching for some of his father's donkeys that have gone astray. They are not finding them, and Saul wants to turn back, so his father will not worry about him. But his companion suggests that they consult a "seer," a "man of God" named Samuel, who lives in that town. At this point in the text the writer decides to introduce a kind of historical explanation in parenthesis:

> *(Formerly in Israel, anyone who went to inquire of God would say, "Come, let us go to the seer"; for the one who is now called a prophet was formerly called a seer.)*

This explanation, that it is only the terminology that has changed, might seem to solve the seer-prophet issue, but that is hardly the case. Once again here, as we have seen frequently, the Bible does not speak in a single voice. In other passages we can find significant tensions between prophets and seers, although the overlap between the two persists, so it is fair to say that both prophets and seers continued to exist through the period of the Old Testament.[4]

As we will see in a moment, the prophet-seer connection is further complicated when we discover that both are related to kingship. In the book that bears his name, Samuel anoints Saul as Israel's first king. But what are we to make of the following account, in which Saul falls into a "frenzy" and seems to become both a seer and a prophet? Here the prophet Samuel is instructing Saul. I have indicated alternate translations of some key phrases in brackets:

> *"After that you shall come to Gibeath-elohim, where there is a garrison of the Philistines; and there, as you come to the city, you will meet a band of prophets coming down from the high place with harp, tambourine, flute, and lyre before them,*

prophesying. Then the spirit of the LORD *will come mightily upon you [*NRSV: *possess you], and you shall prophesy [be in a prophetic frenzy along] with them and be turned into another man. Now when these signs meet you, do whatever your hand finds to do, for God is with you. And you shall go down before me to Gilgal; and behold, I am coming to you to offer burnt offerings and to sacrifice peace offerings. Seven days you shall wait, until I come to you and show you what you shall do.*"

When he turned his back to leave Samuel, God gave him another heart; and all these signs came to pass that day. When they came to Gibeah, behold, a band of prophets met him; and the spirit of God came mightily upon him, and he prophesied among them. And when all who knew him before saw how he prophesied with the prophets, the people said to one another, "What has come over the son of Kish? Is Saul also among the prophets?" (1 Sam. 10:5–11, RSV)

Study Tip ————————————————————————

The intriguing passage in 1 Samuel 10:5–11 further underlines the importance of consulting more than one translation. I have indicated the different ways in which two key phrases have been rendered in recent versions of the Bible. The New Revised Standard Version uses the words "frenzy" and "possess," while the Revised Standard Version avoids these words. Why? The terms used by the NRSV represent in my view the best translation. It was made by a group of scholars who wanted to correct some words from the older RSV in line with new discoveries about the Hebrew language clarified by the Dead Sea Scrolls, which were not known to the original RSV translators. But do the earlier, "softer" terms ("come mightily upon," "prophesy") also reveal a certain squeamishness about words that might imply trance or chaotic worship ("possess," "frenzy")? This raises important questions about whether the current climate of opinion colors the way scholars translate words and phrases.

In summary, the biblical evidence suggests that an element of mysticism and ecstatic experience do have a place in both Christian and Jewish spiritual life. Nor does this place end with the Bible. Both faiths have long traditions of mystics, seers, and ecstatics. Think of St. Teresa of Ávila, the sixteenth-century Carmelite nun who often fell into trances, or the Baal Shem Tov, founder of the Jewish Hasidic movement, whose followers pranced and sang noisily just outside the doors of synagogues they considered too stilted. A similar ecstatic vein, Sufism, continues in Islam.

It seems clear that the prophets, although different in some respects from the seers, drew on their practices and never separated from them entirely. It should not surprise us, therefore, that the worldwide Pentecostal movement is exhibiting a keen interest in social ministries such as combating inequality and poverty in the tradition of Amos. It is also valuable to remember that the American twentieth-century prophet Martin Luther King, Jr., delivered his farewell sermon, "I've Been to the Mountaintop," in the Pentecostal Mason Temple in Memphis. The mystical and the justice dimensions of Christianity need not be at loggerheads; they can reinforce each other.[5]

Study Tip ————————————————————————

For a compendium of the words of a range of "ecstatic" figures, such as Rumi, Hussain al-Hallaj, Hildegard of Bingen, St. Teresa of Ávila, Jakob Böhme, and various Jewish Hasids, collected and introduced by Martin Buber, see *Ecstatic Confessions: The Heart of Mysticism* (San Francisco: HarperSanFrancisco, 1985).

PROPHETS AND PRIESTS

In addition to their complex link with the seers, the second tension the prophets lived with was their relationship to the priesthood. We have quoted Amos's anticeremonial condemnations above, but he was hardly alone in his blasts. The prophet Isaiah continues these tirades. Here are two versions of one passage, Isaiah 1:13–17. The first one is quoted from *The Message*, a highly idiomatic version written by Eugene H. Peterson, based on the original languages and published in segments from 1993 to 2002. Peterson says that he undertook this work because, in teaching a class on the Bible, he noticed that the students did not seem to sense the gritty punch of the original language.

> *Quit your worship charades.*
> *I can't stand your trivial religious games:*
> *Monthly conferences, weekly Sabbaths,*
> *special meetings—*
> *meetings, meetings, meetings—I can't stand one more!*
> *Meetings for this, meetings for that. I hate them!*
> *You've worn me out!*
> *I'm sick of your religion, religion, religion,*
> *while you go right on sinning.*
> *When you put on your next prayer-performance,*
> *I'll be looking the other way.*
> *No matter how long or loud or often you pray,*
> *I'll not be listening.*
> *And do you know why? Because you've been tearing*
> *people to pieces, and your hands are bloody.*
> *Go home and wash up.*
> *Clean up your act.*
> *Sweep your lives clean of your evildoings*
> *so I don't have to look at them any longer.*
> *Say no to wrong.*
> *Learn to do good.*

Work for justice.
Help the down-and-out.
Stand up for the homeless.
Go to bat for the defenseless.

Here is another, somewhat milder translation of the same passage taken from the New Living Translation:

Stop bringing me your meaningless gifts;
the incense of your offerings disgusts me!
As for your celebrations of the new moon and
the Sabbath
and your special days for fasting—
they are all sinful and false.
I want no more of your pious meetings.
I hate your new moon celebrations and your
annual festivals.
They are a burden to me. I cannot stand them!
When you lift up your hands in prayer,
I will not look.
Though you offer many prayers, I will not listen,
for your hands are covered with the blood of
innocent victims.
Wash yourselves and be clean!
Get your sins out of my sight.
Give up your evil ways.
Learn to do good.
Seek justice.
Help the oppressed.

Study Tip

There are literally dozens of translations of the prophets available online today ranging from highly literal to colloquial. You can access them by typing any verse of a chapter—like Isaiah 1:13—into a search engine, and you will find them listed, sometimes with samples or excerpts side by side. Serious readers of the Bible should be familiar with at least some of these, if only to demonstrate that we are all dependent on the whims and theological preferences of translators and that because languages change and mutate, there is never any final or definitive rendering.

Whatever the translation, however, these prophetic denunciations make the prophets appear to be people who did not want to have anything to do with the holidays, festivals, and sacrifices that reenacted and celebrated the symbolic worldview of ancient Israel. But that would be a mistaken impression. Without these rites and symbols, Israel would not have been Israel. Through them the people recalled their deliverance from Egypt in the Passover. They told and retold the stories of the patriarchs, and they marked their continuity with them through the custom of circumcision. After the Temple in Jerusalem was built, they gathered there for the annual New Year's Enthronement of God. It was through these ceremonial activities that they remembered what God had done for them in the past, and this both located them in the present and gave them hope—even in the worst of times—for the future.

Why, then, did the prophets fire off such polemics against what they knew quite well were rituals essential to the well-being of the people? The answer to this question can be discerned by a close reading of one of the verses quoted above, Isaiah 1:13–14: "I cannot endure iniquity and solemn assemblies" (OXFORD STUDY BIBLE—REVISED ENGLISH BIBLE). The word "and" here supplies the clue. In short, the prophets attacked the hypocritical inconsistency of rituals that had become disconnected from, even contradictory to, the social reality they symbolized. They were in danger of atrophying into form without substance.

In some key personalities, the prophet and the priest overlapped. In Exodus 2:11 Moses is referred to as a "Levite," a priest, and 1 Kings 18:32 informs us that the great prophet Elijah offered sacrifices. Ordinarily, however, the prophets were not priests. The two followed separate vocations. Sometimes there were tensions, but they relied on each other. The prophets often borrowed the language of the priestly rituals for their prophetic utterances. Here again form analysis helps clarify the prophet-priest linkage. Studies of some of the later prophets such as Habakkuk, Nahum, and Joel show that their writings rely heavily on liturgical rituals. The prophets were not religious mavericks chafing under the stifling constrictions of the ceremonies and holidays of their people. The fed on these celebrations, and their messages were shaped by them. But they wanted them to be coherent with God's call to his people to "let justice roll down like waters, and righteousness like an ever-flowing stream."

Jesus, who continued the prophetic tradition into another era, struck the right balance when, in one of his best-known teachings. he told his followers that if they were on the way to the Temple to make a sacrifice and remembered a wrong they had done to a neighbor, they should first repair the rift with the neighbor, but then proceed to the Temple and make the sacrifice (Matt. 5:23–24). It was not an antipriestly gesture when he chased the money changers out of the Temple; it was his effort to cleanse it of the racketeers who were gouging the poor pilgrims.

This critical but appreciative rapport between the prophets with the "religious establishment" of their day enables us to understand our present-day prophets better. Two prophets of the American civil rights movement and the efforts to end the Vietnam War, Father Daniel Berrigan and Reverend William Sloane Coffin, combined their priestly/ministerial roles with their activism. Father Berrigan, a Jesuit, continued to say Mass and lead prayer retreats while he and his associates burned draft records and nonviolently opposed nuclear weapons. Coffin occupied the pulpit of one of America's leading congregations, Riverside Church in New York City. Dr. Martin Luther King, while leading protest marches and demonstrations against racial and economic injustice all over the country, insisted on being back in his pulpit on Sunday mornings. Nuns and priests and one bishop lost their lives in Latin America during the struggle against military dictatorships there. And in recent years, Pope Francis manages to sit at the pinnacle of ecclesial authority as Bishop of Rome and Pontiff of the Universal Catholic Church, while he speaks in clarion tones against poverty and inequality. He is both a priest and a prophet. Obviously some clergy have faced demotion and dismissal when authorities considered their activities too disturbing of the status quo. The lively synergetic relationship between prophecy and the religious establishment, which first appeared among the Hebrews twenty-five hundred years ago, is still in force.

PROPHETS AND KINGS

If the association of the prophets with the priests was often a touchy one, the relationship between the prophets and the kings was even more so. Since, unlike other ancient Near Eastern peoples, the Israelites held that their God, Yahweh, was their real and only king, the status of the earthly kings was always shaky. When after his military successes Gideon's warriors offered to make him a king, he declined (Judg. 8:22). But as the Israelites became less nomadic and more settled, and as the Philistines posed more of a threat during the time of Samuel, the pressure among the people to have a king increased. From the outset of the period of the kings, first in one and then in two kingdoms, from Saul (who reigned 1050–1010 BCE) to Zedekiah (597–586), these rulers are described at times as "sons of God" (by adoption) or "anointed of God," but never as themselves divine. And the attitude of the people toward them may best be described as ambivalent, ranging over the years from downright hostility to qualified adoration. Kingship began on a very questionable note when "the people" (or probably some of them) asked the prophet and seer Samuel to give them a king, so they could be "like the other nations."

So Samuel told all the words of the LORD to the people who were asking for a king from him. He said, "These will be the ways of

*the king who will reign over you: he will take your sons and ap-
point them to his chariots and to be his horsemen and to run
before his chariots. And he will appoint for himself commanders
of thousands and commanders of fifties, and some to plow his
ground and to reap his harvest, and to make his implements of
war and the equipment of his chariots. He will take your daughters to be perfumers and cooks and bakers. He will take the best
of your fields and vineyards and olive orchards and give them to
his servants. He will take the tenth of your grain and of your
vineyards and give it to his officers and to his servants. He will
take your male servants and female servants and the best of
your young men and your donkeys, and put them to his work.
He will take the tenth of your flocks, and you shall be his slaves.
And in that day you will cry out because of your king, whom you
have chosen for yourselves, but the* LORD *will not answer you in
that day.”*

*But the people refused to obey the voice of Samuel. And they
said, “No! But there shall be a king over us, that we also may be
like all the nations, and that our king may judge us and go out
before us and fight our battles.” And when Samuel had heard all
the words of the people, he repeated them in the ears of the* LORD.
And the LORD *said to Samuel, “Obey their voice and make them
a king.” Samuel then said to the men of Israel, “Go every man to
his city.” (1 Sam. 8:10–22,* ESV*)*

This is not a particularly propitious note on which to launch the institution of kingship, especially in a region where kings were thought to be
either divine or directly descended from a divinity. The Israelites never
fully reconciled their belief in Yahweh as their true king and commander
with the idea of an earthly monarch. Nonetheless, kingship was a formative
institution during a critical time in Israelite history, and the core message
of Jesus centered on the imminent coming of the kingdom of God. The
prophets constituted what amounts to a kind of "loyal opposition," and it
is noteworthy that, although they had some major prickly confrontations

with kings, such as Nathan's with David and Jehu's with Jeroboam, they mainly addressed themselves to the people. Even though some promonarchical voices in the Bible claimed that God had also made a covenant with the "House of David," the prophets insisted that it was with the people, not with the kings, that God had forged his covenant at Mt. Sinai. And this conviction remained the foundation stone of the Hebrew worldview.

This radical demotion of absolute royal power to relative authority passed through many ups and downs in world history. The early Christians found themselves in deep trouble when they refused to accept the divinity of the emperors. The popes and the later emperors fought out their jurisdictional disputes for centuries. The Protestant Reformers differed on just how the spiritual and the secular spheres should be delineated, but all agreed that they must be separate. The idea of the "divine right" of kings made a short-lived return in early modern Europe, but some of its major royal protagonists literally lost their heads defending it. Today, even in modern democracies, religion still commands significant symbolic authority. The monarch of England is crowned in Westminster Abbey by the archbishop of Canterbury, and the president of the United States takes the oath of office with one hand on a Bible.

Still, the prophetic breakthrough marks a critical point in the Hebrew monarchy, one whose historical importance can hardly be exaggerated. It resulted in the Jewish version of what historians like Karl Jaspers, Eric Voegelin, and more recently Robert Bellah refer to as "the axial age," the point in the long saga of human evolution at which "man as we know him today" appeared.[6] What they mean is that, since a divine king was no longer the conduit between a transcendent God and the people, a space was opened up for criticism and reflection, a transcendent point of reference by which people could envision political, cultural, and religious change at the most fundamental level. Not only had the "archaic myth" of a flawless connection between divine and human rule now been questioned, but human beings began to see that they were responsible for the construction and correction of their values and institutions. The continuing tension between prophets and kings in ancient Israel provides an indispensable model for those Jews and Christians who see themselves as perpetuating the prophetic tradition. The relationship between our communities of faith and governments should never sour into automatic antipathy, but neither should it become too cozy. Prophets would make bad kings, and kings should not be expected to be prophets. There needs to be a creative tension, the shape of which changes as history moves on. No formula can prescribe exactly what it should be at any moment.

How then should we read the prophets today? Indeed, *why* should we read them? We read them because even though they appeared at a moment in history far removed from ours, what they say is not bound to their time. Their voices confront us unsparingly with the rank injustice of the vast inequality and unnecessary suffering that distort our world today. Speaking to us from a distant past, they are as relevant as this morning's headlines. Rabbi Abraham Joshua Heschel says that the prophets were always "the voice of the voiceless." He suggests that "the task of the prophet is to convey the word of God. Yet the word is aglow with pathos . . . the prophet hears God's voice and feels His heart. . . . His soul overflows, speaking as he does out of the fullness of his sympathy."[7]

Getting to the Final Four

Gospels, Kept and Discarded

Then the Pharisees asked him, "When will the kingdom of God come?" He answered, "You cannot tell by observation when the kingdom of God comes. You cannot say, 'Look, here it is,' or 'Look, there it is,' for the kingdom of God is among you."

LUKE 17:20–21,
REVISED ENGLISH BIBLE
(OXFORD STUDY BIBLE, P. 1153)

Before we begin to read the Gospels, a prior question comes to mind: Why are there just four? Why not five, or seven, or twelve? Why not only one? What does the fact that there are four, and not one or twelve, in the New Testament suggest for the way we should read them now, two millennia after they were written?

We have just four Gospels on what might seem to be rather flimsy grounds. The four were picked out of a small sea of contending gospels circulating among the scattered Christian congregations during the first three centuries of Christian history. Among those that did not make the cut were ones written, allegedly, by Mary, Thomas, and Philip. And one is simply entitled, without much humility, the *Gospel of Truth*. Copies of all these in codices written in Coptic were found by a shepherd in 1946 in an ancient cave at Nag Hammadi in Upper Egypt, preserved for centuries by the darkness and dry air. There were other texts as well. They have all been translated into English and published, and they are available for purchase. But you will not find any of them in your Bible. Why not?

The reason is still not entirely clear. Neither factual accuracy nor historical antiquity of the four that are in the Bible seems to have been a key factor. These qualities were not as essential to ancient minds as they are to ours today. Put bluntly, the criterion for inclusion that mattered most to the scriptural gatekeepers was apparently theology: How do they depict the meaning of Jesus and his relationship to God? The people who made the decisions about what to put in and what to leave out were not as worried about precisely what Jesus is said to have done or taught as they were the *spiritual significance* of his words and deeds. Some gospels passed this muster. Others were found deficient and did not, but that left still others to wander for quite a while in a kind of limbo, neither in nor out. These in-between texts were accepted and read in worship services by some early Christian congregations and among some gatherings of monks, but not by others.

For example, most scholars agree today that the recently unearthed *Gospel of Thomas,* which was barred, is probably nearly as old as our four canonical Gospels, maybe older. So why are the final four tucked securely between those leather covers, while the *Thomas* must settle for a single paperback edition? We will touch on similar questions again when we turn to the Letters of Paul and to the book of Revelation, which had their own zigzag trajectories in and out of the collection of books that gradually found a place in our present Bible. How did all this happen?

CANONIZATION

The process of selection and exclusion is called "canonization." "Canon" is derived from the Hebrew term for "rule" or "rod," like one used for measuring, and gradually came to mean a regulative standard. In other words, those books awarded a place in the "canon" were intended to be normative, to set the gold standard by which the message of the early church would be measured. It took a long while, in some cases centuries, to settle on what was in and what was out. It was still not fully resolved at the time of the Reformation a thousand years later. Luther did not feel the Letter of James belonged in the New Testament and had his doubts about Revelation. Protestants at that time removed the "apocryphal" books from the Bible, while the Catholics kept them in. Consequently, most Baptists and Methodists have never heard of biblical books like Tobit, Judith, Baruch, or Bel and the Dragon, while Catholics hear parts of them read at church. (These apocryphal books are, however, still included in some current versions of the Bible, like *The HarperCollins Study Bible*.)

In other words, we are still living with the results of the canonization battles, and for many people today the question is not settled for good. Every person and every church has its own informal "canon." Some books are read and studied, others consistently ignored. When was the last time you heard a sermon on Numbers or the Letter of Jude? The canonizers and gatekeepers are still at work, albeit more quietly.

It is not vital for everyone who reads the Bible today to be conversant with the long, loopy story of canonization. But it is important to realize that it did take place and is not yet over and that the volume we call "The Bible" and hold in our hands is the product of a fractious history, because these realizations give it a deep dimension that intensifies its significance.

People who embrace the verbal inspiration of the Bible are sometimes troubled when they learn about the rough-and-tumble battles over canonization. Still, some have no problem with this tortuous process. Those who believe that the Holy Spirit inspired every word have little difficulty believing that the same Spirit guided the slippery course of both canonization and translation every step of the way: just as God inspired the words, God also guided the process by which those words got to our bookshelves. Therefore both what is in and what is out are there, because that is the way God wanted it.

The point here, however, is that when we read the Bible in the twenty-first century, our appreciation for it is strengthened by reading it along with those who have read it before us, even many centuries before us. Just as my individual "take" on the Bible could be eccentric and therefore should be checked and amplified by the takes of other people, so "our" take on it in our century and our circumstances should be tested and expanded by people who read it in other centuries and other cultures. This is why the "history of interpretation" method of biblical studies has assumed an increasingly important place today. As we have said earlier, it moves us out of the duality of "what it originally meant" versus "what it now means" to *what it has meant*. And it also explains why knowing something about canonization is so fascinating. It enables us to see why, at least for those who did the canonizing, the particular texts we have today were so indispensable, while others were not.

Knowing about the fights over canonization helps explain the view of those people today who are not exponents either of verbal inerrancy or of the divine guidance of its transmission, but still have no problem with the final four. They argue that this quartet was selected for the canon, because these books reflect the emerging consensus of the early church, and that therefore we do not need to pay much attention to the excluded candidates—the losers, as it were—today. They maintain that the New Testament need not reflect every scriptural contender in the arena at the time, for example, the ones that were eventually deemed to be heretical or "Gnostic," such as those with intriguing titles like *The Dialogue of the Savior* or *The Gospel of the Egyptians*. They acknowledge that some of these rejected candidates (like the *First Letter of Clement*) were read in early Christian congregations along with Romans and Galatians, but were eventually denied admission to the Good Book. Consequently, so the logic goes, except for antiquarian interests, we too can safely disregard them.

This seems to be a plausible argument, but it conveniently leaves out what has been rightly called "the politics of canonization," namely, that the various bishops, councils, and synods that actually made these in-or-out decisions were not fully representative of the whole church, and that certain political calculations (East versus West), geographical rivalries (Alexandria versus Jerusalem), and shifting theological currents entered into the debates as well. Feminist biblical investigators also remind us that all these decisions were made exclusively by males, thus casting suspicions on the systematic exclusion of the writings that assign a more prominent role to Mary or refer to God in the feminine. Other students of this contentious process point out that the theological line between the ins and the outs is a blurry one. There are whole sections in the eliminated gospels that also appear in the ones that were included, and there are passages in the included ones that are very similar to ones in the rejects.

Study Tip

Obtain a copy of the *Gospel of Thomas* and compare it with any of the canonical Gospels, noting the unfamiliar elements, the overlaps, and the difference in style. *Thomas* is easily available, and indeed many people with a more mystical inclination have added it to their "personal canon" today. Or you could read the readily available *Gospel of Mary* in comparison to the Gospel of Matthew.

Even after we know something about the history of canonization, however, we are still left with an intriguing dilemma. At the end of this sifting and sorting, there remains the quandary we mentioned above: Why are there four and only four Gospels in today's Bible? The answer to this question can seem peculiar today. While the second-century bishop of Lyons, Irenaeus (d. 202 CE), was pondering the vexed issue, still open and undecided at the time, of how many Gospels there should be, he happened to notice something in the prophet Ezekiel that seemed to answer his conundrum. It was the passage in which the prophet is describing a vision of the "four living creatures" that were drawing the chariot of God. Each creature appeared to be human, but had four faces and four wings. Ezekiel continues:

Their faces looked like this: Each of the four had the face of a human being, and on the right side each had the face of a lion, and on the left the face of an ox; each also had the face of an eagle. Such were their faces. They each had two wings spreading out upward, each wing touching that of the creature on either

side; and each had two other wings covering its body. (1:10–
11, NIV)

For Irenaeus, this was enough. In accordance with his belief that the Old Testament foreshadowed the New, just as there were four creatures in the vision, there should obviously be four—and only four—Gospels. Eventually the "final four" count was accepted.

Further, the figures that symbolize each of these Gospels became their signature icons. Therefore eighteen hundred years later the symbol for Matthew is still an angel; for Mark, a winged lion; for Luke, a winged ox; for John, an eagle. They can be identified in paintings and sculptures all over the world. One exquisite example is the tympanum of Christ in majesty in the Church of St. Trophime in Arles, France. But we see them wherever we look. In a charming painting by Pier Francesco Sacchi (1485–1528), the four Gospel writers all sit around one table, pens in hand. The ox, the lion, and the eagle crouch docilely at the feet of Mark, Luke, and John like household pets. An angel shows Matthew a page from a book. The Holy Spirit in the form of a dove hovers over the whole group. The prophet Ezekiel would probably be surprised that so many centuries after his vision this menagerie-plus-angel was still in business. But what does this plurality of authorship suggest for studying the Bible today?

COMPARING THE GOSPELS

The fact that there are four Gospels and not just one cries out for comparative reading. It makes noting the similarities and differences an obvious way to understand each of them better. And here is where "redaction history" comes to our aid. Don't be put off by the word. "Redaction" simply means "editing," and it is applied when it is known that the writer of a text relied on an earlier written source or sources, which he then edited (redacted) for his own purposes.

Some readers will question the premise. Why should the Gospel writers rely on any previous accounts? Were they not, at least a couple of them, companions of Jesus during his lifetime? Some people even picture them, notepads at the ready, jotting down everything the master said. The consensus of modern historians is that they were not, at least in the historical sense, companions of Jesus. The stenographic theory overlooks the fact that the Gospels report things about Jesus, including words he said, when they were not present. These include the annunciation to Mary, the birth stories, and Herod's exchange with the wise men. They also include Jesus's prayer in the Garden of Gethsemane, which he uttered when the three disciples who were with him were asleep. And there are more examples.

But also, the arithmetic of the companions-of-the-way theory does not add up. Mark, who wrote forty years after the crucifixion, does not claim to have been with Jesus. Further, careful study of his text indicates that he did use both oral and written sources. The other three Gospels were written twenty or more years later, placing the authors at least in their nineties, much older than people lived in those days. Some people claim that at least they could have been in touch with eyewitnesses or with people who knew those witnesses. But how much does that matter?

For some readers of the Bible today it still does. And to find out that the Gospel writers were not at the scenes they describe may at first seem disappointing. I know it was for me when I learned that Matthew was not part of the crowd that heard the Sermon on the Mount and that Mark was not helping gather up the fragments after Jesus fed the four thousand. But, upon further reflection, I have come to believe that this is really good news. Many of us have imagined what it might have been like to have "walked and talked with him" by the Jordan or the Sea of Galilee. We can still do that in our imagination. It can be a good exercise in meditative prayer, and the Jesuits have developed a spiritual discipline that teaches how to do it. But now that the earthly life of Jesus is over, although we can meet him in prayer and imagination and, for many people, in the Eucharist, we cannot encounter him as a historical individual. Also, as it turns out, neither did the writers of the four Gospels. But is this a negative thing?

I think it is not. It puts us closer to the Gospel writers. Like us, they learned about Jesus from people who either knew him or heard and passed on the stories he told and the ones that were told about him. And this is our situation too. We are in the same boat as the four Gospel writers. We can still "meet Jesus" in the ways mentioned above, but for learning about the "historical Jesus" we have to rely on other people. Therefore, in getting to know Jesus and the meaning people attached to his life, we need to *identify with* the Gospel writers and to "learn of him" as they did. And we can be grateful that, although each writer saw him as utterly fundamental to the Christian message and to their own lives, and indeed to all of human history, each had a slightly different "take." And if they had different takes, then so can we. In other words, we can be thankful that, as we began to notice even in the book of Genesis, the Bible—and in this case the Gospel section of the Bible—is not univocal, but polyphonic. It is a coat of many colors, as is the Christian movement, and new tints and shades are still being added.

The problem is that a certain nervousness about varying, even differing, views on the significance of Jesus also arose quite early. The same centralizing and homogenizing forces that would soon lead to the attempt to impose a single creed also went to work on the disparities in the Bible itself, and in the Gospels at the heart of the Bible. This jumpiness about the perceived dangers of diversity led to the attempt to iron out the differences among the four Gospels to yield a single narrative, which later became known as a "harmony."

The earliest of these harmonies was stapled together by a scholar named Tatian the Assyrian (120–180 CE); he called it the *Diatessaron*. But this blending continued to appear into the Middle Ages. Even more were attempted during the Reformation when ordinary people began actually to read the Bible, and some theologians feared that being confronted with diverse portraits of Christ might create unsettling confusion. There have been numerous efforts to smooth out the differences among the Gospels ever since, and various stabs at harmonization still roll off the presses today. Needless to say, most film versions of the life of Christ also resort to harmonization, since exposing moviegoers to dissimilar takes on Jesus would be hard to do on screen. Pier Paolo Pasolini (1922–75) confronted this issue head-on in filming perhaps the best movie about Jesus ever made, *The Gospel According to St. Matthew.* He did it by explicitly confining himself to that Gospel alone.

Undoubtedly the motivation to craft harmonies is sincere, but they have an unintended negative effect. In attempting to forge one "Gospel," editors must lay aside all consideration of the special setting in which each of the Gospels was written and the differing cultures for which they were intended. But this tears the Gospels out of their real history and invents a whole new ersatz homogenized text. Except possibly for children's biblical stories, the effort to squeeze out the obvious inconsistencies between the Gospels robs readers of the refreshing realization that, as we have said, a diversity of interpretations of who Jesus was and what his significance is marked the earliest years of Christianity.

It is especially critical to be aware of this diversity today. Since Christianity is spreading around the world so quickly, our received "Western" theologies, including the ways we interpret Jesus, are being questioned. The key question is how to "contextualize" the message, so that it can be communicated within the parameters of African or Indian or Chinese culture. This process is already under way, and a range of diverse theologies is emerging. But just as we are learning to appreciate these new interpretations and the reality of multiple theologies, any attempt—however well intended—to paint the nascent years of Christianity as more homogenous than they were amounts to a disservice. Contemporary readers of the Bible are well advised to avoid these paste-up jobs and, instead, to discover what can be learned from comparing and contrasting Mark with Luke or Matthew with John. This will not only open a window on the world from which these Gospels emerged, but also better prepare readers to understand the place of the Gospels in the church and in the world in our day. It is good that, at least in the New Testament itself, no one tried to paste all these Gospels into a single one the way they did with the sources of Genesis and other Old Testament books.

Study Tip ———————————————————————————————

A good way to compare the Gospels is to consult a chart laying out the parallel passages next to each other in a four-column format. Such a chart is included at the beginning of the New Testament in *The HarperCollins Study Bible*. In a group study, three or four people could have their Bibles open, each to one of the Gospels, and read aloud in turn. If one is studying alone, the best way to compare and contrast the Gospels is to use *Gospel Parallels: A Comparison of the Synoptic Gospels,* edited by Burton H. Throckmorton, Jr. (Nashville, TN: Nelson, 1992). It is not a harmony. Its arrangement of the actual texts of the Gospels into parallel columns allows readers to see how the different writers cut, rearranged, and nuanced the basic message. It also includes footnotes on similar passages from noncanonical sources. See also Elaine Pagels, *The Gnostic Gospels* (New York: Random House, 1979).

With these useful approaches to the Bible in hand we now turn to the Final Four themselves.

Looking Over the Shoulders of the Writers

Matthew, Mark, and Luke

You have heard that it was said, "You shall love your neighbor and hate your enemy." But I say to you, Love your enemies and pray for those who persecute you, so that you may be children of your Father in heaven; for he makes his sun rise on the evil and on the good, and sends rain on the righteous and on the unrighteous. For if you love those who love you, what reward do you have? Do not even the tax collectors do the same? And if you greet only your brothers and sisters, what more are you doing than others? Do not even the Gentiles do the same? Be perfect, therefore, as your heavenly Father is perfect.

MATTHEW 5:43–48

Imagine yourself looking over the shoulder of Matthew sometime between 80 and 90 CE as he composes his Gospel. The Renaissance artist Michelangelo Caravaggio painted a striking canvas of the scene as he visualized it. Matthew sits at a desk, quill pen in hand, and writes. His bare, dusty feet protrude toward us. Behind him an angel stands, whispering in his ear. This is how one brilliant artist envisioned the tableau, and he makes a telling point with it. For centuries Christians have held that the Gospels are in some sense "inspired," suggesting that they carry a special spiritual significance; in the painting this is symbolized by the angel. This would have been clear to those who viewed this painting at the time. Angels are messengers from God. On the other hand, when we try to think what Matthew might actually have looked like as he wrote the Gospel, something is missing from the Caravaggio painting.

It is now recognized that Matthew drew on earlier written sources, the Gospel of Mark in particular, in penning his own Gospel, but also on a source that scholars call "Q" (for the German word *Quelle*, meaning "source"; we will return to this below). What is missing in Caravaggio's scene are those other documents scattered on Matthew's desk, something the Renaissance artist, of course, did not know about. But it is a good illustration of how various current modes of biblical research can illuminate our grasp of the Bible.

In this chapter we will touch mainly on the "redaction history" approach, demonstrating its helpfulness by concentrating on Matthew's Gospel, but comparing it where relevant to the other three, Mark, Luke, and John. We will also draw on some other methods. In preceding chapters we have demonstrated how recent research not only need not diminish our appreciation of the spiritual significance of the Bible, but can enrich it. In the case of Genesis, Exodus, and Joshua, for example, source analysis, archaeology, and genre study enhance our comprehension.

Now, in reading the Gospels, we will see that a variety of approaches can be helpful. In addition to redaction history, we will touch on the history of interpretation, translation theory, comparative manuscript analysis, and Roman Empire studies as well. None of these approaches is hard to understand. All make a distinctive contribution, and together they can be highly beneficial in enabling us to read the Gospels more fruitfully today. Therefore, let us see what we can learn from the harvest of painstaking biblical studies over the past decades.

The first three Gospels are called "synoptic," because of the common perspective they share on the life of Jesus. But, as we will soon see, although the perspective may be common, it is not identical.[1] Take Mark, for example. Since it was written some twenty years before Matthew, why is Matthew placed first in our four Gospels? The answer is probably because Matthew starts the story earlier, namely, before Jesus was even born, with his ancestral genealogy. For some readers, lists of forebears may at first seem a bit tedious. But they serve an important purpose, and once we see what it is, they can turn out to be fascinating.

Matthew begins: "The account of the genealogy of Jesus the Messiah, the son of David, the son of Abraham" (1:1). The next fourteen verses list *thirty-seven* names, from Isaac through Matthan, concluding with "Jacob the father of Joseph the husband of Mary, of whom Jesus was born, who is called the Messiah" (1:16). Why does Matthew lead us through this tangled ancestor chart? He does so because he wants to speak mainly, but not exclusively, to his fellow Jews, for whom lineage is crucial. This is why he presents Jesus as the rightful heir of Abraham and David and mentions them both in his first sentence. The genealogy is not a historical document, like one you might find in a county archive, for example. It is symbolic, a metaphor. The fact that it includes some Gentiles as well as Jews demonstrates how preoccupied Matthew was with the relationship between these two peoples, who he believed now found themselves, through Christ, in the same enlarged "people of God." He wrote, of course, at a time when Jews probably constituted a majority, though a quickly diminishing one, of the nascent "Jesus movement."

The question of the proper relationship between Christians and Jews is still with us today, and this is one reason why the increasing cooperation between Jewish and Christian scholars in biblical studies, both Old and New Testament, has been a signal advance. Still there is much more to do, and the current fascination with the Jewishness of Jesus falls short of what is needed. Two thousand years of rabbinical reflection have passed since Jesus's life, much of it centered on the scriptures Christians call the "Old Testament." There have been times when some people have questioned this usage, especially when it seemed to imply, at least for some Christians, that the New had displaced the Old. But if we think of the "old" in Old Testament as meaning "original," this does not suggest any displacement. Further, we should bear in mind that the only "Bible" the writers of the New Testament knew of was our Old Testament, the Hebrew scriptures. In keeping with the emphasis in this book on the history of interpretation and listening to interpreters outside confessional circles, clearly rabbinical commentaries on both parts of the Bible should be integral to the conversation.

A STABLE IN AN EMPIRE

With the opening line of the second chapter of Matthew, we suddenly find we are in new territory. It begins "in the time of King Herod." Quite abruptly we are no longer dealing with legends and symbolic genealogies. King Herod, known in history as Herod the Great, is no fairy-tale sovereign. He was a puppet monarch, installed by the Romans as "king of the Jews," who ruled from 37 until 4 BCE. Luke further specifies this historicity when he writes in the second chapter of his Gospel: "In those days a decree went out from Emperor Augustus that all the world should be registered" (2:1). (Some versions make it "taxed," which is probably better, since that is just what the universal registration was intended to do.)

Also in that opening verse Matthew identifies Bethlehem as Jesus's birthplace. Many scholars doubt that Jesus was really born in Bethlehem and believe this part of the story amounts to a kind of poetic license Matthew took, so that the birth would fulfill some ancient prophecies. But the fact remains that Jesus lived his life under Roman colonial rule. What the apparently passing references to Herod and Augustus noted above do is lift the life of Jesus out of any mythic realm and plop it into the thick of secular history, and the history of the Roman Empire in particular.[2]

Scholars of the Bible have known this from the beginning, and the use of secular history to fill in the context of biblical events is not new. But in recent years it has become more precise. Especially in the case of the Gospels, it has been advanced by a more refined archaeology and by sometimes sensational document finds. Other breakthroughs in the study of Roman imperial history, including the empire's tax policies, its military arrangements, and its funereal practices, have helped fill in the gaps between the verses. It is easy to see why this knowledge makes such an invaluable contribution to our understanding of the Gospels. Jesus's life began at a time when an empire-wide "registration," which was of course for the purpose of collecting taxes, was taking place. He was frequently asked about taxes (remember the famous story of the coin with the image of Caesar on it). His early mentor, John the Baptist, was executed by an official of the empire. Jesus himself was crucified by a task force of its legions. We will return to the "empire studies" approach to the New Testament in our chapter on Paul.

Other methods and approaches have illuminated the context of Jesus's life and ministry. Feminist scholars, for example, have made breakthrough contributions. Jesus was surrounded by women from before his birth until his resurrection appearances. He once said that prostitutes would enter the kingdom of God before the pious Pharisees (Matt. 21:31). But who were these prostitutes? Social historians have now established that in the Roman-occupied Palestine of his time the brothels mainly served the legions, and that the young women in them were the daughters of the poorest families, who were forced to sell them in this ancient example of trafficking in order to stave off starvation.[3]

Specialists in examining grave and tomb inscriptions have uncovered new information about the religious beliefs current in first-century Palestine. Add to this that recent investigations of ancient Near Eastern agriculture and viniculture have enlarged our understanding. The many biblical stories and parables about wheat fields and fig trees make more sense when we know something about the agronomy. Each of these types of biblical studies adds its own small pieces to an emerging jigsaw puzzle that enables us to know more about the world in which Jesus lived than any previous generation has.

THE MAGI

When we read the Gospels in light of the history of the Roman Empire, however, we find ourselves not only in the land of phalanxes and gladiators, but also in an environment of superstition and fantasy. During the past few decades, historians of the Roman Empire have not concentrated as exclusively as they once did on the military and political facts; they have also probed the social customs, popular delusions, and folk beliefs of the time. What they have found sometimes casts a new and often surprising light on our images of those days.

For example, when the Christmas season approaches each year and we see the trio of gift-bearing rajahs clustered around the holy family in front yards and public squares or hear "We Three Kings" chiming incessantly over department-store loudspeakers, one piece of such ancient history might prove disconcerting to some. The "magi" mentioned in Matthew's Gospel (Matt. 2:1–12) were not kings. They were probably not even wise men. They were more like astrologers or the palmists who hang signs that say "Readings" outside their doors in certain parts of American cities.

The historians who study the social practices of imperial Rome and its provinces have found that astrology at the time was a highly disputed art. In some cultures, such as in that of ancient Persia, diviners were accorded great deference; rulers depended on them for advice. In the Greco-Roman world, many intellectuals lampooned their pretensions. The New Testament scholar Warren Carter has rounded up some of the denunciations these Roman intellectuals made in his *Matthew and the Margins*.[4] He points out that Tacitus labels their claims "absurdities." Seneca ridicules them for having foretold the death of the emperor Claudius "every year, every month" for many years.

Jews, in general, tended to be skeptical of magicians, fortune-tellers, and clairvoyants. They had heard about the pharaoh calling in his court sorcerers to oppose Moses. They knew about the contests their prophets had had with the false prophets. Isaiah, writing during his people's captivity in Babylon, ridicules their captors' reliance on divinations. He warns the Babylonians that they are in for bad times (and they were; they were soon to be conquered by the Persians) and that defeat is something they "cannot charm away." In a taunting and ironic voice he tells them:

> *Stand fast in your enchantments*
> *and your many sorceries. . . .*
> *Perhaps you may inspire terror. . . .*
> *Let those who study the heavens*
> *stand up and save you,*

those who gaze at the stars,
and at each new moon predict
what shall befall you.
See, they are like stubble,
the fire consumes them. (47:11–14)

Here Isaiah is representative of a common opinion among his people. Those "who study the heavens" are the objects of mockery and scorn.

But in spite of a real ambivalence about soothsayers, who were officially spurned by the prophets, apparently some people harbored a feeling that these diviners might just have something. Following the official Jewish line, King Saul had banned "the mediums and the wizards" from his kingdom. But when he was under pressure before the battle of Gilboa, the temptation to consult one of these sibylline expellees was just too great. He snuck out under cover of night and consulted a medium who is now often referred to as "the witch of Endor" (1 Sam. 28:3–10, rsv). There is no better place in the Bible to see the continuing conflict between the official religion of kings and prophets, on the one hand, and the beliefs of many of the common people (and of kings under stress), on the other.

This is an admixture that has continued into our own time. Some Americans were surprised, but probably not shocked, when it was revealed toward the end of Ronald Reagan's presidency that his wife had regularly consulted a San Francisco–based astrologer named Joan Quigley. In 1987 Mrs. Reagan apparently convinced the president, who had planned to introduce the International Nuclear Forces Treaty on television in prime time, to do it in the afternoon instead, on the advice of her astrologist's star charts. Although there was a little head wagging about this news, most people could not really object, because so many sneak an occasional glance at the daily star-based horoscope predictions published in their newspapers. Surveys reveal that millions of people, many of them churchgoers, faithfully consult these runic gems over their scrambled eggs and coffee. Nancy Reagan had lots of company.

The Roman rulers also had mixed feelings about astrologers. Turning again for aid from historians of ancient Rome, we find that Nero, who was eccentric in many ways, also took omens from the heavens so seriously that he became terrified when a comet appeared in the sky, fearing it was a portent of his demise. The emperor Tiberius became so worried about the predictions of astrologers that he expelled the lot of them from Rome in 19 CE. His successors Vespasian and Domitian did the same thing.

There can be little doubt that the same suspicion, apprehension, and ambivalence were present in Jesus's time. Obviously King Herod did not dismiss the reports of the magi as nonsense, but their knowledge seems to have been piecemeal at best. When they arrive in Jerusalem, they rather naively inquire around about the whereabouts of this new "king of the Jews," whom they have come to venerate. When King Herod hears about these strangers in town and the buzz they have set off, he panics. After all, he is already king of the Jews, although not respected as such by many of his own people, who regarded him as a usurper and only part Jewish.

For all their wisdom from the stars, the magi don't seem to know much. They don't appear to have a clue about who this new king is or where he is. When they ask Herod, he assembles his counselors who, according to Matthew, do not search the stars, but consult the Hebrew prophets (especially Micah; see below) and tell him the visitors from the east have come to the wrong address. The location is not Jerusalem, the hub of religious and political power, but the insignificant "little" town of Bethlehem. Probably considerably relieved, at least for the moment, Herod passes that information onto the magi, and they proceed there, but still have to be guided by the same star they had seen when it first arose.

Why does Matthew play the inexact and incomplete evidence from the celestial bodies off against the words of the Hebrew prophet? Who were these magi anyway? The most important point to notice here is that the magi were not Jews. They were Gentiles, and Matthew wants to alert his readers that this new king will not be just "king of the Jews," but will be the one through whom Jews and Gentiles will at last share a common way to God. He underscores this by mentioning the prophet Micah, who foresees this reconciliation in his prophecy (Micah 4:1–5).

But in the last days it shall come to pass, that the mountain of the house of the LORD shall be established in the top of the mountains, and it shall be exalted above the hills; and people shall flow unto it. And many nations shall come, and say, Come, and let us go up to the mountain of the LORD, and to the house of the God of Jacob; and he will teach us of his ways, and we will walk in his paths: for the law shall go forth of Zion, and the word of the LORD from Jerusalem.

And he shall judge among many people, and rebuke strong nations afar off; and they shall beat their swords into plowshares, and their spears into pruninghooks: nation shall not lift up a sword against nation, neither shall they learn war any more.

But they shall sit every man under his vine and under his fig tree and none shall make them afraid: for the mouth of the LORD of hosts hath spoken it.

For all people will walk every one in the name of his god, and we will walk in the name of the LORD our God for ever and ever. (4:1–5, KJV)

But, not being a literalist, Matthew pastes onto this citation some words about Bethlehem from the next chapter and even part of a verse from 2 Samuel 5:2 that suggest the one born there will be a ruler. Incidentally, in that same chapter of Micah (5:12–13) one can find sharp words against sorceries and soothsayers, who are consigned to the same perdition as idols and Canaanite cultic objects. Matthew's choices of citations to quote were selective, and consistency may not have been his strongest trait.

How did these somewhat ineffective sibyls get promoted to kings? The coronation is strictly a product of a much later lively Christian imagination, and also of the political influence of monarchs who wanted to be identified with them. Some scholars speculate that this crowning may have been inspired by Psalm 72:11, which says of God that "kings shall fall down before him" (KJV), but that is a guess. In any case, the magi were eventually even endowed with names, Melchoir, Caspar, and Balthasar.

Also, the Bible nowhere says there were three (although it lists three gifts: gold, frankincense, and myrrh). According to some Eastern Orthodox traditions there were twelve magi. And most of us have heard stories about "the other wise man." But I am sure, regardless of the evidence, as I did as a boy in my bathrobe and paper crown, we will go on belting out "We Three Kings of Orient Are" at Christmas events. The hope lives on that although kings and rulers have not always submitted themselves to God, one day they will.

Who the magi were is not an issue of weighty consequence in biblical studies. I have included it here to illustrate how inquiry into nonbiblical ancient history can often connect the dots and fill in the colors of biblical narratives. I have not mentioned it to make anyone uncomfortable about continuing to place these traditional figures in their Christmas manger scenes. They will still be there in mine. When I was about ten, my younger brother placed a toy dinosaur among the cows and sheep in our family's crèche. Before our pastor came to visit, my mother told him to remove it and later asked the pastor to explain that there were no dinosaurs in those days. But the pastor told her to let him put it back in with the sheep and cattle. Jesus, he explained had come to redeem all history, past, present, and future, so having the tyrannosaurus among the cows and sheep was, theologically speaking, absolutely correct. Maybe the kings should be there too. Traditions play an indispensable role in our spiritual lives. Just as we learned to look beneath the sediments of legend that cover the exodus to discern a powerful narrative of liberation, we can do the same with the embellishments that have grown up around Christmas. Underneath all the tinsel, the story is true.

THE STORMY CAREER OF JOHN THE BAPTIZER

After the birth stories, the slaughter of the innocent children, the flight to Egypt, and the return to Nazareth after Herod's death, Matthew suddenly drops Jesus and turns his attention to a strange character who wears camel's skins and a coarse leather belt, eats locusts and honey, and wanders through the wilderness preaching God's impending judgment.

John the Baptist (more correctly the "baptizer") had apparently revived a dormant Jewish custom and was submersing people in a river to prepare them for the wrath to come by cleansing them of sin. Evidently, even some of the priestly elite and Pharisees were seeking him out. John appears to be the prototype for a kind of radical preacher who appears now and then on the fringes of organized religion, but attracts a following. Think of Savonarola or Rasputin, at least in style, if not in substance. Matthew portrays John as the kind of seer/prophet who foretells the future, and indeed he speaks of the coming of one who will have a "winnowing fork in his hand" and who will "clear his threshing floor and gather his wheat into the granary; but the chaff he will burn with unquenchable fire" (3:12).

Matthew might well have gone on with the biography of this intriguing, if somewhat scary, character. But he does not. John fills the slot of an opening band at a rock concert. He is still on stage when Jesus appears at the Jordan River to be immersed. What happens there, however, now requires us to compare Matthew with the other Gospels and also to dip briefly into a historical technique involving comparing the oldest existing manuscripts. It is called "text criticism," but again, to avoid the negative connotations, I prefer to call it simply "manuscript comparison."

The need for comparison arises, because often several old manuscripts of any given Gospel are still extant. They have exotic names, attributable to the person who discovered them, the museum they are now in, or the place where they were found. Thus Codex Vaticanus is in the Vatican Library; Codex Sinaiticus was found in the St. Catherine Monastery in the Sinai Desert; and Codex Bezae was found by a man named Theodore Beza in the monastery of St. Irenaeus in Lyons in the sixteenth century. No manuscript, however, dates to any earlier than 140 CE, most of them are later, and the intriguing problem is that they often do not agree with each other. This means that patient researchers have to compare them with each other to decide which one to translate for any edition of the Bible. Inevitably the theological preferences of the translators enter into the decisions they make.

We can illustrate this with a fascinating dispute among scholars about what happened at the baptism of Jesus. Although it hinges on differences between the manuscripts' versions of one phrase, the words spoken by God as Jesus emerges from the waters, it is a significant one, at least for some people. It concerns an old debate about whether Jesus *was always* the Son of God (according to John's Gospel, even before the creation of the world) or whether, as "adoptionists" claim, he *became* God's son at some point in his life. Here is how Matthew describes this important scene, Jesus's baptism:

> And when Jesus was baptized, he went up immediately from the water, and behold, the heavens were opened and he saw the Spirit of God descending like a dove, and alighting on him; and lo, a voice from heaven, saying, "This is my beloved Son, with whom I am well pleased." (3:16–17, RSV)

The problem arises when we compare this depiction with the one given by Luke (3:21–22) and then also compare conflicting manuscript evidence. The version by Luke that appears in our Bibles today agrees substantially with Matthew's, as does the one in Mark. But in several old manuscripts, in both Greek and Latin, the voice from heaven says something noticeably different: "You are my Son, today I have begotten you." In the RSV this discrepancy is mentioned in a discreet footnote at the bottom of the page. Further historical research has shown that the writer of the Gospel may have taken the words from a legal formula of the time used in adoption proceedings, and this is the phrase indicated in the footnote. So just what is going on here? Did Luke (or at least this manuscript of Luke) suggest that Jesus was God's *adopted* son?

For people not particularly concerned with the dispute between adoptionists and anti-adoptionists (and this would probably include most Christians today), this is hardly a pressing issue.[5] But at the time the oldest manuscripts of the Gospels were being copied and, in some cases, edited, it mattered a great deal. The relationship between Jesus and God was in hot dispute, and a variety of opinions were held in the early congregations. Might the first copyists/editors have decided to push the argument along by a slight tweaking of the words? Whether or not that happened, this ap-

parent tempest in a copyist's teapot confirms a point we have been empha-
sizing throughout this book: that a wider variety of theological views than
most people know about existed in the nascent Christian movement, and
they persisted until the (unsuccessful) attempt of the creed writers to sup-
press them.

In any case, after the baptism, Jesus begins his life work, and John
begins to fade from view. We do not hear about him again until chapter
14, when we learn that he has been arrested by Herod and subsequently
beheaded after a wild party featuring an exotic dancer, whose name is not
given, but who was the daughter of Herod's wife, Herodias. Herod is so
entranced by her dancing, he promises to give her anything she might ask
for. Prompted by her show-business mama, the daughter asks for the head
of John the Baptist (14:3–12).

Is this yet another case of men blaming sex and women for their own
faults? It probably is. Matthew got the story from somewhere. But the Jewish historian Titus Flavius Josephus (37–100 CE) tells us that the real reason Herod wanted John out of the way was that he saw him attracting a
following and concluded that he was a political threat. When Jesus learned
about the death of a man he had once followed (the Bible does not say for
how long), he immediately went, as mobsters used to say, "on the lam." He
left Nazareth, where he was well known, moved to Capernaum, and maintained a low profile for a while.

Snatches of John's story are reported in all four Gospels, but this is an
example of something that attracts our attention because it was not
dropped out. Given the exalted representation of Jesus in these sources, it
might have been tempting to the writers not to say much about such a
controversial figure and to minimize the fact that Jesus for a time had
belonged to his disreputable movement. That all the Gospel writers over-
came this temptation (though the Gospel of John deals with it only in
passing) strongly suggests that the core of the John the Baptizer story is
historical. Maybe there were still people who would have remembered
him, and he could not simply be left out.

In Jesus's own trajectory, his "John phase" suggests he was a young
Galilean who was searching for spiritual reality; he was attracted for a

time to this fiery desert preacher, was baptized by him, but subsequently left to strike out on his own. It gives us a rounder and more approachable Jesus. Like many young people, then and now, he was on a quest and was willing both to try things out and to move on when he felt it necessary.

After he recounts the story of Jesus's baptism, Matthew tells us Jesus began his ministry in Galilee and called his disciples. But then Matthew immediately moves to devote three whole chapters to the centerpiece of this first part of his Gospel and the foundation stone of Jesus's teaching, the Sermon on the Mount.

THE SERMON ON THE MOUNT

Study Tip ——————————————————————

To grasp the import of Jesus's Sermon the Mount, found in Matthew 5–7, it would be useful to read it together with Luke's version, sometimes called the Sermon on the Plain, found in Luke 6:17–49. If you are studying in a group, it would be valuable to imagine how various of these well-known verses might be heard by people from different segments of the social spectrum.

When we come to the Sermon on the Mount, it is not difficult to see why so many writers have called it one of the masterpieces of world literature, moral vision, and spiritual discernment. It also appealed to the young Gandhi's growing belief about economic inequality and nonviolence. Take, for example, the idea that if a man has two coats, let him give one away. This idea, the liberation theologian Gustavo Gutiérrez points out, carries a different resonance for someone who has no coat than it does for someone who has a closetful. But here is the part that made the strongest impression on Gandhi, Dorothy Day, and Martin Luther King:

*You have heard that it was said, "You shall love your neighbor
and hate your enemy." But I say to you, Love your enemies and
pray for those who persecute you, so that you may be children of
your Father in heaven; for he makes his sun rise on the evil and
on the good, and sends rain on the righteous and on the unrighteous. For if you love those who love you, what reward do you
have? Do not even the tax collectors do the same? And if you greet
only your brothers and sisters, what more are you doing than others? Do not even the Gentiles do the same? Be perfect, therefore,
as your heavenly Father is perfect. (5:43–48)*

The words are elegant and have become integral to common English
idiom, but when we try to understand what they *actually* say, we come to
one of those points where another school of biblical studies is not only valuable, but essential, namely, "translation theory." Translation theory is based
on the old, but accurate observation, "There is no such thing as translation,
just interpretation." This sounds harsh and may be overstated. But its truth
lies in the fact that language is a living and changing chimera that never
just stays put. Translating the Sermon on the Mount into English provides
a continuing example of the challenge such fluidity presents. The version
that we read in our English Bibles is of course translated from the Greek in
which Matthew wrote it, but there are two issues to cope with here.

First, most scholars agree today that, although Jesus most likely said
everything we find in this discourse at one time or another, he may not
have said it all at once or in one place. Presenting it as a continuous address and locating it on a mountain (to remind readers of Moses) may well
have been handy editorial devices. It is probably a collection of sayings
gathered by Matthew into one uninterrupted session.

Second, Jesus did not first articulate these sayings in Greek. Most biblical specialists agree that he spoke Aramaic, a dialect derived from Hebrew and Arabic. So if Jesus spoke in Aramaic, and Matthew wrote in
Greek, how did the Sermon on the Mount, or the sayings that may have
been compiled into it, get from one language to the other? The answer

most biblical scholars give today is that it was part of Matthew's other source, Q, mentioned above. Still, by the time Matthew has it on his writing desk, Q is already a Greek document. But who did that original translation from Aramaic into Greek? We will never know.

Not only does Q contain no footnotes, remember that it does not even exist except as a hypothetical source, and some students continue to doubt whether it ever existed. But researchers, including Burton Mack, have now placed all the Q material together in a published book.[6] It has been reported, perhaps facetiously, that once this volume appeared and could be held in one's hands, Dr. Mack exclaimed, "See, now they cannot deny that it exists. Here it is. And it has a Library of Congress number!" For a more detailed discussion of the language Jesus spoke, see my Appendix.

In any case, the stubborn fact is that the oldest documents we have of any of the Gospels are in Greek. The translator must decipher the Greek version and "translate" (or interpret) it into English. Easy enough, one might say (if one knows both English and Koine, the Greek dialect of the New Testament). But remember that ancient Greek, including Koine, was also a living language when Matthew was writing. It had already evolved from the language of Homer and Plato. Also, many different local dialects of Greek coexisted at the time. Matthew, or whoever translated/interpreted the Sermon on the Mount (or the sayings collected in it) from Aramaic, had prickly choices to make (this is where translation theory comes into play). As we have just seen with the baptism, these earliest translators may well have shaded some of those choices in light of their theological preferences.

So far we have the Greek text to be rendered into English, but now comes the hard part. Given the fluidity of what they have to work with, English translators cannot avoid making some hard decisions. Take, for example, "Blessed are the meek, for they will inherit the earth" (5:5). Nearly all translators agree that the Greek word translated "meek" definitely did not mean what it does in colloquial English today. It did not conjure up a milquetoast or a doormat. Warren Carter adds that it also did not mean "gentle," "mild," or "passive." It meant simply "powerless." The meek are those who are held down and humiliated by the powerful.[7] So if there is such widespread agreement that the word "meek" does not convey the meaning of the original, why do translators stay with it? This is where translation theory comes to the fore again. They stay with it, despite its misleading connotation, because earlier translations, especially in this case the King James Version, have it that way, and it has become a tradition that is hard to challenge. How many thousands of Sunday school students (including me) have memorized the Beatitudes using the word "meek"? But maybe it is not too late to correct this egregious mistranslation. New versions of the Bible are constantly appearing, and it is time for this change to be part of the next one.

THE MINISTRY OF THE MESSIAH

After the Sermon on the Mount, Matthew launches into the description of the short but historically decisive ministry of the Nazarene healer and teacher. To trace the arc through Matthew's eyes, again let us imagine ourselves watching him write, but noticing the other documents scattered on his desk. As I said above, it is widely acknowledged today that Matthew consulted some written sources. So the writing table at which he sat was not empty. One of the sources he used was the Gospel of Mark, whole sections of which he simply incorporated letter for letter with no changes. But watch carefully. There are some verses in Mark that Matthew changes or just excludes. So now the plot thickens. The intriguing questions become *which* verses did he eliminate and—even more interestingly—*why*?

We begin with the question of "which." Here are some examples of verses in Mark that Matthew simply left out:

1. Mark 1:43, in which Jesus seems to speak harshly with the leper he has just healed: "After sternly warning him he sent him away."

2. Mark 3:5 and 10:14, in which Jesus is depicted as angry.

3. Mark 1:24 and 3:11, in which Mark says that the demons recognized Jesus.

4. Mark 3:21, the famous passage in which Jesus briefly returns home, but his friends think he has gone insane, and the scribes from Jerusalem claim he has been seized by a demon.

5. Mark 10:17–18, in which, when he is called "Good Teacher," Jesus replies that no one should call him good, because "No one is good but God alone."

Matthew eliminated all these verses. He was obviously not a literalist or a fundamentalist and apparently kept his red pencil busy. He felt no compunction to preserve the letter of the text of Mark he had before him.

But the *why* question remains. When we add up these strikeovers, what does it say about Matthew's own purpose? Who was he trying to reach? And what picture of Jesus was he trying to get across that he thought these verses in Mark might obscure or distort?

This is where historical research into the period in which Matthew was writing supplements redaction history. It seems that when he sat down at his desk about 90 CE, some sixty years after the crucifixion and twenty years after Mark, disputes had already arisen about who Jesus was and whether he had been a thoroughly and consistently good person. So, as he combed through the Gospel of Mark, Matthew kept an eye out for sentences that might conceivably convey some negative impression. Seeing the choices he made etches a clearer profile of Jesus's life, at least as Matthew wants us to see it. But why is he so sensitive about the portrait he sketches that he is willing simply to scratch out parts of what Mark says?

To answer these questions we need to step back from peering over Matthew's shoulder and look around at the world in which he found himself toward the close of the first century CE. It was a chaotic time. The Roman legions had brutally suppressed the Jewish revolt in 70 CE just twenty years before Matthew was writing. Most people still considered

Christians to be one of the many rival sectarian movements within Judaism. Christians themselves argued over how much of the law of Moses they were supposed to follow and to what extent they had been freed from it by the gospel. They also disagreed on the exact nature of his relationship to God.

Matthew could hardly escape these controversies. He refers to himself as a "scribe," and he was apparently a member of a "school" of scholars comparable to the much later rabbinical houses of study featured in the stories of Isaac Bashevis Singer. The difference was that Matthew's school consisted of followers of Jesus who were of Jewish heritage and who did feel obligated to Mosaic law, but believed they should interpret it in light of Jesus's life and teaching. They considered him to be the promised Messiah and felt that the light of his Spirit was continuing to guide them in their interpretation of the law. For Matthew, the problem was not just his fellow Jews who did not accept Jesus as the Messiah, but his fellow Jewish Christians. Some of them felt strongly drawn to the law that had linked their ancestors to God for generations and felt reluctant to reinterpret it very much. Others seized upon the new freedom they believed Christ had brought and thought that when there was a clash between law and gospel, the latter should prevail.

Now let us get a more rounded view of the ministry of Jesus by returning to "redaction history" and taking it one step farther, namely, comparing Matthew to Luke. Luke also relied on Mark's earlier Gospel as well as on other sources. Hence, if we compare what Luke kept and left out with what Matthew kept and left out, profiles of the preferences and purposes of these two writers begin to emerge, and our image of Jesus—seen now from two angles—comes into better focus as well. It is a bit like reading two biographies of a recent prominent political figure.

I mention this to emphasize again that the fact that we have four Gospels and not just one is a huge plus. Each was written by a different person with a particular audience in mind, and these readerships varied in geographical location, cultural context, and religious background. Although all the Gospel writers agreed on the centrality of Jesus in the story they were telling, they held somewhat differing views of his significance. Also, since they were all addressing different groups of people in a variety of geographical locations, they shaped their separate Gospels to speak to these disparate groups in a way that would both convey their own interpretations of the meaning of Jesus and connect with the mentality of each population. It is important for contemporary readers to recognize this, because it demonstrates that, from the earliest years of their history, different clusters of Christians and differing perceptions of the meaning of Jesus already coexisted. Variety is not a newcomer to Christianity. It was there from the outset.

With this insight in mind, one can read Matthew with considerably more satisfaction. After the opening portions, the book goes on with the engrossing account of Jesus's healings, parables, and teaching. In chapter 9 Jesus calls a tax collector named Matthew to follow him. This is not the same Matthew as the one who wrote the Gospel, who never claims to be a disciple (although for years many thought they were the same person). The incident is noteworthy, however, because the tax collector Matthew (who did become a disciple) invited Jesus to what turns out to be something of a feast at his home, to which he has also invited many of his fellow tax collectors. Jesus attends and is immediately disparaged by his enemies for the unsavory company he is keeping. According to 11:19 he is even accused of being a "glutton and a drunkard." The phrase "as he [Jesus] sat at dinner" (9:10) actually means "as he reclined at dinner." It seems like a small point, but in Christian art we never catch a glimpse of the Master stretched out on a couch enjoying what was undoubtedly a sumptuous spread. Again, translation studies and some knowledge of the customs of the era fill out our picture of Jesus.

As we follow Matthew's version of Jesus making his way to Jerusalem, we can continue to profit from a multidimensional perspective by comparing and counterchecking his account with the way the other Gospel writers describe—or leave out—the same incidents. When he does finally arrive, however, an incident occurs that many historians consider a critical turning point. Apparently the four Gospel writers agree because, unlike with some other events in his life, all four describe Jesus's "cleansing" of the Temple (Matt. 21:12–13). I place the word in quotation marks, because it does not appear in the text and, more important, because I agree with those who maintain that it was much more than a mere cleansing. It was, in fact, a temporary occupation not unlike those staged by the "Occupy" movement in recent American history.

Study Tip ———————————————————————

Read and compare the four descriptions of the so-called cleansing of the Temple: Mark 11:15–19, 27–33; Matthew 21:12–17, 23–27; Luke 19:45–48; 20:1–8; and John 2:13–16.

———————————————————————————

The Temple narrative is one in which the findings of biblical scholarship are especially valuable. For many years the standard Sunday sermon interpretation of this event was that Jesus felt offended by the merchandising going on in the Temple court and wanted to purify it of such commercialism. One preacher even used this text to thunder against bake sales in the church foyer. But this is a serious misreading. As a first-century Jew, Jesus accepted the sacrificial worship conducted by the priests in the Temple and even advised the people he healed to "go show yourself to the priest and make an offering" (Luke 5:14; 17:14; Mark 1:44; Matt. 8:4). Then why did Jesus exhibit such anger and even, whip in hand, turn over tables?

He gives the answer himself. "Is it not written," he says, " 'My house shall be called a house of prayer for all the nations'? But you have made it a den of robbers" (Mark 11:17). Jesus became enraged not that the Temple courtyard was being used to sell things, but that innocent people were being fleeced. Jesus was in no sense railing against Temple worship, as some misinformed Christian commentaries have suggested. He was not even chastising all the merchants who sold the sacrificial animals. He went after the crooks. Notice that Mark specifically says he overturned the table of those "who sold doves." As historians of the period have shown, the pilgrims who bought doves were the ones who were too poor to buy sheep or cattle.[8]

Jesus was demonstrating what, centuries later, liberation theologians would call a "preferential option for the poor," and numerous Christians who read this passage have been inspired to follow Jesus's example. They were sometimes labeled troublemakers or subversives. The four church-women who were raped and murdered by uniformed soldiers in 1980 in El Salvador are prime examples. Oscar Romero, archbishop of San Salvador, was murdered while saying Mass the same year. His crime was that he spoke out in his pulpit against the death squads. Less than a decade later, on November 16, 1989, six Jesuits who taught at the university in San Salvador and openly supported the struggle of the common people against the dictatorship met a similar fate. All these, and many more, paid the price for what their understanding of the message of Jesus seemed to require of them. Their deaths drove the underlying insight of liberation theology home: discerning the kingdom of God in our midst is not, as Jesus said, a matter of mere "observation." It requires a degree of raw personal exposure to the message that goes beyond arms-length examination.

History yields many examples of temporary disruptions of a sanctuary in the cause of justice. Protests and reforms often begin in religious venues. When an Augustinian monk named Martin Luther posted his complaints against the papacy and the indulgence system in Wittenberg, he tacked them up on the door of the cathedral itself. The Scottish Reformation started in Edinburgh when an angry woman hurled a stool at the head of a preacher who was "praying out of a book." The early New England Quakers interrupted church services to make known their peacemaking message. The colonial authorities treated them harshly, but today they are universally admired for their efforts to advance reconciliation. Gandhi led nonviolent bands of "untouchables" into the Hindu temple precincts from which the higher castes banned them. Then in 1960s America hundreds of black Christians staged "pray-ins" in segregated churches.

There is a more recent instance. On February 21, 2012, five young Russian women, members of the group called "Pussy Riot," staged an unannounced performance in Moscow's Cathedral of Christ the Savior. Their song took the form of a prayer to the Mother of God, beseeching her to rid their country of Vladimir Putin, whom they consider to be a dictator.

Church security officers hurriedly stopped the prayer-in-song, but the women claimed that they had aimed their protest at the Orthodox Church leader's support for Putin during his election campaign.

Three members of the group were arrested and tried for "hooliganism motivated by religious hatred." They were sentenced to two years in prison. In the late winter of 2014, however, Putin commuted their sentences in a public-relations gesture before the Sochi Winter Olympics. But had these young women been guilty of inciting religious hatred, as the court held? Or were they continuing the tradition of using dramatic gestures at sacred sites to communicate a serious message, a practice that goes back to the Hebrew prophets and to Jesus himself? It seems that the honored practice of a brief interruption of the serenity of a holy place in the interest of a holy cause still lives on.

There is something else to learn from Matthew's description of the Temple episode. It provides an especially sharp example of his effort to revise and cut Mark's account, in this case to soften it, when he felt it was needed. Notice that the narrative in Mark (11:15–17) is longer than Matthew's. Mark has it this way:

> *Then they came to Jerusalem. And he entered the temple and began to drive out those who were selling and those who were buying in the temple, and he overturned the tables of the money changers and the seats of those who sold doves;* and he would not allow anyone to carry anything through the temple. *He was teaching and saying, "Is it not written, 'My house shall be called a house of prayer for all the nations'? But you have made it a den of robbers." (11:15–17)*

I have placed a key phrase in Mark's version above in roman, because it clearly claims that Jesus took at least partial control of the immense Temple complex. Further, without a doubt he was supported by his disciples, since he could not have monitored all the entrances alone. Why is it that Matthew consigned this heavily freighted utterance from Mark to the scrap basket?

For an answer we go back again to Roman imperial history. The Temple described in these passages was immense, and it was not just a place of worship. It was also the headquarters of the despised Jewish priestly elite, who, to the dismay and anger of most of their fellow Jews, had acquiesced to the Roman rulers and were profiting handsomely from their sycophancy. In addition, the Temple served as a regional bank, with large deposits, where mortgages and loans could be negotiated. It was this financial, political, and imperial command center that Jesus and his disciples temporarily and symbolically occupied.

And remember, Matthew was writing while the devastating Roman defeat of the Jewish rebellion and the razing of Jerusalem and its Temple in 70 CE, in which thousands were killed, were still smoldering in people's memories. Like Luke, Matthew wanted to stave off any further repression by putting on the best possible front to the Roman overlords. He did not want them to think that Christians posed a threat to the *Pax Romana* ("the Roman peace"). His was part of a concerted effort by many early Christian writers to distance themselves from any hint of Jewish national rebelliousness.

But once we understand Matthew's editorial strategy and think of the earlier and probably more historically accurate description of the Temple incident Mark gives, again a different picture of Jesus emerges. After the confrontational street theater he had staged a bit earlier during his entry into the city, which was a provocative caricature of the Roman imperial triumphal marches, the legions were already wary. Now this noisy fracas within the Temple walls, right under their noses, was too much. They knew that this man had to be terminated before his movement got completely out of hand, and the sooner the better.

There then follows in Matthew the familiar but chilling denouement. The powers that be hatch a plot to kill Jesus. He probably knows. While he dines in Bethany a woman anoints him, and he tells his appalled disciples, "She has prepared me for burial" (26:12). He then celebrates a Passover seder with these same confused followers and is betrayed by Judas, arrested by a Temple posse, tried before the Roman procurator, tortured, mocked, and executed by crucifixion, a death penalty reserved for those judged to be a threat to imperial security.

Study Tip

> At this point I want to insert what may seem to be an odd piece of advice in a book on how to read the Bible: close the Bible and listen to the best rendition possible of J. S. Bach's *St. Matthew Passion*. One of my teachers called it "the fifth Gospel." That may be too big a claim, but since it combines the words of the biblical text with some of the finest music ever composed, careful listeners (maybe with Gospel pages open) can gain a full appreciation of the spiritual power of what is Matthew's magnum opus as well as Bach's.

After the Passion narrative comes the account of the risen Christ meeting his followers in a whole new way. Here there arises another example of how current biblical research both complicates and enlarges our reading of the Gospels. It involves the account of Easter morning in the Gospel of Mark, written about twenty years before Matthew. We have already glanced at what might be called "manuscript comparison" in our discussion of the words from heaven at Jesus's baptism. There, however, it involved only one short phrase and resulted in a theological dispute that might seem unimportant to modern Christians. In Mark, however, it touches on one of the central tenets of Christianity, the resurrection.

The "manuscript" issue in connection with Mark is also unlike the one we discussed in relation to Genesis, because in Mark it is not a matter of attempting to plot the different sources that make up the book. Remember, those were *theoretical* sources, and none of them, like "J" or "P," actually exist anywhere as separate documents. With Mark we face just the opposite problem. Several early manuscripts of the text do exist, but they differ with each other, in some cases quite substantially. Consequently, the way they are studied requires careful scrutiny of the earliest manuscripts in which Mark appears. Also this is not a matter of comparing the differing viewpoints as we did with Genesis. The puzzle that the various manuscripts of Mark put before us is a tougher one: Which parts actually belong in the text at all?

To understand what is meant, readers should turn to the last pages of the Second Gospel (the end of chap. 16) as they appear in the New Revised Standard Version and notice something unique about them. Mark is the only Gospel, indeed the only book in the entire Bible, that—like some postmodern novel—concludes with *alternate endings*. You can make this singularity even more vivid by opening a copy of the King James Version to the same chapter, where 16:9–20 are not differentiated in any way.

In both versions, chapter 16 begins when the Sabbath was over, and Mary Magdalene, Mary the mother of James, and Salome bought spices, so that they could go and anoint his body (16:1). The body of Jesus had been placed in a borrowed tomb, that of Joseph of Aramathea. But since he had been crucified on Friday, the following day was Saturday, the Jewish Sabbath, when pious Jews were not permitted to move about the city and only those caring for the body of a deceased person were allowed to touch corpses. Further, the shops would all have been closed, and the passage says they had to buy the aromatic spices before they could fulfill their obligation as women to anoint a body that was already beginning to decompose. The narrative then proceeds to tell of their finding that the stone that had sealed the tomb had been rolled away and their discovery of a young man dressed in a white robe (16:4–5). He tells them Jesus is not there, but has risen (16:6). Mark 16:8 reads: "So they went out and fled from the tomb, for terror and amazement had seized them; and they said nothing to anyone, for they were afraid," after which the account breaks off unexpectedly.

For centuries scholars have known that this is where Mark originally ended and found it a startling, even disturbing way to end both the chapter and the whole Gospel of Mark. The question is: Why this abrupt conclusion without closure? Theories have abounded. Did Mark die before he could finish it? Was the last page lost from an early manuscript, and then this "alternate" ending found its way into later manuscripts? What is a poor translator to do? Some versions, like the KJV, ignore the issue. It simply adds the longer ending on after v. 8 with no explanation. The RSV puts the endings at the bottom of the page in smaller typeface; and the NRSV labels them and puts additional text in a footnote.

Then there were helpful souls who believed that Mark simply could not have meant to leave everyone in suspense, so they did their best to finish the Gospel for him. A source from nine hundred years later names a certain monk, Agaron, as the writer of our present extended conclusion. A few have even suggested that perhaps Mark himself got sick or had to move away temporarily, then finished it later. This last theory has very few supporters, mainly because the Greek style of the writing from v. 9 on differs so radically from that of the body of the Gospel and uses words that never appear elsewhere in it, which implies that someone else wrote the last verses.

The scholarly battle around these various theories has raged for centuries, and there is an excellent summary of them in the entry on Mark in the *Catholic Encyclopedia,* which is available online. In it the writer traces the appearance of the last verses of chapter 16 in early manuscripts, but also lists those in which it does not appear. The latter outweigh the former. This relentless sleuthing through reports of what the differing Greek, Coptic, Armenian, and Latin scrolls and codices say can cause readers' eyes to glaze over, but the conclusion seems on balance to indicate that whoever wrote the bulk of the Gospel did not write the added longer ending. (In a brave effort to end the article on a positive if not terribly realistic note, the writer of the *Catholic Encyclopedia* entry speculates that maybe one day the original ending, presumably by Mark, will be found in a cave somewhere under the desert sands. But at this writing, it has not turned up yet.)

But even with Bach's last "amen" we have not reached the end. As the music fades and we close the Gospel story of Jesus, the question Jesus put to his disciples at Caesarea Philippi insists on being answered: "Who do you say that I am?" (Matt. 16:15). For some years now participants in the

Jesus Seminar have tried to uncover who Jesus "really was" from the over-
lay of tradition and emendation. Using the Gospels as human documents
and not inerrant revelations, they also combined historical accounts, archaeology and even comparative anthropology to find out what can be said
about the "Jesus of history," relying only on evidence and methods available to anyone. As far as it goes, their work has been outstanding, even
brilliant. It is not fair to say they were asking the wrong question. They
were asking a *different* question. In any case they have not answered Jesus's
question, because *it is not a historical question*. But what kind of question
is it?

Dietrich Bonhoeffer, who was murdered by the Gestapo in a concentration camp just before the end of World War II, posed the question in its
most unavoidable form. Sitting in his cell on April 30, 1944, aware that he
would probably never get out, he wrote to his friend Eberhard Bethge:

> *You would be surprised, and perhaps even worried, by my theo-
> logical thoughts and the conclusions they lead to; and this is
> where I miss you most of all, because I don't know anyone else
> with whom I could so well discuss them to have my thinking clar-
> ified. What is bothering me incessantly is the question what
> Christianity really is or indeed who Christ really is, for us today.*[9]

Bonhoeffer's question, "Who is Christ for us today?" is a good one,
including the "us" and the "today," with which to end our discussion of
the Gospels and some of the research tools that open them to us more
clearly. The question is important, because ultimately none of these finely
honed tools can answer it. It requires a personal response. Like the kingdom of justice and healing that Jesus demonstrated and taught, it cannot
be answered "by observation," even of the keenest and most rigorous sort.
It demands something much deeper.

The account of the resurrection appearances in the Gospel of Luke
presses this question in different language. Having come to the grave to
anoint his body, the women who had followed Jesus encounter two men
"in dazzling clothes," who ask them, "Why do you look for the living

among the dead? He is not here, but has risen" (24:5). Matthew adds that the women and the other disciples are then told to follow him to Galilee (28:7, 10). There it is no longer Jesus, but the disciples who must continue the liberating work he had been doing and carry his message about a kingdom "in the midst of you" to the world. The game had changed.

8

On the Road
with Paul of Tarsus

The Epistles

What then shall we say to this? If God is for us, who is against us? He who did not spare his own Son but gave him up for us all, will he not also give us all things with him? Who shall bring any charge against God's elect? It is God who justifies; who is to condemn? . . . No, in all these things we are more than conquerors through him who loved us. For I am sure that neither death, nor life, nor angels, nor principalities, nor things present, nor things to come, nor powers, nor height, nor depth, nor anything else in all creation, will be able to separate us from the love of God in Christ Jesus our Lord.

ROMANS 8:31–39, RSV

Pity poor Paul. As we mark the two thousandth anniversary of the apostle's life, his reputation has hit a very rough patch. His critics rehearse a catalog of allegations, calling him a small-minded legalist who insisted that people obey the existing authorities no matter what, a misogynist who warned women to be silent in church, a reactionary who instructed slaves to obey their masters, and a prude who inveighed against homosexuals. Further, he is accused in some circles of distorting the gentle love ethic of the Nazarene and turning it into a rigid, dogmatic religion.

But things may be changing for the traveling tentmaker from Tarsus. Every one of these accusations is now being questioned and often discarded. As we turn to his Letters, which make up a large chunk of the New Testament, it is critical to realize that one of the most illuminating new approaches to biblical studies focuses mainly on them. It is called the "empire studies" approach. As the term suggests, its basic premise, as one of its principal advocates says, is that "the Roman Empire is not just the *background* of Paul's letters; it is the *foreground*."[1] Applying this interpretive principle cuts through layers of inherited readings and enables us to see this controversial apostle in a fresh way.

The core of empire studies is not complicated. Indeed, one can wonder why this approach has only emerged with any seriousness in the past two decades. The answer might be that as the voices of Christians in the global south, those who have been the objects of modern imperial ambitions, begin to play a larger role in Christianity, the massive influence of empires in shaping people's lives has assumed more salience, and they bring this painful recognition to their reading of the Bible. In this chapter we will explore how empire studies cast a whole new light on a couple of his key Letters.[2] To discern what these millennia-old letters might mean for us today, however, we need to supplement empire studies with two other methods. We have to understand what their original purpose was and to be aware how they have been both used and misused in the centuries since they were written.

To start with Paul himself, let us recognize that, unlike Abraham or Moses, he is unambiguously a "historical" figure. Not even his sharpest detractors claim he never existed (although some may wish he hadn't). Many people consider him, next to Jesus, the most influential figure in the history of Christianity (although, again, many wish he were not). Paul, or Saul as he was called first, was born in Tarsus, on the southern coast of modern Turkey on the shore of the Cydnus River. The city's other claim to fame is that it is where Antony and Cleopatra first encountered each other and started their ill-fated love affair, but that was thirty years before Saul was born.

PAUL'S WORLD

The most important thing we can say about Saul's birth, early in the first century CE, is that Tarsus was in a Greek-speaking part of the Roman Empire. The young Saul, unlike Jesus, spoke Greek as his first language, and he wrote all his Letters in Greek. This is not just an item of casual interest. Paul is rightly credited with building the bridge over which the essentially Hebrew ideas of early Christianity passed from Palestine into Hellenistic Europe. It has been plausibly argued that without Paul the Jesus movement might have remained a reforming sect within Judaism. When we read Romans, Galatians, or Thessalonians, it is useful to remember that when Paul wrote them (between 53 and 62 CE), the Gospels had not yet been written. Also in reading the Letters of Paul it is essential to realize that all the recipients of these letters, without exception, were not just living under the rule of Rome, but were also living within a political and religious culture energetically promulgated by the empire and, where necessary, forcibly imposed by that same regime. Both Paul and those who received the letters were constantly aware of this situation. As empire-studies historians remind us, Rome was not just a backdrop. It was a force field.

Saul was also Jewish, in his own eyes very Jewish indeed. Here is how he puts it in his Letter to the Philippians in the somewhat colloquial New Living Translation:

> I was circumcised when I was eight days old. I am a pure-blooded citizen of Israel and a member of the tribe of Benjamin—a real Hebrew if there ever was one! I was a member of the Pharisees, who demand the strictest obedience to the Jewish law. (3:5)

We know about Saul/Paul from two biblical sources. The first is his own Letters. The second is the account of his life and travels given in the Acts of the Apostles. In comparing these sources (which do not always agree with each other), it is useful to recall what we have said about genres in the section on form analysis in our chapter on the prophets. These two sources—the Letters and Acts—represent two quite different genres, and they should be read in a different manner. They were composed for different purposes. In the Letters Paul was trying to sort out difficulties that had arisen in the tiny congregations he had either started or helped to start. They speak to a specific small group of people, and it is hard to imagine that Paul would have expected them to be read, examined, and commented on thousands of years later. In perusing them we often have the feeling we are listening in on one side of a long-distance phone call. For example:

> I urge Euodia and I urge Syntyche to be of the same mind in the Lord. Yes, and I ask you also, my loyal companions, help these women, for they have struggled beside me in the work of the gospel, along with Clement and the rest of my co-workers . . . (Phil. 4:2–3)

Who in the world were Euodia and Syntyche, who seem to have been having a spat, and what was it about? We will never know.

THE ROAD TO DAMASCUS

As a pious young man, at some point Saul went to Jerusalem probably to study the Torah with its prominent rabbis. But while he was there he apparently learned something about the energetic new "Jesus movement," and it troubled him fiercely. What was it that got under his skin? It seems these "Jesus people," who continued to identify themselves as Jews, worship in the Temple, and mark the Jewish holidays, were eating together with Gentiles and thus violating the kosher rules, at least as they were interpreted by the strictest enforcers of the dietary code. Empowered by the officials of the Temple, Saul set out for Damascus to take the offenders into custody. But something happened on the "road to Damascus" that has transformed that phrase into an idiomatic equivalent for a sudden, jarring change of life.[3]

Here we must deal with two serious misunderstandings about this turning point in Saul's life. First, he was not intent on persecuting "Christians"—in fact, that word had not yet been invented—and clearly he was not the least bit interested in any Gentiles who were following this Nazarene. With whom the *goyim* were eating, he could not care less. His cap was set only against Jews, in particular those Jews who were brazenly flouting the sacred protocol. Also, when he was stopped in his tracks by a blinding light and heard the voice of Jesus, he was not "converted" in our sense of the word, this despite those artistic masterpieces that depict the "conversion of St. Paul," the most celebrated of which is by Caravaggio.

Second, he assuredly did not "convert" from Judaism to Christianity. Rather, Paul (that is what he henceforth called himself) experienced his personal equivalent of a "call" from the same God who had previously called the prophets before him. His commission, as he slowly learned after this life-changing encounter, was to become a prophet both to the Jews and the Gentiles, to inform them that, through Jesus Christ, they now both belonged to the same commonwealth. This was an epochal change, one that Paul's prophetic predecessors had proclaimed God had promised would one day come to pass. That time, Paul believed, had now come, and he set out on voyage after voyage to make this good news (Gk. *evangelium*) known. The message is expressed in lyrical words in the Letter to the Ephesians, in which he seems to be addressing Gentile followers of Jesus, but it is the same message he was delivering to the Jews in the many synagogues he visited as well:

> *Therefore remember that at one time you Gentiles in the flesh,*
> *called the uncircumcision by what is called the circumcision,*
> *which is made in the flesh by hands—remember that you were at*
> *that time separated from Christ, alienated from the common-*
> *wealth of Israel, and strangers to the covenants of promise, hav-*
> *ing no hope and without God in the world. But now in Christ*
> *Jesus you who once were far off have been brought near in the*
> *blood of Christ. For he is our peace, who has made us both one,*
> *and has broken down the dividing wall of hostility, by abolishing*

in his flesh the law of commandments and ordinances, that he
might create in himself one new man in place of the two, so mak-
ing peace, and might reconcile us both to God in one body through
the cross, thereby bringing the hostility to an end. And he came
and preached peace to you who were far off and peace to those
who were near. (2:11–17, RSV)

PAUL'S MESSAGE

Much has been made of the fact that, when Paul arrived in any city, he
first went to the local synagogue to deliver this message. But if he was supposed to be a messenger to the Gentiles, why did he do that? There are two
answers. The first is that, as we have noted above, his message was to both
Jews and Gentiles. To the Jews he said, in effect, "Fling wide the gate. The
promised time has come to welcome the Gentiles into the commonwealth
of Israel." To the Gentiles he said, "Welcome. You are now no longer
strangers, but fellow citizens."[4]

But the second reason he hastened to the Jewish meetings is that, as
recent studies, especially inscriptions in synagogues, have ascertained,
there were many, perhaps thousands, of non-Jews who were attending synagogue services. This is mentioned explicitly in the Acts of the Apostles:
"So Paul stood up, and motioning with his hand said: 'Men of Israel and
you who fear God, listen'" (13:16, ESV). Who were these "God-fearers"?
They were Gentiles of Paul's time who had become restless and dissatisfied
both with the weakening polytheistic system of the Hellenistic Roman
world, which for many had become sheer superstition, and with what to
many seemed the callousness and spreading decadence of the age. They
were drawn to the ethical monotheism and clear moral principles of the
Jews. In some cities, whole sections of the larger synagogues were set aside
for these spiritual searchers who, given the lack of clarity about just what
Paul meant by "fearing" God, might better be called God-seekers or God-
respecters. But most, although they wanted to be close to Judaism, drew
back from actual conversion, due no doubt, at least for the men, to their

hesitation about circumcision. Some may also have had reservations about the dietary restrictions.

For this growing wave of "God-seekers," Paul's message must have come as welcome news. Now, because of what God had done in Christ, they could become part of the covenant community without subscribing to these practices. They could "take the best and leave the rest." Naturally, however, to many Jews, who associated their faith with hundreds of years of traditional rules and ritual practices, these newcomers must have seemed like freeloaders. Further, in Jewish teaching, the eventual integration of the Gentiles was believed to be a sure sign that the messianic age had begun, so opening the gate also implied recognizing Jesus as that messiah. But most were not prepared to make that move. This cluster of issues was what eventually (not right away) divided the nascent Jesus movement from what became rabbinical Judaism. And we have lived with that division ever since.

After his startling experience on the road to Damascus, Paul traveled to what he calls "Arabia" (Gal. 1:17). He does not say for how long. But here we must question another long-standing idea about him. When I first learned about Paul in Arabia, the image I conjured up was of his squatting in silence on the sand, maybe near an oasis, for a very long time in silent meditation to let his Damascus road experience sink in. But historical geographers have now begun to clarify the meaning of this brief passage. "Arabia," it seems does not just refer to the long peninsula that now bears that name. It designated a much larger region, including the area just east of Damascus. After his radical change of heart, Paul may have reverted to what had been his family's business of fabricating and selling tents, probably mostly for the use of the wealthy and the Roman legions. So he became, in effect, a traveling salesman (similar incidentally to the early life of Muhammad), traversing the cities and towns of Arabia, like Petra. Some scholars calculate that he stayed at this trade for seventeen years, driven perhaps by both the need to earn a living and an inner restlessness, before returning to Damascus.

We do not know exactly what Paul was doing during this time, and he does not tell us. But what we do know, both from standard ancient histories and from empire studies, is that "Arabia," as part of the Roman Empire, was agitated by clashing ethnic and religious loyalties, which Paul could not have missed. As he trekked from place to place, still under the searing spell of his encounter with the risen Christ, he had many long months to ponder what it meant both for his own people of the covenant and for the suffering and divided world outside the confines of his Jewish sphere. Everywhere he met the cult of the divinized emperor, proclaimed by inscriptions, many of them still discernible today, as a "savior" who had brought "peace and blessings" to "all humankind." The cult was especially popular in the eastern provinces, where Paul was traveling and where people were accustomed to god-kings.

CLASHING WORLDVIEWS

Here is an example of a proclamation issued in 9 BCE, one of hundreds that might be quoted, by the assembly of the province of Asia to honor the emperor Augustus. It illustrates the profuse use of religious language that would no doubt have infuriated Paul:

> *Whereas the providence which divinely ordered our lives created with zeal and munificence the most perfect good for our lives by producing Augustus and filling him with virtue for the benefaction of mankind, sending us and those after us a savior who put an end to war and established all things; and whereas Caesar [Augustus] when he appeared exceeded the hopes of all who had anticipated good tidings, not only by surpassing the benefactors who had been born before him, but not even those to come have any hope of surpassing him; and whereas the birthday of the god marked for the world marked the beginning of good tidings through his coming . . .*[5]

The assembly and its governor then went on to proclaim that from then on the new year should henceforth begin with Augustus's birthday. Although this particular document dates from decades before Paul's mission, it and others like it continued to gather strength and were in full flowering during his lifetime. Roman governance and the religious culture it sponsored were inseparable. They relied utterly on each other. The imperial religion, centered in the cult of the divine emperor, was assiduously cultivated by the state, and the cult bolstered and undergirded imperial rule. But there was also something else.

In addition to the emperor cult, Rome maintained its rule by means of an elaborate patronage policy integrated into a rigid hierarchical system. The emperor and his court dispensed valuable privileges and the immense riches and lands gained by their wars to people who were then expected to be deferential to them in carrying out imperial policies. Then these recipients of patronage handed down favors to the next level with the same expectation of submissiveness, and the trickle-down process continued to the lowest strata of the empire. Patronage provided the glue that bound imperial subjects to their immediate superiors, to the emperor, and to "Roma" as a religious and political entity. It was a pyramidal structure that created, indeed required, dependency on layer after layer of higher-ups. Thus patronage and the imperial cult worked together, and every man, woman, and child anywhere in the empire, whether a citizen or not, was subject to both aspects of this imperial regime. It was the all-encompassing grid within which Paul found himself, and against which—as we will see below—he preached and organized an alternative.

During his "silent years" in Arabia and then even more so during his three later hectic journeys around the Mediterranean, Paul became increasingly aware that he was living in an era of clashing worldviews. Both made sweeping universal claims. On the one side loomed the powerful imperial cult and the debilitating patronage system, enforced by imperial law and the legions. On the other was the view of history Paul himself embraced. It traced its beginnings back to the very creation of the world and the divine promise to Abraham that through him all the nations of the world would be blessed. It continued with the deliverance of the Israelites from Egypt and entrance into their promised land and then the coming of the Messiah in the person of the crucified and risen Christ.

This world vision had no legions and no means to enforce its way of life. But Paul was confident that in God's good time, which for him was soon, the imperial system, which he called "this present evil age," would topple and the reign of God would be established on earth as it already was in heaven. It would be a universal reign that would include all peoples. This was the vision that gradually grew in Paul during his seventeen years of traveling through Arabia as he made and sold his tents, witnessed the repressive rule of Rome, and wondered what he should do with the rest of his life. Eventually he returned to Jerusalem and at last met and conferred with some of the original followers of Jesus, like James, who still lived there. Only then was he ready to set out on the arduous travels that took him by land and sea to places that are familiar to us in part because of the letters he later wrote, like Philippi, Corinth, Galatia, Ephesus, and Rome. In each of these he announced the imminent arrival of a new world age, initiated by the crucifixion and resurrection, that would displace the rotten remnants of the present one.

It is important to underline here that, despite much that has been said and written to that effect, the clash of worldviews that Paul saw was not one between Judaism and Christianity. After his Damascus road experience Paul remained a Jew, summoned now to announce the fulfillment of God's promise, made through Abraham and the prophets, to unite all peoples in a new dominion of justice and shalom. His message was not anti-Jewish, but anti-imperial. Given the irreducible disparity between these two empires, the Roman one, ruled over by a divine imperator with his enervating patronage system, and the kingdom of God, Paul devised two strategies.

First, he heralded the coming of a new reign of justice and love that would displace the harsh and ruthless Roman one, which—in any case—Paul believed was already teetering and fated for destruction. In announcing the victory of the One whose kingdom would soon come, Paul daringly appropriated some of the same words the Roman underlings employed to characterize the emperor, words like "savior, "peace bringer," "source of blessing for all humankind." Then, as both Jews and Gentiles responded to the message, he helped them develop alternative gatherings, to which he gave the name *ekklesia,* a civic term used for the assembly of citizens in the *polis,* the Greek city-state. This was decidedly not a "religious" term; it was a political one. Paul knew perfectly well what temples and shrines were, but he was not interested in building them or in creating a new religion. What he organized was a kind of "shadow" structure, a regime in exile that would already be in place when the one Rome had built fell, as he was sure it soon would.

But in addition to announcing the *evangelium,* or "good tidings" (the same phrase used in the message about Augustus in the proclamation quoted above), Paul had a second strategy. He also established an elaborate alternative to the humiliating patronage system. He organized the *ekklesia* as networks of mutual aid. Within these citizen assemblies, equality obtained between men and women and among those who had joined as slaves or tradesmen, Jews or Greeks. Responsible people (deacons) were appointed to share the goods of the group, making sure no one went hungry. Among the scattered assemblies, or congregations, gifts and money were exchanged, the better off ones assisting the poorer ones. Paul himself carried donations collected during his trips back to Jerusalem, which was one of the poorest of the congregations. An extensive web of horizontal giving and receiving arose, which liberated the citizens of the new era of shalom from the clutches of the Roman patronage system. No wonder that when the local magistrates heard this radical message and saw these new associations arising, they viewed both as treasonous, which is why Paul was beaten, jailed, and eventually executed.

But during the period from the Damascus road encounter, which took place in about 33 CE, to his return to Jerusalem in 51, all this was still in the future. Then, however, there he began a series of hair-raising trips around the Mediterranean interrupted by shipwrecks, arrests, and beatings, but sometimes by warm welcomes. For this chapter of his life the best sources are his own Letters. The account of his travels narrated in the Acts of the Apostles can be helpful, but is supplementary. In reading these texts today in the light of current biblical research, it is vital to remember that the Letters constitute what historians call a "primary source" while Acts is a "secondary source." Therefore we read them in a different way. The Letters were written by Paul himself on the run during the 50s and early 60s. Luke wrote Acts decades after the incidents it describes, probably between 80 and 90 CE. In many ways the chronology and details of the two sources coincide, but not always, and where they do not, historians rely on Paul.

(A fascinating issue for biblical researchers is that at one point in Acts, the author switches from the third person to the second-person plural and begins to speak of "we." For many years these "we passages" were taken to indicate that from this point Luke had actually traveled with Paul and was therefore an eyewitness. But more recently students of this text have come to believe, on linguistic grounds, that Luke has simply incorporated someone else's diary into his book.)

As we read the Letters, we cannot avoid thinking about the indictment of Paul mentioned in the opening paragraph of this chapter, about Paul the bigot, chauvinist, misogynist. As we do we need to remember that Paul, like all of us, was a person of his era. He shared many of its customs, scruples, and perhaps even some of the biases of that time. But, even granting all that, are the current condemnations valid?

WOMEN'S SILENCE IN THE CHURCHES

Let us begin with Paul the woman hater, or at least the patriarch who wanted to keep women in their place. Those who want to depict Paul in this way rely on a couple of citations, but invariably single out one verse as their proof-positive text:

> The women should keep silent in the churches. For they are not permitted to speak, but should be in submission, as the Law also says. (1 Cor. 14:34, ESV)

A great deal of argumentation has roiled around this controversial verse, much of it highly repetitive. Briefly, the debate centers on whether Paul actually wrote these words or whether they are an interpolation, penned into a copy of 1 Corinthians after the letter had left Paul's hand. Those who argue against the interpolation theory point out that there are no existing documents without this verse. On the other hand, the verse appears in different places in different manuscripts, suggesting that it might have been inserted by copyists who decided on their own where it should be. In other words, there is real evidence that some of the earliest copies of 1 Corinthians have been tampered with.

Those who claim that this verse is a later add-on and that Paul could not have written it also point out that, in addition to evidence of tampering, these words are utterly inconsistent with virtually everything else Paul says and does with reference to women. Time after time Paul commends his women co-workers, like Phoebe (a deacon); Tryphaena and Tryphosa, named in Romans 16:12; and Junia, whom he calls "eminent among the apostles" in Romans 16:7. It is inconceivable that these women were not supposed to speak in the churches.

Admittedly, this is the kind of scholarly dispute that can become baffling and tedious, and in the end today's readers must make up their own minds. For what it is worth, I find the case against Pauline authorship of this verse quite convincing. But I also realize that for people who regard every syllable in whatever translation of the Bible they are using as directly inspired by God and inerrant, regardless of what the old manuscripts say, the case against Pauline authorship carries no weight. Some inerrancy advocates warn of a slippery slope. If we grant that this verse was tucked in later, they argue, then how many other verses might fall under suspicion? That way, they claim, lies the undermining of all scriptural authority and ultimately results in relativism.

This contention is understandable, but in the end unpersuasive. There are in fact different manuscripts of biblical books in existence, and some of the ways they differ are important. We have discussed this in connection with the alternate endings of the Gospel of Mark. Once again the net result of the patient work of biblical researchers is to demonstrate that our Bible does not speak in a monosyllabic way. It is a single book of many voices, and this is a welcome discovery, one that mature readers cannot afford to ignore.

The only reason to dwell on the dispute about Paul and women is that ironically those who accuse him of rampant male chauvinism as well as those who want him to uphold male dominance in the church agree with each other that he did in fact tell the women to shut up in church. They rely on this one verse as well as a scattering of other references (some of them in the Letters Paul did not himself write) to argue against the ordination of women or welcoming them into any significant leadership positions. But for both these parties, their case is faltering. Opposition to women's leadership in Christianity (and in other faiths as well) is crumbling. We now have women priests, ministers, rabbis, and bishops. And I think Paul, who relied so heavily on women co-workers in the early church, would heartily approve.

BE SUBJECT TO THE GOVERNING AUTHORITIES

Another charge brought against Paul is based on seven verses from Romans 13, in which he appears to support obeying all constituted authorities without reference to how unjustly they are exerting their power:

> *Let every person be subject to the governing authorities. For there is no authority except from God, and those that exist have been instituted by God. Therefore he who resists the authorities resists what God has appointed, and those who resist will incur judgment. For rulers are not a terror to good conduct, but to bad. Would you have no fear of him who is in authority? Then do what is good, and you will receive his approval, for he is God's servant for your good. But if you do wrong, be afraid, for he does not bear the sword in vain; he is the servant of God to execute his wrath on the wrong-doer. Therefore one must be subject, not only to avoid God's wrath but also for the sake of conscience. For the same reason you also pay taxes, for the authorities are ministers of God, attending to this very thing. Pay all of them their dues, taxes to whom taxes are due, revenue to whom revenue is due, respect to whom respect is due, honor to whom honor is due. (13:1–7, RSV)*

It is impossible to estimate how many times this passage has been cited to justify a vast range of horrendous officially sanctioned abuses, including the denial of human rights under apartheid and the garnering of popular German support for the criminal Nazi regime. Even though Paul lived in a different age, what motivated him to write these words, if indeed he did write them?

The dilemma only deepens when we consider that in so many other places in his writing Paul speaks of the "powers of this evil age" and predicts their imminent collapse. Also remember that Paul himself obviously did not obey his own dictum. He was publicly whipped more than once and imprisoned at least three times by the "governing authorities." He wrote three of his Letters, Philippians, Colossians, and Philemon, in prisons. Yet he says we should dutifully obey? Such obvious contradictions have caused many investigators to question whether the words in Romans are actually Paul's. To quote just one of many of these scholars, James Kallas writes in the leading journal in the field: "Paul could not have ascribed such an exalted status to Rome without being not only hypocritical and servile, but untrue to his whole theological position." Kallas therefore concludes in plain words, "This is not Paul."[6]

Some of the same kinds of arguments against the authenticity of the verse silencing women in the churches have been marshaled against the authenticity of these submission-to-the-authorities verses. Some linguists believe the whole last section of Romans reads like a document by another writer that was then appended to Romans to benefit from Paul's authority. But this is a highly disputed point. There may be a reason other than hypocrisy or servility that Paul really did write these verses.

By employing a meticulous empire-studies method, one historian has uncovered the noteworthy fact that, at just the time this Letter was written, the Jews of the city of Rome had fallen under suspicion of sympathizing with their Jewish compatriots in Judea who were causing the legions endless troubles. One ancient historian says there were "tumults" in the city of Rome, and the emperor Claudius had expelled many of the Jews. But since at that time "Jews" included the "followers of Christus," who were seen as a Jewish subsect, Paul may have feared that the tiny Christian congregations there might have been in genuine danger. When we add to this information the recognition that Paul thought he was writing to a specific congregation at a particular time and not for all Christians anywhere in the world then or now, these verses are nothing like the "theology of the state" they are too often made out to be. He may simply have been advising the recipients to avoid unnecessary or premature martyrdom. Like Martin Luther King, when he saw the forces arrayed against him and hundreds of peaceful marchers when they tried to cross the Edmund Pettus Bridge in Selma, he was simply making a painful, but necessary strategic decision. (Days later, supported by a court order, King and those with him did cross the bridge and proceeded to Montgomery.)

PAUL AND GAY PEOPLE

Finally, there is the accusation against Paul the homophobe. During the present dispute over the appropriate place of gay and lesbian Christians in the churches, the following verses from Romans are quoted time after time:

> *For this reason God gave them up to shameful passions. Their women exchanged natural intercourse for unnatural, and in the same way also the men, giving up natural intercourse with women, were consumed with passion for one another. Men committed shameless acts with men and received in their own persons the due penalty for their error. (1:26–27)*

But the question is this: If Romans 13 cannot be widened into a "theology of the state," can these two verses (sometimes paired with selected Old Testament texts) be stretched into a "theology of sexuality"? Once again, viewing Paul, and this Letter in particular, through the lens of Roman imperial history helps to clarify his intent. First, in that world and at that time sexuality was understood largely as an expression of power, and almost always of unequal power. Men held power over women, free citizens over slaves, adults over children. Rape, nonconsensual activity between masters and servants, and pederasty were rampant. The tone and context of Paul's condemnation of what he calls *porneia*, translated above as "shameful passions," indicate that he did not have affectionate or committed affection between consenting adults in mind. In surveying the corrupt power relations of "this fallen age," he saw that the injustice and brutality wielded by those in power also expressed itself through sexual behavior. And at the pinnacle of power perched the imperial court and family, whose sexual exploits were well known to everyone.

In his book *Liberating Paul: The Justice of God and the Politics of the Apostle,* Neil Elliot surveys some of the commentaries made at the time by writers familiar with the decadent goings-on of the ruling elite.[7] According to the Roman historian Suetonius, when the emperor Tiberius retired and moved to the island of Capri, he imported a large number of male and female sex slaves in part for his own use, but also because he was a notorious voyeur who took delight in watching various combinations of sexual activities. The next emperor, Gaius Caligula, did not wait for retirement to indulge his appetites. Again according to Suetonius, he hosted elaborate dinners and would pull the wives of his guests unto nearby rooms where he noisily raped them. He topped off his debauched career by establishing an imperial brothel in which the wives and sons of the nobility were forced to serve as prostitutes. This is the same Caligula who insisted on his own deity and ordered a statue of himself erected in the Temple in Jerusalem.

No wonder, then, that Paul condemns idolatry in the same paragraph with *porneia*. He considered them both to be part of the same depraved system that was doomed to imminent destruction. Paul does not disguise the fact that this system enraged him, and he was especially concerned that the members of the embryonic congregations he was guiding should not be drawn into its clutches.

Second, Paul does not seem to have derived his view of sexuality from the gospel he was proclaiming. He relies on his understanding of what he calls "natural." Researchers have determined that this idea comes from handbooks of medical treatment available at a time, when it was not yet recognized in some quarters that some people have a "natural" preference for others of the same sex. Paul knew nothing of long-term committed relationships between men or between women.

In view of this historically informed reading of Paul, more and more churches today are placing a "welcoming and affirming" sign on their doors. And in those churches (as in the one I attend) gay and lesbian people bring their children to morning worship and Sunday school, sing in the choirs, take up the collection, and more and more frequently stand in the pulpit. Most long for just what everyone else wants: respect, appreciation, and loving long-term relationships, including marriage. Even Pope Francis declares that he is not in a position to judge them. Yet in many churches these people still sometimes hear the words from Paul thrown at them like fiery darts. But I think this ugly chapter in Christian history is ending, and those dart throwers will be remembered solely the way we remember those tiresome opponents of abolition and racial justice who in times past marshaled isolated verses to support their cause.

To conclude this summary of Paul and homophobia, I agree with the New Testament scholar Robin Scroggs, who writes that the relationships gay and lesbian Christians now nourish within the Christian community bear no resemblance whatever to the festering and dehumanizing liaisons the apostle condemns. Scroggs therefore concludes that, although the Bible is indeed authoritative, based on the difference in context between then and now, what the Bible says about homosexuality and life in today's churches have nothing to do with each other; therefore these Pauline verses simply should not be used in discussions about the place of gay and lesbian people in our pews and pulpits today.[8]

PAUL'S LETTERS TODAY

What does all this mean for how we should read the Letters of Paul today? I agree with those Bible teachers who suggest it may be best to read them in the order in which they were written. Like any other human being, Paul learned from experience, modified some of his ideas, and incorporated new insights. Sometimes he even stops himself in the middle of a sentence and starts over. Some well-meaning scholars have tried to make Paul over into a systematic theologian. But despite the fact that he does write eloquently on such key themes as the nature of God and Christ, the meaning of salvation, and the meaning of human life, Paul was just not systematic.

Still, by reading his Letters in chronological sequence, we can follow the arc of his thinking and notice how it changes and develops. This means we start with 1 and 2 Thessalonians, written about 52 CE, and then go on to 1 and 2 Corinthians and Galatians, written between 53 and 56. He wrote his masterful Letter to the Romans around 57. The shorter letters—Ephesians, Philippians, Colossians, and Philemon—are all dated to around 62. The Letters to Timothy and Titus (63–64), attributed to Paul, may not be from his own hand.

Study Tip

The scholar Kevin Edgecomb, relying on the most recent research, has assembled a useful chart showing in what year and at what point in Paul's life each Letter was written, where he was when he wrote it, and how the Letters relate to each other. This resource can be accessed at http://www.bombaxo.com/paulchron.html.

As we read both Paul's own words in his Letters and about Paul in Luke's Acts of the Apostles today, two millennia later, it is important to bear in mind something that neither Paul nor Luke could envision. Christianity (a word neither ever uses) was moving from its infancy as a reforming sect in Judaism (another word not in use at the time) to the next and supremely critical phase in its life. The Jewish Greek-speaking Paul, although he was not alone in the work, thus laid the foundation for the next two thousand years of Western history, during which the faith he taught circled the globe. Paul took the risky step of interpreting the message of and about Jesus to the Greco-Roman world. His adventurous project means that in its earliest years Christian faith became "a religion made to travel." Anchored in its Hebraic sources, it embraced the language and thought forms of a pivotal era in Western history, and it became the cultural wellspring of a whole civilization. Paul of course could not foresee all this, but we read him today with that history—with all its strengths and weaknesses—in our minds.

But it is critical to our understanding of Paul to read him not only with his own task in mind—how to include the nations (Gentiles) in God's promise to Abraham—but in the light of our present challenge in a world vastly expanded from Paul's. He built a bridge from Jerusalem to Athens. It was an assignment fraught with hazards and pitfalls. But in some ways, as Paul's descendants, ours is even more complex. He facilitated the rebirth of biblical faith in one very foreign culture. But today Christianity faces the challenge of making itself real in dozens of cultures, each of them in its own way different from Paul's and from ours. Today *ekklesia* are multiplying in Africa, Latin America, the Asian rim, and in mainland China. None of these areas has lived through the formative period of the church fathers, the medieval synthesis, or (except for Latin America) the Reformation and Counter-Reformation. If the Christian faith was indeed "made to travel," it must now become as much a part of religious cultures that have drawn for centuries on the Lotus Sutra and the Mahabharata, not on Homer, Aristotle, or St. Augustine. The challenge Paul faced was daunting. Ours may be even more so. He had one big bridge to build. We have several.

I doubt that Paul will ever cease to be controversial. He was in his own time; he still is in ours. But Paul is never dull. If in reading his Letters we can imagine ourselves in multicultural Ephesus, profit-hungry Corinth, or the teeming and dissolute imperial capital of Rome, we can begin to understand and appreciate him. But if, with due allowances for the different time and setting, we read him in our own twenty-first century, we may appreciate him even more.

If we had to choose one fragment of the apostle's writings to send along in a space vehicle to another planet or solar system, what would it be? I think most people would agree. When he wrote to the congregation at Corinth about 53 CE, that tiny cluster was living through some severe internal tensions. It seems some members believed that if they could "speak in tongues" or display other marvelous gifts of the Spirit it would somehow put them way ahead of their brothers and sisters. Paul had nothing against spiritual gifts and even says that he can speak in tongues better than the rest. But he pleads with the Corinthians to have a sense for priorities, to recognize what was of supreme importance and what was not. "If I speak in the tongues of men and of angels," he writes, "but have not love, I am a noisy gong or a clanging cymbal" (1 Cor. 13:1, RSV). He then goes on to sketch one of the most eloquent paeans to love to be found in any literature. Love, he says, is patient and kind, not jealous, boastful, or arrogant.

These words are frequently read at weddings, and they may be the only passage from Paul nonchurchgoers ever hear. Unfortunately, some patronizing scholars shake their heads. "It was not originally meant for weddings," they sigh. But the pedants forget a point I have emphasized in this volume. Yes, *what it meant* is important to know, but *what it has come to mean* is also important, and it is hard to imagine anything as urgent in our world today as the celebration and practice of love.

So let us pack our space capsule with these verses and hope that the creatures on some alien star who come upon them will recognize their power and truth. "So faith, hope, love abide, these three; but the greatest of these is love" (1 Cor. 13:13, RSV).

Surviving a Turbulent Trip

The Book of Revelation

The revelation of Jesus Christ, which God gave him to show his
servants what must soon take place; he made it known by sending
his angel to his servant John.

REVELATION 1:1

Has this ever happened to you? Your plane has taken off successfully
and has now reached its cruising altitude. You expect the seat-belt sign to
go off, but the pilot's voice crackles over the loudspeaker. "Please keep
your seat belts securely fastened," he says. "We might experience some
turbulence." The same advice is pertinent for anyone who opens the book
of Revelation, except the correct word here is not "might," but "will." Revelation is turbulent. It is graphic, lurid, and violent, a long way from the
comforting tones of Psalm 23 or Paul's homage to love in 1 Corinthians. It
churns with blood, disaster, and vituperation. Here is a random sample:

> The first angel blew his trumpet, and there came hail and fire,
> mixed with blood, and they were hurled to the earth; and a third
> of the earth was burned up, and a third of the trees were burned
> up, and all green grass was burned up. (8:7)

There is more. In addition to its often brutal and vitriolic voice, Revelation claims the unlikely distinction of being the part of the Bible that,

more than any other, many thoughtful people, both past and present, have believed does not belong there at all. As we will see in a moment, it barely squeaked into the canon and today, after centuries of argument, remains the most disputed and disagreed-upon text in all of scripture. Do we really want to board this flight? Having once gotten on, will we ever land safely?

I think the answer is yes. For all its blood and gore, Revelation is a trip worth taking. If in reading it we follow the principles for coming to grips with the Bible already described, we may even have an enjoyable and informative journey. Admittedly reading Revelation can produce some queasiness in the stomach. But, like some other bumpy excursions, it more than repays the effort. One good reason is that Revelation illustrates, perhaps better than any other biblical book, how two more recent schools of biblical scholarship can enhance its spiritual value for us. Just as we found in Genesis a valuable example of source analysis and with Exodus explored the challenge of biblical archaeology, Revelation affords an excellent opportunity to demonstrate two more methods of study. The first is called simply "history of interpretation." It takes off where the historical and textual studies end, then traces the history of what readers in various ages and settings have made of a text. Its premise is that the meaning of any writing is not locked within the words on the page, but is the result of both those words and what readers have invested in them. It adds to the duality of "What did it mean then?" and "What does it mean now?" an additional dimension: "What *has* it meant, to whom?"[1]

A second method that is especially appropriate for Revelation is called "effect history." The scholars who adapt this approach build on the hard work the textual analysts, archaeologists, and history-of-interpretation students have done, but they move to the next level. They ask the question most thoughtful readers wonder about: "What difference has it made?" "What effect, if any, has this book or this portion of the Bible had on actual human life?" It is a perfectly natural thing to ask, and some wonder why it has taken so long for a rigorous way of responding to it to evolve.

Therefore, in considering Revelation, we will retrace the way these two strategies build on earlier ones and then add the new component. We will:

1. Seek to identify the writer and place him in his cultural and religious context (the historical method).

2. Chart the structure and the story line from start to finish, so that—as in some long-distance flights—we can see where we are on the map (the narrative-theory and literary-critical methods).

3. Ask why, despite all the disputes, early church leaders eventually placed it in the Bible (the canonical-history method).

Then, however, we will turn to the kinds of questions the "history of interpretation" and "effect history" probe by:

1. Sampling a small cross section of readers/interpreters representing different ages, genders, races, and classes (history of interpretation).

2. Discussing how Revelation has been used in the past and how it is presently being interpreted, deployed, and applied to undergird different, often opposing causes (effect history).

3. Finally, ask the bottom-line question: What meaning, or meanings, does the powerful and baffling text hold for us today?[2]

AUTHORSHIP

Revelation was written by a political prisoner named John who had been exiled to the rocky island of Patmos, the Guantanamo of its era, just off the western coast of present-day Turkey. He was an inmate in an island detention center where people who were considered a threat to the national security of the Roman Empire were incarcerated. We do not know the exact nature of the infraction that landed him there, but it was on that stony shoal with its fifteen square miles of pebbly hills that he composed Revelation.

Who was this John? He wastes no time in introducing himself, first in the third person (1:1) and then in the first person (1:2, 9–11). The first verse appears at the beginning of this chapter. In 1:2 John writes that he is the one "who testified to the word of God and to the testimony of Jesus Christ, even to all that he saw." Then he says in 1:9–11:

> *I, John, your brother who share with you in Jesus the persecution and the kingdom and the patient endurance, was on the island called Patmos because of the word of God and the testimony of Jesus. I was in the spirit on the Lord's day, and I heard behind me a loud voice like a trumpet saying, "Write in a book what you see and send it to the seven churches, to Ephesus, to Smyrna, to Pergamum, to Thyatira, to Sardis, to Philadelphia, and to Laodicea."*

But which John is this? Some early Christians thought he was the same one who wrote the Fourth Gospel, but "John" was a common name at the time, and the John of this book never claims to be an apostle or the Gospel writer. Also the vocabulary and style of the two books differ so graphically that most scholars believe they were two different Johns. Does that matter?

I do not believe it does, but even to question whether they were the same person is still not welcome in some circles. Some years ago, when I was a lecturer on a study trip that included a visit to Patmos, I was asked to talk about John of Revelation. When I alluded briefly to the possibility of two separate Johns, none of the European or American passengers blinked, but the Greeks on board bristled. I quickly detected the source of their irritation. In their view there was only one John, and he was both the Greek-speaking author of Revelation and an original apostle of Jesus. They resented having his impressive credentials questioned.

Since then I have never made a point of this dispute. Whoever this "John" was, he wrote a mesmerizing book that has attracted a vast array of detractors and admirers for two thousand years. Everyone knows that controversy sells books, and if John were alive today, he might be pleased with the mixed reviews his book has received, if—that is—he was interested in selling books.

There is another reason the "John" in the title of Revelation is a touchy subject. For centuries the authority of any text often depended on who people believed had written it. Authorship was proof of authenticity, and the modern idea of attaching the individual writer's name to a work had not yet arisen. Affixing the name of some famous or revered person gave it a better chance. This is why there were so many writings floating around the ancient world that were attributed to the original apostles of Jesus, even though the vast majority of them were not actually written by them.[3]

But today our view of the spiritual authority of a religious text or teaching has changed. Now more and more people are reluctant to accept the authority of something simply because of its alleged author. They now tend to give credence to a text for one of two reasons. Either they know it has had a long history of acceptance in a religious community or, more frequently, they find it speaks to them, it "rings true," no matter who wrote it. Authorship in most fields has declined as a measure of authenticity or worth. As modern literary critics say, the text must stand on its own.

This is why, when it became widely known that Moses had not in fact written the first five books of the Bible, it did not undermine people's attachment to them as much as some feared it might; for most readers it has not diminished their value. The same is true for other parts of the Bible. It is now agreed that Jeremiah did not write Lamentations and that David did not compose all of Psalms. Scholars realize that Paul did not write all the Letters credited to him, but that has not reduced their spiritual validity. Not much is known about the John who wrote Revelation. There is little doubt that he was of Jewish origin and knew the Hebrew scriptures, especially Ezekiel, Zechariah, and the later Jewish apocryphal literature. Scholars who spot grammatical mistakes in the text suggest John probably learned Greek, the language in which he wrote the book, later in life.

Readers of Revelation today should be prepared to discover that its writer is not a particularly benevolent person. He is angry, indeed furious, incensed at the pride and cruelty of the Roman Empire. He sheds no tears over its coming disintegration. On the contrary, he finds it just, appropriate, and richly deserved. John is not an exemplar of Christian charity or of loving one's enemies. The tone of his scorching indictment and vivid warnings of the awful fate in store for Rome is reminiscent of that of some of the Hebrew prophets or the poet of Lamentations when they inveigh against those they believe are the enemies of God. In this way Revelation is one of the books in the Bible that tell us not how we *should* feel, but reminds us of how we often *do* feel. Like John himself, it is human, all too human.

John's purpose in writing Revelation was to encourage his beleaguered brothers and sisters in faith during a period of persecution. It was meant to reassure them that, although things now looked dim, ultimately God's love and justice would triumph. The plot revolves around a coming political paroxysm, the certain demise of the mighty empire that kept him in chains, but John amplifies his account with lavish Technicolor dragons and vials of flame. It is true that a convulsion like this might well have sounded to the people of Rome like the end of the world, or at least of "civilization as they knew it." But to the oppressed minority of Christians whom the Roman officials were hounding at the time for disloyalty and treason, the end of the empire was something most of them undoubtedly longed to see, and good riddance.

STRUCTURE

In following the convoluted plot of Revelation, it is helpful to know that many scholars believe it was first written as a drama to be read or acted out on a stage. In group study, it might be a good idea to arrange a dramatic reading. A group in a local church in the town I live in did this a few years back, complete with costumes and music (neither, it must be added, claiming to be drawn from the first century). The audience was absorbed, if a little bewildered at times. Overall it was a minor hit. But don't imagine that such a staging ever happened in the early centuries of Christian history in one of those open-air amphitheaters the Romans loved. The Christians would never have risked such public exposure. Rather, they probably read it in their homes, with the shades drawn. Nonetheless, reading it as a drama moves the plotline along well.

INTERPRETATIONS

Revelation has frequently been read as a vivid description of how the world will end. Given its astral and cosmological imagery, this is an understandable interpretation. But it is misleading. It is true that the book now stands as the last text in the Christian canon, just inside the back cover, before the maps and the index. Consequently, many people like to pair it with Genesis as the two bookends of human or even cosmic history, the first telling how it all started, and the last revealing the dazzling details of how it will all end. The truth is that for centuries many people did read it this way and were often lured into wacky predictions about an end of the world just around the corner, all of which turned out to be mistaken. Curiously, the fact that this repeated failed prophecy has been going on for a thousand years has not deterred people from continuing to try. The coming of the year 1000 witnessed a special outburst of these forecasts, but even today hardly a year goes by without a preacher somewhere warning us all that the end is near.[4]

Other readers, however, did not see Revelation as a description of the coming end of the world, but of the coming end of the Roman Empire. It is ironic that for many readers Revelation's position at the end of the New Testament should endow it with special significance. During the centuries-long quarrel about whether it should be allowed in the Bible at all, which we will turn to below, editors often placed it last not to underline its special authority but, on the contrary, to signal how questionable it was. They made it a kind of appendix.

AUDIENCE

For whom was this text intended? The first answer is that it was meant to hearten John's fellow followers of Jesus who in some parts of the empire were already undergoing sporadic persecution by the Roman authorities or those who in other areas were fearful that it would begin soon. But there is another dimension. John not only attacks the ruthless empire; he also fiercely criticizes some of his fellow followers of Christ. Why?

Clearly, the Christians were responding in different ways to the harass-
ment, and there were disputes among them about what the right response
should be. Often the argument focused on the imperial altars, and what to
do about the "pinch of incense" and the loyalty oath that were required,
sometimes on pain of death. Some said, in effect, "Look, this is just a *civic*
ritual. What's the big deal? We know Emperor Domitian is not God, but we
accept him as the emperor. Why not honor him as such? Why, even the apostle Paul has taught us to obey the earthly governing authorities, because they
have been put there by God. If you need to cross your fingers behind your
back when you venerate him, go ahead. It's better than being fed to the lions."

It was a sensible argument. But many other Christians, including
John, did not buy it. They claimed that the Roman emperor was a usurper
and that his claims to divine status were blasphemous. They were afraid
that one small compromise would lead to others. This was not just a political issue, but also a spiritual one. They insisted you cannot serve both
Christ and Caesar; you must make a choice. It is a familiar quarrel and has
gone on wherever minority groups, not just Christians, are persecuted.
How much can we accept before we draw a line? When does being true to
your principles harden into self-destructive stubbornness? Jews under the
Nazis argued over these questions, and people caught in oppressive situations still debate it today. If you give in on something small, can you save
yourself for what is more important?

When I worked with the church in East Germany during the Com-
munist rule there, the question came up around the "Youth Dedication"
ceremony (*Jugendweihe*), which all young people were expected by the
government to participate in at age fourteen. Some pastors opposed it as
an attempt to displace Christian Confirmation. Others disagreed and
contended that it was a civic duty that all citizens, including Christians,
owed to their country. The dispute was never settled.[5]

DATING

The dating of Revelation continues to be disputed. Some scholars put
it as early as the gruesome reign of Nero, who died, probably by his own

hand, in 68 CE. Others place it later, under Vespasian, who died in 79, or Domitian, who succeeded him. For various reasons, I prefer Domitian. This is not because I find him attractive. Domitian was one of the least appealing of the Roman emperors. He claimed to be *dominus et deus* ("Lord and God"), a divine ruler. Incessantly jealous and suspicious, he lived in fear that someone would try to displace him; he was especially nervous about the Christians, who claimed to serve another Lord and would not worship at the imperial altars he had scattered over the landscape.

An early Christian history records that he arrested some people he thought were heirs of King David, worried that they might stake a claim to the purple. Once when he became suspicious of his cousin Flavius Clement, who was also the husband of his niece, he accused him of "atheism" and had him executed. Oddly, the term "atheist" in this context meant having Jewish or Christian sympathies, since neither of these groups honored the traditional Roman gods. Finally Domitian's close associates had had enough. They assassinated him on September 16, in the year 96 CE. Few people grieved.

Knowing something about this unsavory emperor is not only fascinating; it helps us understand the context of John's religious and political drama. Clearly, under Domitian and his fellow emperors, religion was inseparable from politics; this is why John was considered sufficiently dangerous by the Roman authorities under Domitian to confine him to a gulag. Guides to present-day Patmos will happily show you the very cave where John was kept. They should not be taken literally. Their colleagues in Israel will also show you three different locations where Jesus was baptized. But they should not be dismissed out of hand either. Legends enhance a story, and who knows? Some may carry a grain of truth.

SCOPE

The narrative of Revelation is epic in scope. John daringly places the imminent collapse of Rome within a narrative of world history in which one empire after another—Egypt, Persia, Babylonia—rises and falls.

Mighty Rome's turn, he says, is coming, and soon. Further, John positions this dirge for fated empires against the backdrop of an even larger cosmic struggle between the forces of domination and violence, on the one hand, and the energies of love and mutuality, on the other. The current actors in this drama were God and Caesar, but Caesar was really reenacting an old script. The dramatic tension in John's production of the old story revolves around the question: Who is in ultimate control of the world? This is history writing on the grand scale.

LANGUAGE

Large parts of the book seem to be written in an exotic code. Why? The answer is not hard to come by. John, as a political prisoner writing for a persecuted minority, cleverly composed the book in an argot his intended audience, or at least some of them, would understand, but outsiders would not. He did not just invent the madcap images. He drew on symbols and myths of the Jewish literature that emerged in the period between the two testaments that we refer to as "apocalyptic." He used this eerie, often uncanny, imagery to deepen the resonance of what he wrote, the way a filmmaker adds a musical score to heighten what appears on the screen. John was undoubtedly a Christian with a Jewish background (like many Christians of the time), and his intended audience consisted of the same kind of people. He therefore uses symbolism from the current Jewish religious literature both he and they would understand. But it would have knitted the brows of the Roman censors. If they had intercepted any copies of this text, they might well have dismissed it as yet more crazy Jewish superstition, not particularly harmful to their powerful *Pax Romana*.

The problem is that this feral symbolism also knits our brows today and has given rise to whole cottage industries of deciphering. Volumes have been given over to futile, often bizarre attempts to crack it. G. K. Chesterton once wrote that, although John "saw many strange monsters in his vision, he saw no creatures so wild as his commentators." He was right, but the obscurity is indeed both puzzling and tempting. What are we to make of the "four horsemen of the apocalypse," the "battle of Arma-geddon," the various seals (including Ingmar Bergman's dreaded "seventh seal") that are broken open and pour out flame, the "woman who sits on seven mountains" (that one is not too hard to decode), and the Alpha and Omega? There is one character some readers expect, but he does not ap-pear on these bloodstained pages, namely, the Antichrist. He may be al-luded to, but his only explicit mention by name is in 1 and 2 John. This is probably just as well, since readers of Revelation will have enough iniquity to cope with without his explicit presence.

Admittedly, all this sounds daunting, and we will return to these mys-tifying figures later. But in the meantime, people who have survived *Star Wars, Dracula, The Blob, Avatar,* and *Frankenstein* should hardly recoil at a few winged monsters, walking dead, and eruptions of fire. Those who have been hearing warnings about the decline of the West and the rise of some other civilization, maybe China or the Islamic world, should not be unfamiliar with hearing a bell being tolled for an allegedly declining em-pire. John wrote for his time and place. He undoubtedly had no idea we would be reading his words two thousand years later. But far from being old and fusty, Revelation, both in its message and its style, sounds strik-ingly up-to-date, if also strikingly unwelcome.

STORY LINE

Here, then, is a rapid run-through of the saga this early science-fiction spectacular tells. It is a drama in seven acts. I advise readers to read the passages indicated along with what follows.

Act I (1:9–3:22): John sets the scene, then addresses the play to seven early Christian congregations, all in Asia Minor. He commends some of them and upbraids others, but his point is that they should all persevere during this persecution and that they had better know what is lying in store for them, but that they will be vindicated in the end.

Act II (4:1–8:1): John spreads out the cosmic background by taking us to the Court of Heaven (similar to the opening scene in Job). The purpose is to assure us that, despite all the awful things that are about to unfold, God is still in charge. The act ends with the curious "silence in heaven for about half an hour" (8:1). Might this have been an intermission when those in the audience could have enjoyed some refreshments or sought out the restrooms?

Act III (8:2–11:19): Now the trouble begins. The plot thickens or, better still, boils over. The churches are being harassed. Trumpets are blown. There is a call to repentance. Voices speak from the heavens.

Act IV (12:1–14:20): The tide begins to turn. The heavenly righteous defeat the minions of evil. Their victory signals the ultimate victory of these tiny powerless congregations. Even though it might appear improbable now, someday they "will overcome."

Act V (15:1–16:21): This part is not for the tenderhearted. Things get ugly. God's angels begin pouring out great bowls of wrath on the proud oppressors and sending plagues to decimate them (a scenario any Jew would have immediately recognized from the frogs and boils of the exodus story).

Act VI (17:1–20:10): Now God's legions finally win the battle. "Babylon" is a code word that Jewish readers or listeners would have immediately known meant "Rome." The coming liberation from imperial captivity would echo the previous one from Egypt. Now Christ, the gentle lamb, is triumphant, not Caesar, the raging beast.

Act VII (20:11–22:5): In the grand finale, the titanic struggle between God and Evil, the cosmic confrontation, is ended not by human beings being carried off to heaven, but by a "New Jerusalem" taking shape here on earth.

Note that after the drama ends, at v. 20, the playwright himself, as many playwrights like to do, briefly steps onto the stage, implores Jesus to come again soon, and ends with a benediction. The curtain falls.

When this trial by fire is over, today's audience might have two questions. First, why does a phantasmagoria like this appear in the New Testament at all? And second, why should a sensible twenty-first-century person bother with it or risk exposure to it?

CANONIZATION

The answer to the first question, why this book is in the Bible, begins with the recognition that it is a perfectly good question and that Christians, and others, have been pressing it for almost two thousand years. During the early centuries of Christian history, a fierce debate raged about which books should or should not be read during public worship in the congregations scattered around the Mediterranean Sea, and Revelation was one of the most controversial. Eventually lists of approved books appeared, ones that would become what is now called the "canon." Some books, like the *First Letter of Clement,* which is dated to about 96 CE and was allegedly written by the traditional fourth bishop of Rome, were widely used at first, but then excluded. This fate eventually eliminated the *Gospel of Thomas,* which, however, has experienced an impressive "second coming" in recent years in part because its theology appeals to a current inward-looking mystical mood. Since the discovery of the ancient library in a desert cave near Nag Hammadi in Upper Egypt in December 1945, which includes fifty-two texts, scholars now suspect there were once dozens, perhaps even hundreds, of such gospels and letters. Many of these documents at one time enjoyed some circulation among Christian congregations, but in the end did not make the cut. Once they were eliminated, ecclesial (and later imperial) authorities demanded they be destroyed. Undoubtedly many were. But others were hidden and have only recently come to light.

The history is further complicated by the fact that respected early Christian writers circulated different, sometimes contradictory lists of approved books. For example, the canons of two Christian thinkers, Marcion and Valentinus, who both wrote in the middle of the second century CE, do not agree with each other. When Irenaeus, bishop of Lyons, issued his list in 180 CE, he did not include some of the books that are now in our New Testament, such as Philemon, James, 2 Peter, 3 John, or Jude. There seems to have been precious little consensus. But among the most disputed texts, sometimes in and sometimes out, Revelation stands out as the most debated.

Revelation was hardly known in the earliest church, and by the time it appears in Christian commentary in the second century, it is already hotly disputed, in part because some insisted it was written by the apostle John, but even then others vehemently denied it. Eventually this argument took the form of a West-versus-East feud. Revelation was widely accepted in the West, but rejected in the East. Still, it lingered in its canonical limbo. In 692 an official synod exacerbated the controversy by issuing two decrees, one including Revelation, the other excluding it. Only quite gradually and over the course of centuries did the Eastern Orthodox Church recognize it as canonical. This hardly ended the quarrel. Neither Luther nor Calvin had much regard for it, in part because they doubted John the apostle had written it and therefore it lacked apostolic credentials. In his translation of the Bible into German, Luther consigned it to an appendix.

Does this convoluted record of Revelation's rocky road to canonization make any difference to today's readers? I think it does, if only because not a few contemporary readers harbor serious doubts about whether it belongs, but they sometimes feel uncomfortable voicing them. "After all," they reason, "it is *in the Bible*." But the real question is, how did it get there? Why should Bible readers today be hesitant about questioning the appropriateness of including Revelation when thoughtful Christians have been pondering the same dilemma for millennia?

Thinking about this pushes reading the Bible today to a new level. Any group or individual studying it should be familiar with the history of canonization of any particular book. This information can easily be found in any standard Bible dictionary.[6] The reason is that ascertaining why a book was placed in the Bible and even where it is placed can sometimes tell more about a given book than many other things can.

Imagine a meeting of early Christian scholars and bishops who are trying to decide on what belongs in and what does not. What criteria did they use? Are those criteria still valid for us today? Remember that inclusion in the canon did not necessarily signify a book's historical accuracy (which is something that became important only in a later age), its authenticity, or even its inspirational value. It meant only that a text sufficiently represented the developing consensus of what the Christian message was about and could therefore be read in public worship.

Given this standard, however, Christians today might reflect on whether we are in effect engaged in an ongoing informal "canonization." We do not tear pages out of the Bible (although Thomas Jefferson famously took barber shears to the parts he did not like). But there are books in the Bible that are almost never read in public worship, and others that have become a kind of "top twenty" that one hears all the time. Even the use of a lectionary does not prevent this selectivity from happening, since most lectionaries list several passages that can be read on a given Sunday and allow worship leaders to choose among them. Canonization is anything but a boring subject. It is often the story of furious arguments and angry fallings-out. Knowing something about it enables us to see the Bible not as a volume dropped from the clouds, but as the product of a long and often divisive process, one that is still going on.

Was the canonization of Revelation, then, just a big mistake? Reflective and faithful people can differ about this, but I think the answer to this perennial query is that, first, Revelation does indeed belong in the Bible. One reason it does is that its being there pushes us both to the second question we raised above (Why should anyone today bother with it?) and to the bottom-line query we put to any biblical book we open today: What, if anything, does it say to us now?

To respond to these questions, let us bring in something we mentioned earlier in this chapter, namely, the history-of-interpretation approach to biblical texts. Many people have found that being familiar with how a book has been read is often a useful entrée into how we might read it today. Here is a scattered sampling of how this book has been interpreted.

HISTORY OF INTERPRETATION

Victorinus of Pettau is an otherwise little-known Greek bishop whose only claim to fame is that about 300 CE he wrote (in Latin) the first full-length commentary on Revelation. His work was largely overlooked for centuries, but has received more attention in recent decades, because he suggested that the book is not about the end of the world, but about the theological and moral struggles the Christian church was and would continue to be faced with. Thus, in discussing chapter 12, he identifies the woman with the church and the dragon with the devil. Here is the original text in Revelation:

> And a great portent appeared in heaven, a woman clothed with the sun, with the moon under her feet, and on her head a crown of twelve stars; she was with child and she cried out in her pangs of birth, in anguish for delivery. And another portent appeared in heaven; behold, a great red dragon, with seven heads and ten horns, and seven diadems upon his heads. His tail swept down a third of the stars of heaven, and cast them to the earth. And the dragon stood before the woman who was about to bear a child, that he might devour her child when she brought it forth; she brought forth a male child, one who is to rule all the nations with a rod of iron, but her child was caught up to God and to his throne, and the woman fled into the wilderness, where she has a place prepared by God, in which to be nourished for one thousand two hundred and sixty days. (12:1–6, RSV)

Victorinus reads "the woman" as Mary, who was then becoming both more widely venerated and more closely associated with the church. He sees the dragon as the devil, which accords with much pre- and early Christian symbolism. Consequently, he discerned in Revelation an ongoing struggle between angelic and demonic forces both within and outside the church. But Victorinus also allowed for a very literal and imminent coming of the kingdom of God. The result is an interpretation that suggests both moral-symbolic and literal-historical readings, a tension that, as we will see below, continues to split interpreters today.

Not long after Victorinus, an interpreter called Tyconius (late fourth century) solidified his predecessor's mainly moral-symbolic reading, but denied any historical or predictive meaning to the text. He would have been aghast at the literalistic fundamentalist readings that have become so widespread in our own day. He is the interpreter who most influenced the vastly more influential St. Augustine and St. Jerome. They, however, added the triumphalist idea that Christians should not look forward to a coming kingdom because it was already here: it was the church. This reading of Revelation continued for centuries to be the officially accepted one until the next influential interpreter appeared.

That interpreter was the twelfth-century Calabrian abbot Joachim of Fiore (1135–1202). He did not entirely discard the moral-symbolic reading, but he insisted that Revelation was nothing less than a description of what he called the *plenitudo historae* ("the fullness of history"): "the key to things past, the knowledge of things to come; the opening of what is sealed, the uncovering of what is hidden." Joachim saw history as divided into three sweeping epochs, that of the Father (largely the Jewish segment), that of the one Son (since the arrival of Jesus Christ), and—dawning in his time—the age of the Spirit. For a time Joachim's biblical interpretation claimed a wide following among churchmen. But when some of his followers began to preach that in this new age the sacraments, the priesthood, and even the pope would become superfluous, the hierarchy started to have doubts. When other followers of Joachim taught that St. Francis of Assisi was the principal herald of the new epoch, this became too much to take, and the imaginative abbot's writings were eventually declared heretical.

By then, however, this historical-predictive and antipapal reading of Revelation had won a wide audience, and it became one of the factors contributing to the Reformation, which in turn increased its popularity. It did not take long for the idea of the pope as the embodiment of the Antichrist to emerge. Usually without ever having heard of Joachim, today's fundamentalist writers who have flooded the market with books full of end-time predictions (to which we will return below) are nonetheless his descendants.

Luther himself in his commentary of Revelation chooses the historical route in his decoding of the symbols. He was especially interested in the three woes announced by the eagle: "As I watched, I heard an eagle that was flying in midair call out in a loud voice: 'Woe! Woe! Woe to the inhabitants of the earth, because of the trumpet blasts about to be sounded by the other three angels!'" (8:13, NIV). Luther divined in the first woe the ancient heretic Arius. It is hard to understand how he came to this seemingly far-fetched reading.

When we come to the second woe, however, it is easier to see how, assisted by an active imagination and his well-known capacity for exaggeration, he could read Muhammad's followers and the threat of Islam into an ancient text:

> Then the sixth angel blew his trumpet, and I heard a voice from the four horns of the golden altar before God, saying to the sixth angel who had the trumpet, "Release the four angels who are bound at the great river Euphrates." So the four angels were released, who had been held ready for the hour, the day, the month, and the year, to kill a third of mankind. The number of the troops of cavalry was twice ten thousand times ten thousand; I heard their number. And this was how I saw the horses in my vision: the riders wore breastplates the color of fire and of sapphire and of sulphur, and the heads of the horses were like lions' heads, and fire and smoke and sulphur issued from their mouths. (9:13–17, RSV)

Given the sensational military victories of the Muslim armies, and the hysterically exaggerated rumors of their power, one can see how Luther arrived at this reading.

As for the third woe, Luther had no problem decoding it:

> And I saw a beast rising out of the sea, with ten horns and seven heads, with ten diadems upon its horns and a blasphemous name upon its heads. (13:1, RSV)

It was of course the papal empire, plainly in his view the "evil empire" of the day.

By the time the Reformation reached England the conceit of seeing the pope as the beast or the Antichrist had become commonplace. This made it easier to sanction the separation of the (true) Church of England from the (false) Church of Rome. But as the reform took a more radical turn, the anti-Roman interpreters found themselves hoist by their own petard when the radical Congregationalist separatists and Baptists found the established Church of England to be the beast and themselves to be the faithful remnant.

EFFECT HISTORY

The line between the history-of-interpretation approach (sometimes called "reception criticism") and effect history (*Wirkungsgeschichte*), which I mentioned above, is not a clear one. When a given interpretation begins to make an impact on the larger religious, social, or political history, then it has an "effect." In the case of Revelation, perhaps more so than most other biblical books, this means we need to be aware of more than its original context and purpose. We also need to recognize the way it has been used for centuries and is still being used today. It also means that serious readers of the Bible, but especially of Revelation, should not avoid questions about how it is deployed by often contradictory interpreters today. We hardly need to be reminded that the Bible can be used in stupid, destructive, and hateful ways. The unpleasant reality is that Revelation has been used and is still being used for such purposes today. It provides a splendid if troubling example of "effect history."

In 2009 two prominent biblical scholars, William John Lyons, of the University of Bristol in the United Kingdom, and Jorunn Økland, of the University of Oslo, Norway, published a collection of essays, entitled *The Way the World Ends: The Apocalypse of John in Culture and Ideology*, applying "effect history" to Revelation.[7] Unlike some scholarly tomes, this book is highly readable and accessible to nonspecialists, a fine example of "effect history" for lay readers. One of the writers, for example, describes the immense popularity of the *Left Behind* series of sixteen novels written by Tim LaHaye and Jerry B. Jenkins.[8] Lest anyone doubt that the fascination with how the world will end that inspires so many readings of Revelation is no longer a force in modern America and in some other parts of the world, let it be known that these books were bestsellers and were devoured by upwards of sixty million people.

Jenkins and LaHaye claim to have based their work on the Bible, Revelation in particular, and most of the people who bought them apparently thought they were getting a fictionalized account of what the Bible itself says. The truth is, however, that the books take off from a very peculiar and quite modern variant of Protestant fundamentalism characterized by two features, each with a complex name: dispensationalism and premillennialism. It is not surprising that most Americans, including most Christians, are not familiar with these technical terms, and most of the novels' readers probably were not either. But each term does designate a religious sensibility that is both still present in American culture and still shaping much of the way Revelation is read, so it is important for readers of this highly contentious text to understand them.[9]

Dispensationalism is a branch of Protestant fundamentalism that teaches that history is divided into seven phases from the creation to the end, and God deals with the world in different ways in each of these "dispensations." Here we can make out the long shadow of Joachim of Fiore, whose three stages—Father, Son, and Spirit—have now morphed into seven, a favorite biblical number. The theory holds that we are now in the final stage, therefore we are in the "last days," and the physical second coming of Christ to set up his rule on earth will occur soon. Dispensationalists cherry-pick verses from biblical books in both Testaments, wrench them from their contexts, and reassemble them to try to make their case. They especially like to apply their decontextualized method to Revelation.

Premillennialism is a variant of dispensationalism. Recalling the mention in Revelation of a thousand-year (millennium) reign of God on earth, this interpretation rejects the idea that Christ will return at the end of a peaceful era. Instead, it teaches that he will return before it begins (hence the "pre"). In this first phase of a two-stage second coming, Christ will gather up all those who are faithful to him in what is called the "rapture." These fortunate folks will be conveyed into the divine presence without having to die. What will follow will be a period of unprecedented suffering and dislocation on earth, which they call the "Great Tribulation." Only then will the millennium and the Last Judgment follow.

The immense popularity of the *Left Behind* novels tells us something about the current spiritual culture, especially in America.[10] Despite a surface secularism, a layer of biblical literalism lurks just below the surface. A recent survey indicated that 44 percent of Americans say they believe there will one day be a battle of Armageddon. About 49 percent believe in the Antichrist, and fully 60 percent in a Judgment Day. Add to this substratum the desperate uncertainty of our times, with its spasms of revolutions and coups, its terrorist attacks and its economic anxiety, which often makes people yearn for some reliable guide to what it all means and to what is coming next. Because the Bible still occupies such a prominent place in the cultural imagination, many people have at least heard that Revelation is literally about "what must soon take place" (as John himself describes it). But they are frustrated by their inability, despite trying, to make sense of this perplexing book. It is understandable that they turn to an easy-to-read paperback that promises to tell them what Revelation (and some of the other apocalyptic books) say is coming.

Further, when one realizes that the cultural influence of the Bible today goes along with a gnawing suspicion of current scholarship, readers most often fall back on a literalistic understanding of Revelation. In addition, they think it is an infallible, if puzzling, predictor of what is "soon to come," not in the time of John or of any of the innumerable panicky end-time movements that have appeared since then, but in our own time. This reading in turn generates endless efforts to seize on today's headlines in the light of the "four horsemen" and the "battle of Armageddon." Religious television shows parade "expert" after "expert" in Bible lore before the cameras to delve into where the Great Beast and the Antichrist are making their current appearances. The analyses range from Russia to China to the Islamic world. But since much of our news comes from the troubled Middle East, where the books of the Bible originated, that region offers limitless possibilities for such bogus scholarship.

REVELATION TODAY

Is Revelation significant for us today? The answer is that it is, but that in order to clarify that relevance readers must not underestimate what we are up against, namely, a massive and destructive misinterpretation of its relevance. We must remind ourselves that Revelation is not a horoscope. Even though John himself invited this kind of reading by using phrases like "what must soon take place" (1:1) and "surely I am coming soon" (22:20), his book is not concerned with predicting what will happen in the twenty-first century, and he would be astonished to see that it is read that way. It is not the biblical equivalent of Nostradamus or a crystal ball. Rather, it is a hugely ambitious attempt to craft a full-scale philosophy or theology of the entire sweep of human history, viewed from the perspective of an early Christian writer from a Jewish background named John in the context of what he and his fellow Christians were facing in the final decades of the first century. When we realize that at that time most of the writing about the meaning of history was expressed in myths and symbols, it is understandable that he chose the same idiom.[11]

The meaning John discerns in what, many years later, the writers of the American Declaration of Independence would call "the course of human events" is a titanic contest between the spirit of domination and violence, on the one hand, and the spirit of mutuality and peace, on the other. For John, the first spirit has manifested itself in the empires of the past, such as Assyria and Babylon, and it was in his time incarnate again in the Roman Empire. But John was sure that in the long run the "empire" of love, which the Hebrew prophets and Jesus had called the kingdom of God, would win out. Still there would be some tough times to endure between now and then, and John's message to his fellow Christians was to "hang in there" or "hold out." He encouraged them not to be seduced by the wiles of the Roman colossus, which he referred to as "the Beast" or as Satan. But this Rome has nothing to do with the Roman church, which had barely come into existence, or the papacy, which had not yet appeared.

But John also excoriates those fellow followers of Jesus who he believed had succumbed to the Beast. As we have seen, this reflects a nasty argument going on about how far those who testified that only Jesus was worthy of worship should compromise and acquiesce to the empire's sporadic efforts to get them to acknowledge the divinity of Caesar. Some held that doing so was really just a civic duty, perhaps like singing the national anthem or pledging allegiance to the flag. Others insisted that compromise was a slippery slope. Even just performing a seemingly meaningless and routine gesture might be an opening wedge that could pry them away from their fundamental loyalty to Christ and his new empire of peace and healing.

John emphatically sided with the resisters, and his denunciation of those who chose to compromise is neither irenic nor conciliatory. He is clearly infuriated. He lashes out at them, and his language is not restrained. He even allows himself to imagine the ghastly punishment these betrayers might expect when Christ reigns instead of Caesar. Perhaps without his being aware of it, his gruesome descriptions of these retributions seem at odds with his belief in a kingdom of mercy and compassion. But John is only human, and his own life situation makes his livid language understandable, if not forgivable.

The dilemma John addresses, how people whose highest loyalty is to God, should respond to the demands of a state to which they are also expected to be loyal, is one that Christians have never escaped and never fully resolved. Even when Christianity became fully legal two centuries after John wrote Revelation, the problem remained. Some followers of King Jesus chafed under the cozy alliance that soon developed between the official church and the empire, so much so that many left for the clear desert air and founded what became known as the monastic movement. During the sixteenth-century Protestant Reformation Christians who insisted on following Jesus's command not to take up the sword and therefore refused to serve in armies were condemned and executed by the more prominent Reformers such as Calvin and Luther. But Mennonites and Quakers resisted and continue to do so today. In some countries the right of conscientious objection to military service has been legally recognized, though those excused are required to perform alternate service. The U.S. Supreme Court recognized a citizen's right not to salute the flag in 1943, but the right to refuse to pay taxes to support war has never been allowed.

John grappled with this persistent challenge as it presented itself in the first centuries of the common era. He chose the hazardous course of refusing to compromise at a time when the price for such disloyalty sometimes meant death. And he had little patience with those who chose what he no doubt considered cowardly, the easy way out. It is impossible to say what percentage of the Christians in John's day took his side and how many took the other option. It is quite possible, maybe even probable, that John represents a minority. But the view he voices with such energy has been heard and heeded frequently over the centuries. Indeed, it is precisely his minority status that is the key to reading his words today because, although they can galvanize a persecuted minority, when they fall into the hands of the religiously or politically powerful, these same words can become lethal weapons.

His writing may well have inspired some early Christians to "hang on," but when the emperor Constantine ended the persecution and the sword fell into the hands of Christians, the dark side of Revelation became evident. Now a new and imperialized church, basking in the emperor's favor and benefits (including financial ones), began to wield the sword against other Christians whom they viewed as theologically incorrect. The first Christian to be martyred by his fellow Christians was one Priscillian of Ávila, a bishop who, following a judgment by his fellow bishops, was beheaded with a small number of his disciples in 385 CE. He was the first, but hardly the last. One historian estimated that in the three hundred years that followed, imperial authorities in close cooperation with church officials put some twenty-five thousand Christians to death for their deficiency in creedal orthodoxy. It is painful to recall that even John Calvin, the revered founder of the Reformed tradition in Christianity, thought the views of Michael Servetus so dangerous he agreed to his execution in Geneva in October 1553. Servetus was burned at the stake, although Calvin is reported to have preferred the quicker method, beheading.

But is it fair to blame Revelation, with its scenes of righteous and bloody punishment, for these deaths? Context is critically important:

John was a man *against whom* the sword was being wielded, and he was writing from that perspective. Today, although most Christians do not find themselves in that situation, in other parts of the world many still do. And for them Revelation speaks directly to what they are facing.

Another critical point to keep in mind in reading Revelation is that John is a *Jewish* follower of Jesus (he never uses the word "Christian"). He sees himself standing in the succession of Hebrew prophets like Isaiah and Jeremiah. He is deeply familiar with the literature of the Jewish religious tradition and mines it extensively in his writing. He is especially drawn to the more imaginative Jewish literature we now call "intertestamental," which was produced after the last canonical book of the Hebrew scriptures but before the New Testament came into being. (These texts are populated by fearsome figures like dragons and beasts, and John follows suit in Revelation.) John had a special fondness for the book of Daniel. In fact, this sometimes extravagantly dramatic story was so important to him that one scholar has suggested recently that in order to come to grips with Revelation, one should have the book of Daniel close at hand.

John would have been puzzled by the idea that he was writing for what would eventually be a "new" testament. He would have been repulsed by the very idea of such a thing. As a Jew, what we now call the "Old Testament," together with recent Jewish myths and some other ancient sources, was quite enough to make the case that Jesus was indeed the promised messiah and that the same God who had created the world and assigned the Israelites their special task was the God of all ages and all people. In this sense his theology of history is radically universal.

We have already charted the rocky road to inclusion in the New Testament that Revelation had to negotiate. Now we have to ask why was it so tortuous? The answer lies precisely in John's being part of a double minority, belonging both to a highly suspect faith and a minority within it of those who would not bow their heads to Caesar. The reason Revelation was originally so disputed, continued to be, and still is can be explained by the fact that people read it from so many different places in the social hierarchy. It is like a powerful drug that can be a medicine for some, but a poison for others. Taken by those who suffer from oppression, it can inspire them to believe that their anguish will not last forever. But when it is ingested by people who fear that their privileged perch is threatened, it can be used as a clumsy rhetorical bludgeon.

Fittingly, the book ends with two contradictory images. The first, symbolized by "Babylon," is an unsparing warning about the pride and pretense of all empires, past and present (18:10–19). But it is followed a few chapters later by another vision, that of a "New Jerusalem," a world of peace and beauty where every tear is wiped away. Like the entire Bible, it is a diptych of the best and the worst of human possibility. Here, first, is the doomed empire:

> Terrified at her torment, they will stand far off and cry:
>
>> "Woe! Woe, O great city,
>> O Babylon, city of power!
>> In one hour your doom has come!"
>
> The merchants of the earth will weep and mourn over her because no one buys their cargoes any more—cargoes of gold, silver, precious stones and pearls; fine linen, purple, silk and scarlet cloth; every sort of citron wood, and articles of every kind made of ivory, costly wood, bronze, iron and marble; cargoes of cinnamon and spice, of incense, myrrh and frankincense, of wine and olive oil, of fine flour and wheat; cattle and sheep; horses and carriages; and bodies and souls of men.
> They will say, "The fruit you longed for is gone from you. All your riches and splendor have vanished, never to be recovered." The merchants who sold these things and gained their wealth from her will stand far off, terrified at her torment. They will weep and mourn and cry out:
>
>> "Woe! Woe, O great city,
>> dressed in fine linen, purple and scarlet,
>> and glittering with gold, precious stones and pearls!
>> In one hour such great wealth has been brought to ruin!"

Every sea captain, and all who travel by ship, the sailors,
and all who earn their living from the sea, will stand far off.
When they see the smoke of her burning, they will exclaim,
"Was there ever a city like this great city?" They will throw dust
on their heads, and with weeping and mourning cry out:

> *"Woe! Woe to you, great city,*
> *where all who had ships on the sea*
> *became rich through her wealth!*
> *In one hour she has been brought to ruin!" (NIV)*

This is an appalling picture. But it is not the last word. The book ends with the opposite vision, the peaceable city, a cosmically enlarged version of "I Have a Dream":

> *And I saw the holy city, new Jerusalem, coming down out of*
> *heaven from God, prepared as a bride adorned for her husband;*
> *and I heard a loud voice from the throne saying, "Behold, the*
> *dwelling of God is with men. He will dwell with them, and they*
> *shall be his people, and God himself will be with them; he will*
> *wipe away every tear from their eyes, and death shall be no more,*
> *neither shall there be mourning nor crying nor pain any more, for*
> *the former things have passed away." (21:2–4, RSV)*

It is appropriate that the last book in the Bible ends with this condensed précis of the varicolored themes—creation and destruction, cruelty and mercy, the lowest and the highest—that we have encountered throughout it. The "Amen" with which it ends is not only a finis for Revelation, but for the whole Book.

10

How Do We Read the Bible Today?

After we have reached the last verse of Revelation, we are still not finished with the question the title of this book implies: *How should we read the Bible today?* I have suggested that some familiarity with technical biblical studies, from form and source analysis to archaeology, history of interpretation, and empire studies, can illuminate our reading. But the *how* problem remains. W. H. Auden once teased people "who read the Bible for its prose." In this book I have been critical of those who read it in search of answers better left to paleontologists. Then of course there are those who study it in an effort to cast doubts on its value for any purpose today. In other words, people read the Bible with wildly disparate motivations.

I suspect this will always be the case, and I see no reason to object. The Bible does indeed contain some magnificent prose and poetry. As for those who read it in order to discredit it, I would forewarn them that what they are doing has been tried for centuries, but somehow the Bible has survived and even flourished. For those who seek the date of the big bang in Genesis, I can only reiterate what I wrote in the first chapter: I am afraid their search will not succeed, mainly because that is not what the writers of that book had in mind. Here, however, I want to address a more important meaning of the "how to read the Bible" question. It pertains to those—and there are many—who read the Bible with the hope of finding something significant for their own lives or maybe even for the world. Does the Bible itself provide hints for *how* they should read it?

I think it does. In this book we have necessarily bounced from "In the beginning . . ." (Gen. 1:1) to "The grace of the Lord Jesus be with all the saints. Amen" (Rev. 22:21) and from century to century. And in this process something important may have been lost sight of, namely, that for all its dazzling variety the Bible tells a single story. It is a book about the dramatic interaction between God and the world, mainly that part of the world we call humankind. The story comes to us through the imperfect, often badly flawed words and perceptions of human beings. But the drama has a continuing plot and direction. And the voice of the Bible invites readers to become part of the action. But how?

Historical research can help establish what any part of it might originally have meant and what it has meant over the years. But what it means for *us* and what it means *today* are questions of a different kind. They cannot be answered by any of the methods of biblical study we have described or by all of them combined. Whatever the devoted scholars of the Jesus Seminar may have discovered about the historical Jesus, after their work is done, he still remains a historical figure, a personage—however attractive, fascinating, or inscrutable—of the past, not of the present. The same is true for the whole Bible. Clearly, it is invaluable to be familiar with the research techniques and modes of literary analysis that have been brought to bear on the Bible in recent years. Still, after all that exertion is done, the persistent question of what the Bible *means* for us today remains. How, then, do we address it?

The Bible itself offers its own response. The central thread running through the whole sixty-six books is that of the coming of the kingdom of God. In my chapter on the Gospels I pointed out that when asked by the Pharisees when the kingdom of God that he spoke of would actually come, Jesus answered, "You cannot tell by observation . . ." In saying this he was insisting that what is required is personal involvement from a deeper level of the self than objective investigation. There is a philosophical term for this perspective—"existential"—and there are biblical scholars, most famously the German Rudolf Bultmann, who applied it to their method. But the word has become both so fashionable and so esoteric that it hardly serves our purpose here. Is there a better word?

Realizing that it involves some risk, I prefer to call the attitude Jesus calls for "spiritual," but I in no way mean a strictly inward reading. I mean "spiritual" in the sense of the Spirit that makes its presence felt throughout the Bible, from Genesis to Revelation. This is the Spirit that manifests itself in both individuals and groups, in both nature and history, and in the animals and plants we live with every day. It is the Spirit of God that both comforts and disturbs and that cannot be channeled or contained by institutions or doctrines. The point is that if we do not read the Bible with a genuine openness to being spoken to, perhaps upset and shaken by what we find in it, we will have missed the message.

But there is another component in Jesus's admonition about the coming of the kingdom of God. Not only can we not perceive it "by observation"; it is also "in our midst." The phrase at the end of Luke 17:21 has often been badly translated as "within you," and the mistake has been handed on in songs and sayings and even appears frequently in some of Leo Tolstoy's books. But the word Jesus uses is not "within" in an individual sense. It is better translated as "among you" or "in the midst of you." It points to a reality that is not inward in an individual sense, but that suffuses the relationships of people with each other. This suggests another dimension of how we should approach reading and studying the Bible, one that adds an additional reason why the word "spiritual" in its largest holistic sense best conveys this approach: to grasp the meaning of the kingdom of God "for us," it is critical to know who the "us" is. It is imperative that we find out how other people are responding to this same drama. But which other people?

Again we can be guided by the words of Dietrich Bonhoeffer that we found helpful in our consideration of Job. In reflecting from prison about what he had learned from his years behind bars and from the decade since the Nazis came to power, he writes something, he said, "of incomparable value." He had learned to see the world "from below," from the perspective of "those who suffer."[1]

Bonhoeffer also wrote to his friend that since he had been in prison he had read the Old Testament through twice. His words here indicate that he did. They resonate with the whole Bible's repeated emphases on God's favoring the poor, the sick, the brokenhearted, and the outcast. God's law as enshrined in the Torah makes no pretense of being even-handed. Its symbol is not a blindfolded justice with a weighing scale. It leans heavily toward favoring the "widow and the fatherless." This means that in reading the Bible today we need to check our view of it with those who do not share our life situation, with those whom we consider "others." So now the question becomes, who are our "others," the inclusive "us" with whom we need to read the Bible "today"?

Taking our clue from Bonhoeffer, it means three clusters of "other" Bible readers: those who, as he says, see life "from below"; those who read the Bible as adherents of other faiths; and poets, novelists, visual artists, and filmmakers who retell the biblical narratives in a sometimes jarring or juxtaposed manner, often calling conventional readings into question.

"FROM BELOW"

For centuries nearly all the interpretation of the Bible was carried on by men in the educated clerical elite. Women were usually not welcome, and the majority of laypeople were illiterate. It is possible that the most important breakthrough in biblical studies in the past century was not the new quest for the historical Jesus at all, but the fact that, for the first time in history, large numbers of people who had previously been excluded from biblical studies because of their social class, lack of education, or gender began to take part. And because they brought their own experiences to the effort, these newcomers discovered fresh dimensions in the Gospels that even the best trained linguists and archaeologists had never found. They also made these discoveries because they did not just read the Bible objectively or, as Jesus warned, "by observation." Although many were well prepared in the technical tools of biblical research, their "search" was more than an intellectual enterprise. They had something at stake.

The best example of this "reading from below" is the stance toward the Bible introduced by liberation theology, a movement that originated in Latin America; it has been pilloried and denounced, but remains vital in many places in the world, including Asia and Africa. For our purposes it is important to recognize that it grew out of small study-and-action groups called "ecclesial base communities" and is built on a different way of reading the Bible. It is rooted in the effort launched by Latin American Christian leaders fifty years ago to serve large numbers of people with a small number of priests. Groups of laypeople were organized for prayer, sharing food, often singing, and taking action in their communities when it seemed called for. But because these groups began to meet just as the Catholic Church had decided to encourage laypeople to read the Bible, the newly formed groups soon made the study of scripture, especially the Gospels, a focal part of their lives. Still, it is the *way* they read the Bible that is most instructive for us.

For centuries the Catholics of Latin America were discouraged by the hierarchy from reading the Bible. We recognize this today as a serious deprivation, but it brought with it an unexpected advantage. Ordinary laypeople were spared the nasty conflict between modernists and fundamentalists that wrenched apart American and some European churches. Consequently, when at last they were allowed—indeed urged—to read the Bible, they read it without either set of preconceptions. Also, since most of the members of the groups were from the lower levels of their societies, they brought their own pain and destitution to their reading. As one of the principal voices in the liberation theology movement, Father Gustavo Gutiérrez, when asked in a conversation why the movement had grown so rapidly in Latin America, said that it was because the people were both Christian and poor, and they understood their faith through their poverty and their poverty in the light of their faith."[2]

It is worth noting that in recent years some serious questions have been raised about liberation theology even from some of its earliest supporters. They claim that the movement tended to homogenize "the poor," but in fact the excluded and disinherited in any society include those mistreated for a variety of reasons, such as color, physical makeup, gender, language, religion, or sexual orientation. Also its critics suggest that liberation theology is unduly dismissive of popular religiosity, too easily

viewing it as a delusion that prevents marginalized people from recognizing the real sources of their exploitation.

There was once an element of truth in such complaints. But the movement has tried, often with success, to correct these blind spots. But there
is another objection that bears more directly on the theme of this book,
namely, that liberation theology has been too text-bound, seeking its inspiration almost entirely from the Bible and ignoring the liberating potential of folk religion, festivals, and oral traditions. Again, liberation
theologians have tried to respond to this critique, but it serves as a warning to us that, in answering our question about how to read the Bible, we
must be careful not to read it as the only authentic source of faith, but
instead to see it as one among several.

Still, for the more privileged among us, liberation theology's emphasis
on reading the Bible "through the eyes of the poor" has made an essential
contribution. Of course it requires a leap of imagination. But it enables us
to grasp its message in ways we had not noticed before. The underlying
point of trying to read the Bible "from below" is not that everyone needs
to kick over tables or become a martyr. It suggests that we who read the
Bible from a more comfortable position in society need to check our impressions against those who read it from a less secure point of view. Fortunately, there are ample resources available, interpretations articulated by
Christians who read the Bible from that standpoint. (See the Study Tip
below.)

OTHER RELIGIOUS PERSPECTIVES

As Christianity spreads rapidly to areas where other world religions
have lived for centuries, some for millennia, a number of fresh ways of
reading the Bible have appeared. First, Christians outside the old precincts
of Christendom are aware that their faith is that of a minority and will
probably always be. Their neighbors rely on other sacred texts, and the
cultures they share have been shaped by those texts, just as ours has been
by the Bible. Reading in this situation opens up new meanings in familiar
biblical passages.

Study Tip ————————————————————————

There are numerous resources for learning how the Bible is read and interpreted in other settings and from alternate points of view. Miguel A. De La Torre describes many of these in his *Reading the Bible from the Margins* (Maryknoll, NY: Orbis Books, 2013). See also Fernando F. Segovia and Mary Ann Tolbert, eds., *Reading from This Place,* especially vol. 2, *Social Location and Biblical Interpretation in Global Perspective* (Minneapolis: Fortress, 1995). R. S. Sugirtharajah has edited one volume on this subject, *Voices from the Margin: Interpreting the Bible in the Third World* (Maryknoll, NY: Orbis Books, 1995). He has also written a more recent one, *The Bible in the Third World: Precolonial, Colonial and Postcolonial Encounters* (Cambridge: Cambridge Univ. Press, 2001). By far the best book on African-American renderings of biblical stories is Allen Dwight Callahan's *The Talking Book* (New Haven, CT: Yale Univ. Press, 2006).

————————————————————————

As a result of the current meeting of ancient faiths in new ways, numerous adherents of these other faiths have written commentaries and responses to the Bible, something that has hardly ever happened in the previous nineteen centuries. These writers tend to be especially drawn to the Gospels. One example is the Tibetan Dalai Lama, perhaps the best-known Buddhist in the world. His book *The Good Heart: A Buddhist Perspective on the Teachings of Jesus* provides an excellent alternative view of the Gospels.[3] It includes his commentary on Jesus's words followed by a Christian's response to the Dalai Lama's. Thus the format opens the possibility of a serious comparison of what people informed by different traditions find in the same text.

Another Buddhist, the monk Thich Nhat Hanh, has also written a book comparing Christ with the Buddha, *Living Buddha, Living Christ.*[4]

It differs in important ways from the Dalai Lama's work, which demonstrates that within the Buddhist tradition itself there are "others."

The Hindu tradition is immensely variegated, and there is also no single view of Jesus or of the Bible. Some see Jesus, like Krishna, as an avatar of God, easily incorporated into the Hindu pantheon. Others value him as a great ethical teacher. Millions of Indians know that Gandhi admired Jesus, especially his Sermon on the Mount, and so view him with reverence but, like Gandhi, want to "liberate Jesus from the clergy and the church."

Islam is a unique case for comparison since the Old Testament prophets, Mary, and Jesus are already featured in the Holy Qur'an, but most Muslims reject the accounts of the crucifixion based on the conviction that God would not permit one of his prophets to suffer such an ignominious death. Still, this has not prevented many of them from understanding his death as a heroic sacrifice for justice.

Judaism provides another special case, since most of what Christians call "the Bible" (namely, the Old Testament) is also accepted by Jews as scripture, but the ways in which it is interpreted vary enormously. There is also a wide range of understandings of Jesus among Jewish religious thinkers, and these views have changed markedly in recent years. There was a time when any discussion of Jesus was viewed with distrust, but since the emergence of the state of Israel, many Jewish scholars, especially in Israel, have begun to reclaim him as one of their own, but reject the mainstream Christian interpretations of his significance.

Study Tip ——————————————————————————

For non-Christian interpretations, see Gregory A. Barker and Stephen E. Gregg, *Jesus Beyond Christianity: The Classic Texts* (Oxford: Oxford Univ. Press, 2010). As a resource for additional Hindu interpretations, see www.samarthbharat.com/ jesushindu.htm. The Swedish scholar Oddbjørn Leirvik has compiled the best source on Muslim views, *Images of Jesus*

Christ in Islam (Uppsala: Studia Missionalia Upsaliensa, 1999). For a useful chart comparing a range of beliefs about Jesus in different faith traditions, see www.religionfacts.com/jesus/ religious_views.htm.

ARTISTIC INTERPRETATIONS

Finally, one of the most intriguing places to look for the voice of the "other" in understanding the Bible is to the poets, artists, filmmakers, and novelists who have drawn on it to fashion their own interpretations. There are far too many of these to allow for a comprehensive list. Instead, I will mention some of the best resources I have found for becoming familiar with them. Starting with poets, check Peggy Rosenthal's *The Poets' Jesus*.[5] It touches on the work of dozens of poets from before Blake to after Borges, including the Korean poet Ku Sang. Another good source is the book Rosenthal edited with George Dardess and Robert Atwan, *Divine Inspiration: The Life of Jesus in Poetry*.[6] This book ends with a quote by the American poet Denise Levertov (1923–1997):

> *A poet speaking from within the Christian tradition and using traditional terms (though not upholding every orthodoxy) may have more resonance for our intellectual life than is supposed. The Incarnation, the Passion, the Resurrection—these words have some emotive power even for the most secular minds. Perhaps a contemporary poetry that incorporates old terms and old stories can help readers to appropriate significant parts of their own linguistic, emotional, cultural heritage, whether or not they share doctrinal adherence.*[7]

When we turn to films, clearly the Bible has provided a mine of material for countless movies—silent and with sound, black-and-white and in color—ever since the medium was invented. Serious readers of the Bible will undoubtedly be disappointed, incensed, and bemused by most of them. One reason is the problem filmmakers must face about the obstinate question of what they can do about "translating," say, the book of Exodus, with its spectacular miracles, or the Gospels, in which we have four sometimes divergent narratives. As powerful as the film medium is, it is not suitable for portraying the spiritual truth that lies behind the miracle stories or multiple takes on the same scenes in the life of Jesus.

In the case of the miracles, film directors are almost forced into a kind of fundamentalist-literal depiction of Jesus walking on the sea or turning water into wine. The temptation to do so is increased by the ability of directors to employ special effects. These techniques can easily divide the waters of the Sea of Reeds (popularly known as the Red Sea) or, as occurred in one Jesus film, show a grotesquely deformed man instantly transformed into a picture of smooth-skinned health.

As for portraying the divergent views of Jesus in the four Gospels, which we have seen to be highly instructive in rounding out a portrait of him, not even the best directors have attempted to solve it. One thinks of the possibility of using a split-screen technique for showing the different descriptions of the cleansing/occupation of the Temple, for instance. But audiences would probably not stand for it. This produces another kind of quasi-fundamentalism or at least false realism. It implicitly tells viewers, "This is the way it really was," and thus destroys the advantage gained from seeing an event from different perspectives. As I mentioned earlier, the Italian director Pasolini resolved the issue by choosing to base his classic *The Gospel of St. Matthew* on only that one Gospel, that is, explicitly from the standpoint of one of the Gospel writers. However, he did not try to solve the literalism challenge. He used special effects to depict miracles in a completely literal way. The ironical result was that even though his Jesus appeared as a social radical, reflecting Pasolini's own political stance, conservative Catholic and Protestant viewers overlooked that aspect and in general liked the film. The director was especially happy that the pope appreciated it.

A vast trove of biblical films is available. One can go back to the silent era for the earlier cinematic depictions *The Ten Commandments* (1923) or

King of Kings (1931), the latter of which had an accompanying musical score. When sound pictures arrived, the pace of Bible movies slowed, but only temporarily. In the days of stricter production standards, directors discovered they could inject more bare flesh and suggestive action by bringing in Eve, Delilah, or Jezebel. Some producers were even accused of blatantly splicing erotic scenes into religious epics. This reproach prompted Cecil B. DeMille to remark, "I wonder whether my accusers have ever read certain parts of the Bible."

Some Bible films were both theatrical and box-office successes. Some failed. Ironically, sometimes the films that stray the farthest from the biblical account, like Mel Gibson's *The Passion of the Christ,* make the most money. Still directors keep trying. And none of the problems I have mentioned should deter readers of the Bible from dipping into the huge film archive that is on tap. It would be both fascinating and enjoyable to do some comparing of biblical texts to the movie versions.

There are hardly any Old Testament films that are worth serious consideration. With the New Testament, we find that almost all the films focus on Jesus. One exception is Ingmar Bergman's graphic *The Seventh Seal,* inspired by the book of Revelation. But the vast majority of Jesus films are quite bad. Only a few are worth viewing. One is *Jesus of Montreal,* which tells the story of a group of young people in that Canadian city who are asked by a liberal priest to work up a contemporary version of a Passion play. Uncertain as to how to go about their assignment at first, each of the young people gradually begins to identify with his or her character, Mary, Jesus, or Peter, and the action takes some surprising turns. The Temple incident takes place in a TV studio, where an angry Jesus kicks over cameras and klieg lights. The resurrection features the distribution of his body organs to other people.

It can be both exhilarating and daunting to realize how many resources are at hand for reading and thinking about the Bible from perspectives different from one's own. No one needs to become familiar with even a small portion of them. But drawing on them selectively to check and cross-check one's own reading is a bracing and broadening experience. As wide and as deep as the Bible itself is, my interpretation of it can become mired in one cultural or regional track. I need to have that interpretation jogged at times, maybe even upended. This jarring will remind us that when we consider the question, "How should we read the Bible?" there is no single answer.

Conclusion

While I was writing this book, several friends asked me, as they often do, what I was working on now. When I told them it was a book "about the Bible," some looked mildly surprised, others expressed or at least feigned interest, but a few took active exception to my expending my time on such a questionable project.

Their objections took several forms. Some wondered why I would waste even a few hours on an old tome crammed with such incredible and ridiculous fictions. "A collection of Jewish fairy tales," one called it. Others granted that the Good Book might once have had real value, but that was then and this is now. It was archaic and obsolete, of possible interest to undereducated provincials and a few antiquarians, but I should be devoting my energies to matters of more immediate concern. A few scolded me, usually gently. Didn't I recognize how dangerous the Bible was, how much hatred and strife it had engendered over the centuries. Why stir interest in it now? Wouldn't it be better to just let it fade away or, better yet, do something to hasten its eventual but inevitable demise?

There is some truth to each of these criticisms, and in bringing to a close this book on the Bible that, despite them, I did write, they deserve some response. Is the Bible ridiculous and incredible? The answer is, in part, yes, it is. It includes sagas, legends, and tall tales about giants and one about a talking ass. It contains, as Huck Finn wrote about Tom Sawyer's anecdotes, "some stretchers." But the underlying question raised by this complaint concerns the appropriate role of fantasy and imagination in human life. It is simply not true that our culture today is bereft of fantasy and tall tales. We thrive on them. We sop up sagas about intergalactic warfare, vampires, and monsters that emerge from the depths of the sea. We have had an enduring love affair with hobbits. But we rarely ask what values and worldviews these fables impart, and our insatiable craving for them suggests a yen for something that is not fully satisfied.

Both J. R. R. Tolkien (1892–1973), who gave us *The Lord of the Rings*, and C. S. Lewis (1898–1963), who wrote both theology and fantasy, including *The Chronicles of Narnia*, recognized this hunger. The two were both professors of literature and close friends, belonging to a literary society called "The Inklings." Both believed that the modern mind was becoming too flat and pedestrian, cut off from the full range of human potential by a dearth of fantasy, or at least good fantasy. Both were men of faith, Tolkien a Catholic, Lewis an Anglican, who felt that the modern alienation from Christianity had arisen in part from our shrunken capacity for mythic thinking.

If anything, and despite the hobbits, that sterile condition has worsened since the coming of Facebook and Twitter. But it is a difficult malady to remedy. We say we want "the facts, just the facts," but a gnawing thirst for fantasy persists. Tolkien and Lewis recognized it. So instead of trying to expunge the mythic element from the Bible as some modern theologians did, their tactic was to address the problem indirectly. They tried to restore the mythic dimension to the culture in the belief that this would help people grasp the message of Christianity better and thereby deepen our capacity for a fully human life. Taking a hint from them, we can read the Bible today welcoming the fact that it represents a world in which the capacity for the fabulous was still alive.

The charge that the Bible is obsolete, that it may once have been a source of wisdom and inspiration, but no longer is, may also have some merit. Some of our issues are different from those of people who lived in the late Neolithic age. But what makes something archaic? How dissimilar really are we from our ancient and even prehistoric forebears? Why do Sophocles and Shakespeare still resonate with us? Why do we feel a curious kinship with the people who scratched the pictures on the cave walls in Lascaux or with those who positioned the boulders at Stonehenge? Has the fact that our knowledge of the size of the universe or the structure of the genome exceeds theirs made their insights into the human situation obsolete? We may differ from our ancient and prehistoric forebears in some ways, but we are like them in many more. We realize that we are mortal. We struggle with how to live with each other in families, tribes, and—more recently—a whole world. We grapple with disease and aging, and we smart under the stings of betrayal and misunderstanding by those close to us. We brood about how to respond to the fathomless mystery that envelops us. These are the themes the characters in the Bible cope with, sometimes graciously and sometimes in cruel and destructive ways. But they are issues we have not outgrown.

Is the Bible dangerous? Once more, let us concede the accusation. Certain pages in it—sometimes rightly called "texts of terror"—have sparked mayhem, violence, pogroms, and Crusades. In places, as we have seen in the chapter on Joshua, it depicts a God who commands the slaughter of whole populations, including women, children, and animals. Might we have been better off if it had never been written? Should it not be clearly labeled, "Reading this could be dangerous to your health and to everyone else's"?

True. It is in fact dangerous to read parts of the Bible as though they were commands to us today, and this includes the ghastly orders God is reported to have issued to the Israelites when they invaded Canaan. But neither in those times nor in ours have invading armies needed scriptural warrant to rape, burn, and murder. Among many other things, the Bible is an unvarnished witness to the horrific violence of which we have been capable as a species, just as it is a chronicle of sporadic and usually unsuccessful efforts to limit that brutality. At the same time it is an archive of humankind's attempts to face up to the mystery that both surrounds us and wells up unsummoned from within us.

From the beginning, the Bible says, God has shared his power and tried to enlist us in continuing his creation and in caring for it. Instead, we have messed it up badly more often than we have gotten it right. But this is the sometimes magnificent, but more often miserable history of our species, not another one. And we need to be aware of it, however painful, because it is not yet over unless we manage to destroy it for good with nuclear fallout or by continuing to dump millions of tons of carbon dioxide into the air.

On the other hand, as despots and overlords have learned over the years, the Bible can be dangerous for their health. It introduces us to a God who leads an enslaved people out of peonage. His prophets warn the affluent about the toxic dangers their wealth carries with it, and they thunder against those who trample the poor underfoot. Its apostles defy the mightiest empire history had known, and its seers herald the eventual collapse of all tyrannies. When we hear that the Bible is "dangerous," we have to ask, for whom and under what circumstances?

Why should I spend any time writing yet another book about this strange old collection? One answer is that the Bible helps us to know who God is, and for many people, perhaps most, that is enough. But there is another reason. The Bible also helps us to heed the counsel of Socrates to "know thyself," and the wisdom of all the religious traditions teaches that the knowledge of God and the knowledge of ourselves are inseparable.

Whether we like the idea or not, the Bible has shaped our identity as a civilization, with all its extraordinary strengths and horrid weaknesses. For bane or for blessing, actually some of each, it has molded the institutions, values, and worldview not just of Western civilization, but in recent history of the whole world as well. It reverberates throughout our language and literature, our art and music. It has seeped into our synapses and gotten under our skin. It affects the way we think and live even when we are unaware of it. Even those people who devote their careers to trying to discredit the Bible are shaped by it. In short, there is no escaping it, so we need to come to grips with it.

At the personal level, since our civilization constitutes a large part of who I am, the Bible, even before I open it, has entered into my formation as a person. Erik Erikson, the developmental psychologist who invented the term, says my identity is a distillation of both my own experience and that of my family, my tribe, my nation, and my culture. When I internalize images of what it means to be a man, a parent, a husband, a father, I include not only images of my own parents, but their images of their parents, of their parents' parents, and the exemplars they modeled themselves on. As Walt Whitman wrote, "I am large, I contain multitudes."

Plumbing into the Bible may be a bit like classical psychoanalysis. One begins with what is on the surface of the mind, but then peels back layer after layer to expose what lurks beneath. What heaves into view are incidents from early childhood, then young adulthood. But we also discover we are not alone with these memories. We share the scars of our struggles with parents, siblings, lovers, heroes, and villains. These often return to us as stories, and their kinship with biblical sagas is all too evident. The analytical psychologist Carl Jung believed that we all draw on a "group subconscious" that is handed on from generation to generation. Of course, what one uncovers can be troubling, even traumatic. We unearth halfburied memories of abandonment, rage, longing, desperate hope. The uncovering process can be painful, but what I disinter is part of me. Not to know it is not to know myself.

In any case, despite the warnings, I did work on this book. With these final sentences written, it is now out of my hands and in yours. My hope is that at many points you will lay it aside and turn to the Book that this book is about. And when you do, my hope is that you may come to know both God and yourself a little better, since in the end the two cannot be separated.

NEW TESTAMENT

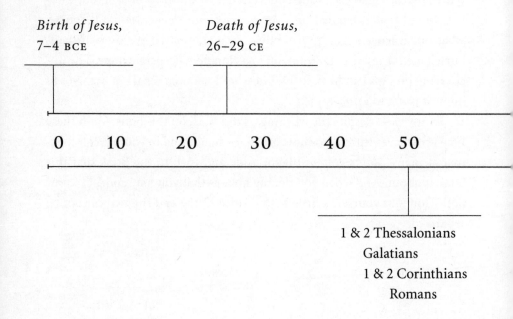

Birth of Jesus,
7–4 BCE

Death of Jesus,
26–29 CE

0   10   20   30   40   50

1 & 2 Thessalonians
Galatians
1 & 2 Corinthians
Romans

TIME LINE

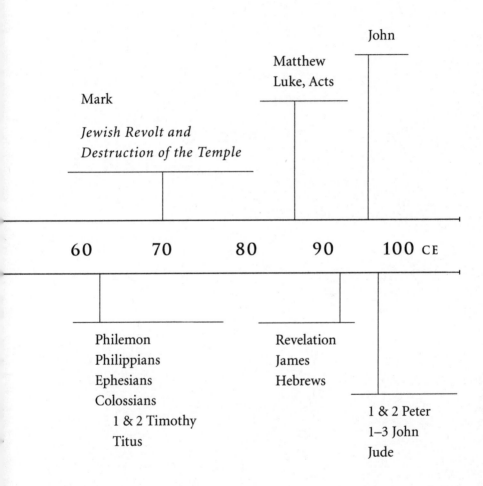

John

Matthew
Luke, Acts

Mark

Jewish Revolt and
Destruction of the Temple

60   70   80   90   100 CE

Philemon   Revelation
Philippians   James
Ephesians   Hebrews
Colossians
    1 & 2 Timothy   1 & 2 Peter
    Titus   1–3 John
                         Jude

Appendix

What Language Did Jesus Speak?

The question of what language, or languages, Jesus spoke was not widely discussed until recent years. When Mel Gibson's blockbuster *The Passion of the Christ* hit the screen in February 2004, the moviegoers who lined up to see it were often surprised that not a word of English was spoken in the whole film. In an effort to lend it a degree of authenticity, Gibson has Jesus and his disciples speak in Aramaic, while the Roman legionnaires converse in Latin. Popcorn-munching audiences had to rely on subtitles to know what was being said. This is a good example of how an event in popular culture can stir a slumbering scholarly pot. A question that had lain dormant for a long time suddenly came to life. People wanted to know what language Jesus really did speak.

It is important to note that at certain points in the Gospels Jesus's own words are preserved as minuscule islands of Aramaic in a sea of Greek. Jesus's cry from the cross, for example, "Eloi, Eloi, lama sabachthani" ("My God, my God, why have you forsaken me?"), is an Aramaic rendering of the words from a Psalm in Hebrew. Once, in a class I was teaching on Jesus, when we read the phrase he used ("talitha cumi") to arouse the little girl her parents thought was dead, an older Palestinian woman who was auditing the class raised her hand. "Yes, yes," she said enthusiastically, "that's what my mother used to say to me to get me out of bed!" Historians of language have noticed that over the years, although new words and expressions are coming in and some older ones are being abandoned, people seem reluctant to change words in rituals or in the idiom they use with children. But where does this get us on the question of what language Jesus spoke?

Researchers have been hot on the trail. But as with most investigations, no unanimous answer has been forthcoming. One such scholar, Mark D. Roberts, has, in my opinion, done the best job in summing up the evidence. His conclusion, albeit advanced with the necessary waivers, was that Jesus primarily spoke Aramaic, a language derived from an earlier form of Arabic, but he probably at least read, and may have spoken, some Hebrew and might also have known some Greek, which was the commercial lingua franca of the eastern Roman Empire in his time. He probably did not speak any Latin. On the other hand, one New Testament scholar told me that, although Jesus may have known a smattering of all these languages, like most working-class Palestinians of the time, he was probably only semiliterate, and thus his knowledge of Hebrew, used mainly in prayer, was scattered.

Of all these opinions, I found Roberts's work most convincing, but as he warns in one of his informative blogs: tread carefully! The question of what language Jesus spoke has now assumed political importance. Some Christians, mainly from the Middle East, whose mother tongue is Arabic, are pleased to discover that he spoke a language closely related to their own. Some other Christians are not happy with the idea that Jesus spoke in an idiom akin to the language of the Qur'an. On the other hand, many Muslims are delighted to welcome Jesus as something of a kinsman. It seems that it is impossible to disentangle current politics from even the most historically remote questions.

Meanwhile historians on the trail of the Aramaic connection continue to visit three tiny Christian towns in Lebanon, Ma'lula, Bakh', and Jubb'Adin, where people still speak a modern version of Aramaic at home, while using Arabic in public. These simple folk are amused by the stream of friendly foreign visitors, armed with notebooks and voice recorders, who visit their villages and seem to hang on their every word, no matter how trivial. The problem is that in the two thousand years since Jesus's time, like any other language, Aramaic has evolved to such an extent that little useful information can be gleaned from these visits.

The ongoing search for the language of Jesus serves as a kind of metaphor for all the historical investigations that focus on his life and times. They can tell us something, but not much, and this includes the techniques I have described in this book. Despite all the toil, as Albert Schweitzer, whose *The Quest of the Historical Jesus* remains the classic in this endeavor, once wrote:

> *He comes to us as One unknown, without a name, as of old, by the lakeside, He came to those men who knew Him not. He speaks to us the same words: "Follow thou me!" and sets us to the tasks which He has to fulfill for our time. He commands. And to those who obey Him, whether they be wise or simple, He will reveal himself in the toils, the conflicts, the sufferings which they shall pass through in His fellowship, and, as an ineffable mystery, they shall learn in their own experience Who He is.*[1]

For Further Reading

The Literary Guide to the Bible (Cambridge, MA: Belknap Press, Harvard Univ. Press, 1990), edited by Robert Alter and Frank Kermode, is an excellent collection of outstanding essays, mainly by literary critics, covering many of the biblical books. It can function as an instructive addition to standard commentaries by providing another way of looking at the texts.

In *Jesus in the World's Faiths* (Maryknoll, NY: Orbis Books, 2005), the editor, Gregory Barker, has selected twenty scholars from five different traditions to share their views of the significance of Jesus. This book contains a well-selected bibliography and is well suited for use in a study group.

Timothy Beal's *Biblical Literacy: The Essential Bible Stories Everyone Needs to Know* (San Francisco: HarperOne, 2009) is a delightfully readable volume that roughly follows the same book-by-book pattern I have used in *How to Read the Bible*. The difference is that Beal's work concentrates on the narratives as such. It is spiced throughout with delightful anecdotes.

For nonspecialists who want to keep abreast of the current discoveries in early Christian archaeology and textual analysis, the monthly *Biblical Archaeology* is an indispensable source (subscriptions: Box 7026, Red Oak, IA 51591–2026).

Paul and the Philosophers (New York: Fordham Univ. Press, 2013), edited by Ward Blanton and Hent de Vries, is surely one of the best and most influential texts on the apostle Paul, important especially because it did not originate in theological circles but among philosophers who have lately "rediscovered" Paul as one of the most significant thinkers in Western history.

For centuries the treatment of "the Jews" in the Passion narratives has constituted a source of tension between Jews and Christians. Mary C. Boys's *Redeeming Our Sacred Story: The Death of Jesus and Relations Between Jews and Christians* (New York: Paulist, 2013) takes a careful and informed look at these troublesome texts and suggests another way to read them.

Most people recognize that there is an approach to reading the Bible, namely, fundamentalism, that is at marked variance from the one I have taken in this book. Torkel Brekke's *Fundamentalism: Prophecy and Protest in an Age of Globalization* (New York: Cambridge Univ. Press, 2012) describes the origins of that important movement and its way of interpreting sacred texts, both in its Christian expression and in parallels drawn from other faiths.

For most of us, if the Bible is not a source of ethical direction, it is not worth the trouble of studying it. Drawing on the idea of an "ethos," the context in which moral decisions are made, Brian Brock, in his careful and well-written *Singing the Ethos of God: On the Place of Christian Ethics in Scripture* (Grand Rapids, MI: Eerdmans, 2007), demonstrates that the Bible, properly understood, does indeed fulfill this responsibility.

It would require several paragraphs to list and describe all the books of the biblical scholar Walter Brueggemann, but all his volumes are worth reading. He is the gold standard for relating careful critical scholarship to urgent and recurrent human problems. His most recent work is *Reality, Grief, Hope: Three Urgent Prophetic Tasks* (Grand Rapids, MI: Eerdmans, 2014).

Allen Dwight Callahan's *The Talking Book: African Americans and the Bible* (New Haven, CT: Yale Univ. Press, 2006) reminds readers of the invaluable insights to be gained by discovering how the Bible has been read and applied by those previously not admitted to the scholarly fraternity.

In his fascinating and aptly titled *The Religious Case Against Belief* (New York: Penguin, 2008), James P. Carse draws on history to make the same distinction between belief and authentic religious faith I discuss in the present volume.

Gary Dorrien's *The Remaking of Evangelical Theology* (Louisville, KY: Westminster John Knox, 1998) follows the important changes going on in a critical part of the Christian world.

A Sociology of Spirituality (London: Ashgate, 2007), edited by Kieran Flanagan and Peter C. Jupp, analyzes the variety of ways the term "spirituality" has come to be used and some of the problems it creates in a variety of settings.

Louis Ginzberg's *Legends of the Bible* (Philadelphia and Jerusalem: Jewish Publication Society, 1992) is a shortened version of the original, which was first published in 1909. Its 650 pages contain captivating stories, myths, and legends spun out by Jewish teachers that take off from the Bible, but then soar into realms of the imaginary.

Peter Gomes, the recently deceased minister at Harvard's Memorial Church, writes insightfully in *The Good Book: Reading the Bible with Mind and Heart* (New York: Morrow, 1996) about some controversial questions in the Bible such as anti-Semitism, homosexuality, and race, but also on topics like evil, wealth, suffering, and the "good life."

Stephen Jay Gould's balanced and eloquent *Rocks of Ages: Science and Religion in the Fullness of Life* (New York: Ballantine, 1999) is in my view still the best single treatment of this much-debated topic.

The *Dictionary of Scripture and Ethics* (Grand Rapids, MI: Baker Academic, 2011), edited by Joel B. Green, is a unique and quite successful effort to relate biblical sources to a range of issues from "abortion" and "accountability" to "war" and "welfare." The connections it makes are not proof-texting, but nuanced and comprehensive.

As Christians and others search for a more solid and effective theology of public life, Eric Gregory's *Politics and the Order of Love: An Augustinian Ethic of Democratic Citizenship* (Chicago: Univ. of Chicago Press, 2008) reaches back to an immensely influential figure and argues persuasively for his relevance today.

Richard Horsley's *Jesus and Empire: The Kingdom of God and the New World Disorder* (Minneapolis: Augsburg Fortress, 2003) is the best single source for understanding early Christianity in the light of its Roman imperial context.

Philip Jenkins's *The Lost History of Christianity: The Thousand-Year Golden Age of the Church in the Middle East, Africa, and Asia—and How It Died* (San Francisco: HarperOne, 2008) describes the thousand-year "golden age" of Christianity in what is now called the global south.

Mark Juergensmeyer's *Global Rebellion: Religious Challenges to the Secular State, from Christian Militias to al Qaeda* (Berkeley, CA: Univ. of California Press, 2008) thoughtfully explores the link between "fundamentalism," nationalism, and disquietude about the secular state.

Karen King's engaging and groundbreaking *What Is Gnosticism?* (Cambridge, MA: Harvard Univ. Press, 2003) makes it impossible to rule out many expressions of early Christianity as simply "heretical."

In *The Meaning of the Bible: What Jewish and Christian Scriptures Can Teach Us* (San Francisco: HarperOne, 2011), Douglas A. Knight and Amy-Jill Levine go beyond the ordinary commentary approach and ask the critical question of what the Bible means for us here and now. They uncover jewels of wisdom and ethical guidance from the full range of the biblical books.

Helmut Koester's *Ancient Christian Gospels: Their History and Development* (Philadelphia: Trinity International, 1992) is still the most complete and accurate overall guide to the welter of early Christian documents that have reshaped our understanding of that period. For a delightful and useful up-to-date source for studying the apostle Paul, see Koester's *Cities of Paul: Images and Interpretations from the Harvard New Testament and Archaeology Project* (Minneapolis: Fortress, 2005). It is a CD-ROM with 900 pictures that carry us to Athens, Corinth, Philippi, and Ephesus, based on the latest archaeological research.

The Japanese Christian writer Kosuke Koyama, in *Mount Fuji and Mount Sinai* (Maryknoll, NY: Orbis Books, 1985), presents a thoughtful comparison relying heavily on Old Testament passages from Jeremiah, the Psalms, Exodus, and Hosea; in addition, he is intimately familiar with and sympathetic to various religions of his homeland.

As the dialogue between Christians and Muslims looms larger, David Levering Lewis's *God's Crucible: Islam and the Making of Europe, 570–1215* (New York: Norton, 2008) reminds us that this conversation has been going on in one way or another for a long time.

For the most recent and comprehensive analysis of the exploding Pentecostal movement, see Donald Miller and Tetsunao Yamamori, *Global Pentecostalism: The New Face of Christian Social Engagement* (Berkeley, CA: Univ. of California Press, 2007). The book includes a fascinating DVD.

Stephen D. Moore, in *Literary Criticism and the Gospels: The Theoretical Challenge* (New Haven, CT: Yale Univ. Press, 1992), demonstrates how various forms of literary criticism open a selection of biblical texts to new understandings.

Are We Rome? The Fall of an Empire and the Fate of America (Boston: Houghton Mifflin, 2007), by Cullen Murphy, draws some fascinating comparisons and contrasts between our own and the ancient world.

Carol Osiek and Kevin Madigan, in *Ordained Women in the Early Church, 30–600: A Documentary History* (Baltimore: Johns Hopkins Univ. Press, 2005), present convincing evidence for a much larger role of women in the history of the church than has previously been recognized.

Joerg Rieger's *Christ and Empire: From Paul to Postcolonial Times* (Minneapolis: Augsburg Fortress, 2007) documents how theological assumptions have been tainted by imperial thinking for centuries. Rieger is also the coeditor with Pui-Lan Kwok and Don M. Compier of *Empire and the Christian Tradition* (Minneapolis: Fortress, 2007).

Lamin O. Sanneh's *Disciples of All Nations: Pillars of World Christianity* (New York: Oxford Univ. Press, 2008) ties the previous history to the phenomenal growth of Christianity in the global south today. This book is part of the invaluable Oxford Studies in World Christianity, of which Sanneh is the editor. See also Sanneh's classic *Translating the Message: The Missionary Impact of Culture* (Maryknoll, NY: Orbis Books, 1989), an in-depth study of both the difficulty and the creativity of translating the Bible into non-Western cultures.

The Greenleaf Guide to Old Testament History (Lebanon, TN: Greenleaf, 1994), by Rob and Cyndy Shearer, is a simple and well-organized guide that, by presenting small portions of the biblical text from Genesis to Nehemiah, takes readers through the entire history of biblical Israel. Not overly sophisticated, it is basic enough to be read by young people, but is also useful to adults.

R. S. Sugirtharajah's *The Bible and the Third World: Precolonial, Colonial and Postcolonial Encounters* (Cambridge: Cambridge Univ. Press, 2001) is possibly the best charting of the various forms of engagement with the Bible in the southern world, including such topics as colonialism, indigenous religions, and liberation theologies.

Charles Taylor's massive but thorough *A Secular Age* (Cambridge, MA: Belknap Press, Harvard Univ. Press, 2007) traces the history of the emergence and acceptance of nonreligious and antireligious thinking, locating its sources well before our contemporary era.

After many years of lagging behind, Catholic biblical scholarship and interpretation have caught up and in some instances surpassed that of Protestants. Carey Walsh's *Chasing Mystery: A Catholic Biblical Theology* (Collegeville, MN: Liturgical, 2014) concentrates on mystical encounters with the divine, but does not avoid the age-old problem of the harrowing experience of the absence of God.

Notes

INTRODUCTION

1. Elisabeth Schüssler Fiorenza, *Bread Not Stone: The Challenge of Feminist Biblical Interpretation* (Boston: Beacon, 1995), p. 104.

CHAPTER 1: SERPENTS, FLOODS, AND THE MYSTERY OF EVIL

1. Stephen Mitchell, *Genesis: A New Translation of the Classic Bible Stories* (New York: Harper-Collins, 1996). A skilled and poetically gifted translator gives us a fresh and informative new look into the first book of the Bible.

2. Nicolas Berdyaev, *The Destiny of Man* (London: Geoffrey Bliss, 1937).

3. Avivah Gottlieb Zornberg, *The Beginning of Desire: Reflections on Genesis* (New York: Schocken, 1995), p. 4. See also Ilia Delio, ed., *From Teilhard to Omega: Co-creating an Unfinished Universe* (Maryknoll, NY; Orbis Books, 2013).

4. Hannah Arendt, *Eichmann in Jerusalem: A Report on the Banality of Evil* (New York: Penguin, 1994). For more on the resurgence of discussion on the "problem of evil," see Susan Neiman, *Evil in Modern Thought: An Alternative History of Philosophy* (Princeton, NJ: Princeton Univ. Press, 2002).

5. Philip Almond, *The Devil: A New Biography* (Ithaca, NY: Cornell Univ. Press, 2014), a recent book on the problem of evil, traces the perennial dilemma of how to reconcile the goodness of God with his omnipotence.

6. Nahum M. Sarna, *The JPS Torah Commentary: Genesis* (Philadelphia: Jewish Publication Society, 1989), p. 94.

CHAPTER 2: FOLLOWING THE FOOTSTEPS OF MOSES

1. John Noble Wilford, "Camels Had No Business in Genesis," *New York Times,* February 11, 2014, p. D13, http://www.nytimes.com/2014/02/11/science/camels-had-no-business-in-genesis.html?_r=0.

2. Thomas E. Levy et al., *Cyber-Archaeology in the Holy Land: The Future of the Past* (Washington, DC: Biblical Archaeology Society eBook 2012), http://www.biblicalarchaeology.org/free-ebooks/cyber-archaeology-in-the-holy-land-the-future-of-the-past/.

3. G. Ernest Wright, *The God Who Acts: Biblical Theology as Recital* (Chicago: Univ. of Chicago Press, 1952).

4. Everett Fox, *The Five Books of Moses* (New York: Schocken, 1995), p. 273.

5. Israel Finkelstein and Neil Silberman, *The Bible Unearthed: Archaeology's New Vision of Ancient Israel and the Origin of Its Sacred Texts* (New York: Free Press, 2001), pp. 62–63.

6. Finkelstein and Silberman, *The Bible Unearthed*, p. 64.

CHAPTER 3: BATTLES AND BURLESQUES IN THE CONQUEST OF CANAAN

1. Regina M. Schwartz, *The Curse of Cain: The Violent Legacy of Monotheism* (Chicago: Univ. of Chicago Press, 1997).

2. Robert Allen Warrior, "Canaanites, Cowboys and Indians: Deliverance, Conquest and Liberation Theology Today," *Christianity and Crisis* 49 (1989): 264.

3. Mario Liverani, "Memorandum on the Approach to Historiographic Texts," quoted in Ian Douglas Wilson, "Conquest and Form: Narrativity in Joshua 5–11 and Historical Discourse in Ancient Judah," *Harvard Theological Review* 106/3 (July 2013): 310.

4. Norman K. Gottwald, *The Tribes of Yahweh: A Sociology of the Religion of Liberated Israel, 1250–1050 BCE* (Maryknoll, NY: Orbis Books, 1979).

5. Schwartz, *The Curse of Cain*, p. 161.

CHAPTER 4: TALKING BACK TO GOD FROM THE GARBAGE HEAP

1. Moshe Greenberg, "Job," in Robert Alter and Frank Kermode, eds., *The Literary Guide to the Bible* (Cambridge, MA: Belknap Press, Harvard Univ. Press, 1987), p. 303.

2. Stephen Mitchell, *The Book of Job* (New York: Harper Perennial, 1992).

3. Harold Attridge, ed., *The HarperCollins Study Bible*, rev. ed. (San Francisco: HarperSanFrancisco, 2006), study note to Job 1:6.

4. Mark Larrimore, *The Book of Job: A Biography* (Princeton, NJ: Princeton Univ. Press, 2013).

5. Elsa Tamez, "Carta al Hermano Job" ("A Letter to Brother Job"), *Paginas* 53 (June 1983): 2.

6. Gustavo Gutiérrez, *On Job: God-Talk and the Suffering of the Innocent* (Maryknoll, NY: Orbis Books, 1987).

7. Dietrich Bonhoeffer, *Letters and Papers from Prison*, ed. Eberhard Bethge (New York: Collier Books, 1972), p. 17.

8. Claus Westermann, "Two Faces of Job," *Concilium* 169 (1983): 18.

9. Arthur Gold, "Complaining to God," unpublished lecture, September 1987.

10. Mitchell, *Book of Job*, p. xxv.

CHAPTER 5: LISTENING TO THE VOICES OF THE VOICELESS

1. Victor H. Matthews, *The Hebrew Prophets and Their Social World: An Introduction*, 2nd ed. (Grand Rapids, MI: Baker Academic, 2012).

2. See Abraham J. Heschel, *The Prophets* (New York: Harper & Row, 1962).

3. Harvey Cox, *Fire from Heaven: The Rise of Pentecostal Spirituality and the Reshaping of Religion in the 21st Century* (Reading, MA: Addison Wesley, 1995).

4. Gary V. Smith, *The Prophets as Preachers: An Introduction to the Hebrew Prophets* (Nashville, TN: Broadman and Holman, 1994).

5. James D. Newsome, Jr., *The Hebrew Prophets* (Louisville, KY: Westminster John Knox, 1986).

6. Karl Jaspers, *The Origin and Goal of History* (London: Routledge, 1953); Eric Voegelin, *Order in History* (Baton Rouge, LA: Louisiana State Univ. Press, 1957); Robert Bellah: *Religion in Human Evolution: From the Paleolithic to the Axial Age* (Cambridge, MA: Belknap Press, Harvard Univ. Press, 2011).

7. Heschel, *The Prophets*, p. 62.

CHAPTER 7: LOOKING OVER THE SHOULDERS OF THE WRITERS

1. For comparing texts with each other, as I have done in this section, see Paul Hoffmann, Thomas Hieke, and Ulrich Bauer, eds., *Synoptic Concordance* (Berlin and New York: De Gruyter, 2014). This new version of the older *Gospel Parallels* is an invaluable source, because it presents the texts in parallel, but also includes a concordance, which makes going back and forth between two volumes unnecessary. See also Elaine Pagels, *The Gnostic Gospels* (New York: Random House, 1979).

2. See Mark Chancey, *Greco-Roman Culture in the Galilee of Jesus* (Cambridge: Cambridge Univ. Press, 2005). Archaeology is playing an ever larger role in allowing us to glimpse the environment into which Jesus was born and in which he ministered.

3. For an excellent example of a contribution by a feminist biblical scholar, see Susan Miller, *Women in Mark's Gospel* (London: Clark, 2004). Another sterling example of a feminist uncovering of Jesus, this time among his own followers, is in Mattila Talvikki, *Citizens of the Kingdom: Followers of Jesus in Matthew from a Feminist Perspective* (Helsinki: Finnish Exegetical Society, 2001).

4. Warren Carter, *Matthew and the Margins* (Maryknoll, NY: Orbis Books, 2000).

5. A thoughtful account of this manuscript controversy can be found in Bart D. Ehrman, *Misquoting Jesus: The Story Behind Who Changed the Bible and Why* (San Francisco: HarperSanFrancisco, 2005), pp. 255–56.

6. Burton L. Mack, *The Lost Gospel: The Book of Q & Christian Origins* (San Francisco: HarperSanFrancisco, 1993).

7. Carter, *Matthew and the Margins*, p. 133.

8. Chris Keith, *Jesus Against the Scribal Elite: The Origins of the Conflict* (Grand Rapids, MI: Baker Academic, 2014). This book gives invaluable insights into the history that led up to Jesus's confrontation at the Temple and eventually his crucifixion.

9. Dietrich Bonhoeffer, *Letters and Papers from Prison*, ed. Eberhard Bethge (New York: Collier Books, 1972), p. 362.

CHAPTER 8: ON THE ROAD WITH PAUL OF TARSUS

1. Richard Horsley, ed., *Paul and Empire: Religion and Power in Roman Imperial Society* (Harrisburg, PA: Trinity International, 1997), p.4.

2. Horsley, ed., *Paul and Empire*, p. 12.

3. See A. N. Wilson, *Paul: The Mind of the Apostle* (New York: Norton, 1997). See also Jerome Murphy-O'Connor, *Jesus and Paul: Parallel Lives* (Collegeville, MN: Liturgical, 2007), a book that argues eloquently against any division or dichotomy between Jesus and Paul. See also Robin Griffith-Jones, *The Gospel According to Paul: The Creative Genius Who Brought Jesus to the World* (San Francisco: HarperSanFrancisco, 2004).

4. Krister Stendahl, *Paul Among Jews and Gentiles and Other Essays* (Philadelphia: Fortress, 1976).

5. N. Lewis and M. Reinhold, eds., *Roman Civilization* (Harper & Row, 1955), 2:64, quoted in S. R. F. Price, "Rituals and Power," in Horsley, ed., *Paul and Empire*, p. 53.

6. James Kallas, "Romans 13:1–7: An Interpretation," *New Testament Studies* 11 (1965): 369. See also Yeo Khiok-khng, ed., *Navigating Romans Through Cultures: Challenging Readings and Charting a New Course* (New York: Clark International, 2004), a splendid example of what a scrupulous history-of-interpretation approach, here for one of Paul's most important Letters, can do to enlarge our understanding of a familiar text.

7. Neil Elliott, *Liberating Paul: The Justice of God and the Politics of the Apostle* (Maryknoll, NY: Orbis Books, 1994).

8. Robin Scroggs, *The New Testament and Homosexuality* (Philadelphia: Fortress, 1983), p. 127, quoted in Neil Elliot, *Liberating Paul*, p. 38.

CHAPTER 9: SURVIVING A TURBULENT TRIP

1. Bernard McGinn, ed., *Apocalypticism in Western History and Culture*, vol. 2 of *The Encyclopedia of Apocalypticism* (New York: Continuum, 1998).

2. Elaine Pagels, *Revelations: Visions, Prophecy, and Politics in the Book of Revelation* (New York: Viking Penguin, 2012).

3. J. Massyngberde Ford, *Revelation*, vol. 38 of *The Anchor Bible* (Garden City, NY: Doubleday, 1975).

4. Richard K. Emmerson and Bernard McGinn, *The Apocalypse in the Middle Ages* (Ithaca, NY: Cornell Univ. Press, 1992).

5. Stephen D. O'Leary, *Arguing the Apocalypse: A Theory of Millennial Rhetoric* (New York: Oxford Univ. Press, 1994).

6. For example, articles on canonization in both the Old and the New Testament canons appear in vol. 1 of *The Interpreter's Dictionary of the Bible*, ed. Keith R. Crim and George A. Buttrick, 5 vols. (Nashville, TN: Abingdon, 1981).

7. William John Lyons and Jorunn Økland, eds., *The Way the World Ends: The Apocalypse of John in Culture and Ideology* (Sheffield: Sheffield Phoenix, 2009). See also Jonathan Kirsch, *A History of the End of the World: How the Most Controversial Book in the Bible Changed the Course of Western Civilization* (San Francisco: HarperSanFrancisco, 2006).

8. Tim LaHaye and Jerry B. Jenkins, *Left Behind* series (Wheaton, IL: Tyndale House, 1995–2007).

9. Paul Boyer, *When Time Shall Be No More: Prophecy Belief in Modern American Culture* (Cambridge, MA: Belknap Press, Harvard Univ. Press, 1992).

10. Michael Barkun, *A Culture of Conspiracy: Apocalyptic Visions in Contemporary America* (Berkeley, CA: Univ. of California Press, 2003).

11. Elisabeth Schüssler Fiorenza, *The Apocalypse* (Chicago: Franciscan Herald, 1976). There is a brilliant chapter on Revelation in Robert Alter and Frank Kermode, eds., *The Literary Guide to the Bible* (Cambridge, MA: Harvard Univ. Press, 1987). See also Lyons and Økland, *The Way the World Ends*.

CHAPTER 10: HOW DO WE READ THE BIBLE TODAY?

1. Dietrich Bonhoeffer, *Letters and Papers from Prison*, ed. Eberhard Bethge (New York: Collier Books, 1972), p. 17.

2. Gustavo Gutiérrez, private conversation with the author.

3. His Holiness the Dalai Lama, *The Good Heart: A Buddhist Perspective on the Teachings of Jesus* (Somerville, MA: Wisdom, 1996).

4. Thich Nhat Hanh, *Living Buddha, Living Christ* (New York: Riverhead, 1995).

5. Peggy Rosenthal, *The Poets' Jesus: Representations at the End of a Millennium* (New York: Oxford Univ. Press, 2000).

6. Robert Atwan, George Dardess, and Peggy Rosenthal, eds., *Divine Inspiration: The Life of Jesus in Poetry* (New York: Oxford Univ. Press, 1997).

7. Denise Levertov, "Work That Enfaiths," in *New and Collected Essays: Where I Live* (New York: New Directions, 1992), p. 257, quoted in Atwan, Dardess, and Rosenthal, eds., *Divine Inspiration*, p. 172.

APPENDIX

1. Albert Schweitzer, *The Quest of the Historical Jesus* (1906; New York: Macmillan, 1961), p. 403.

Index

DISCOVER MORE BY HARVEY COX

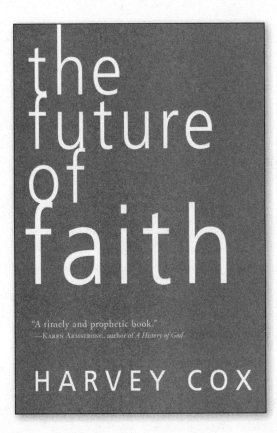

HarperOne
An Imprint of HarperCollinsPublishers

Discover great authors, exclusive offers, and more at hc.com.